MARGINAL MYSTERIES

Unless otherwise specified, all Scriptures are taken from the King James Version of the Holy Bible.

MARGINAL MYSTERIES

For more information contact:
Defender Publishing—www.defenderpublishing.com.

Printed in the United States of America

ISBN 0-9848256-0-6

MARGINAL MYSTERIES

A BIBLICAL PERSPECTIVE

Dr. Noah Hutchings
Dr. Larry Spargimino
Dr. Bob Glaze

Table of Contents

Preface

Jesus drew a parallel to the secret Grecian societies in Matthew 13:11:"He answered and said unto them, Because it is given unto you [the disciples] to know the mysteries of the kingdom of heaven, but to them [the outsiders] it is not given."

The New Testament is a revelation, or making known, the mysteries that were hidden from the knowledge of men from the beginning of time:"If ye have heard of the dispensation of the grace of God which is given me to you-ward: How that by revelation he made known unto me the mystery;...Which in other ages was not made known unto the sons of men, as it is now revealed unto his holy apostles and prophets by the Spirit" (Ephesians 3:2–3,5).

There are many segments of God's great mystery. For example, in 1 Corinthians 15:51 we read: "Behold, I shew you a mystery; We shall not all sleep, but we shall all be changed."

In ancient Greece there were secret societies where religious rites and ceremonies were practiced by the membership. In ancient Greece, there were secret societies where religious rites and ceremonies were practiced by the membership. Those initiated into those societies became partakers of certain knowledge that was withheld from outsiders. These secret organizations, with their hidden meetings, were known as the mysteries.

The revealing of the greatest mystery was by Jesus Himself when He informed Nicodemus in John 3 that a man could be born again without reentering the womb.

The subjects considered in this book, however, are marginal scriptural mysteries. They have only a peripheral bearing on basic Bible doctrine and truth. However, these mysteries have persisted for centuries, and our only desire is to shed as much knowledge on them as possible to determine, if we can, how they stand up in the light of the Scriptures.

The Mystery of the
La Brea Tar Pits

Faraway Animals in a Nearby Place

Can the reader imagine the following animals in downtown Los Angeles: monstrous mastodons and mammoths; thirty-five hundred–pound sloths; saber-toothed cats (also called saber-toothed tigers) with teeth a foot long; three different breeds of bear, one much larger than the modern-day grizzly; bison twice as large as those that roamed the plains of the past two centuries; huge werewolves roaming in packs; along with dozens of other types of animals including African lions, camels, zebras, huge condors flying overhead seeking out the remains of herbivorous animals killed by carnivorous ones? This was a typical scene in downtown Los Angeles only a few thousand (not million) years ago. How do we know? Because the skeletons of all these animals, by the millions, are in the La Brea Tar Pits over which downtown Los Angeles was built. A few of these tar pits have been left open for archaeological purposes.[1]

The discovery of these wonderful treasures goes back to August 3, 1769, when Gaspar de Portola, the governor of lower California, arrived at the site of present-day Los Angeles. His expedition noted extensive swamps and tar pits in the area. Father John Crespi recorded the following information:

---

1. John M. Harris and George T. Anderson, Ed., *Rancho La Brea: Treasures of the Tar Pits* (Los Angeles: Natural History Museum of Los Angeles County, 1985), pp. 1–17.

This afternoon we felt new earthquakes, the continuation of which astonishes us. We judge that in the mountains that run to the west in front of us there are some volcanoes, for there are many signs on the road which stretches between the Porciuncula River and the Spring of the Alders, for the explorers saw some large marshes of a certain substance like pitch; they were boiling and bubbling, and the pitch came out mixed with an abundance of water. They noticed that the water runs to one side and the pitch to the other, and that there is such an abundance of it that it would serve to caulk many ships.[2]

In the late 1700s the residents in the area used the tar for waterproofing, and as a sealer on the roofs of their adobe buildings. In 1828, Antonio Rocha was given 4,439 acres of land—this parcel included what is now known as the La Brea Tar Pits—as a provisional Mexican land grant. The grant, known as the Rancho La Brea (meaning "the tar ranch" in Spanish), stated that the public would continue using as much tar for their personal use as was needed. In the 1860s, Major Henry Hancock obtained a large portion of the La Brea. In the years of the following decade Hancock mined the asphalt and drilled for oil.[3]

Biblical "Slime Pits"

The Bible also mentions what resemble "tar pits." In Genesis 14 we read of a great battle that arose as the result of a rebellion against Chedorlaomer (vs. 4), and that the battle occurred in "the vale of Siddim" (vs. 8). Verse 10 describes the site: "And the vale of Siddim was full of slimepits. . . ."

Interestingly, "slime" is a translation of the Hebrew word *chemar*. The same word is used with reference to the construction of the Tower of Babel (Genesis 11:3) and for the waterproofing used on the "ark of bulrushes" (Exodus 2:3) in which Moses was placed by his mother and later

2. Gretchen Sibley, *La Brea Story* (Los Angeles: Los Angeles County Museum of Natural History, 1969), pp. 26–27.

3. *Trapped in Time: Study Guide to the Fossils of Rancho La Brea* (Los Angeles: George C. Page Museum of La Brea Discoveries), no page or date.

found by the daughter of Pharaoh.

Some believe that the "vale of Siddim" is a reference to the tongue-shaped peninsula that protrudes from the east bank of the Dead Sea near Bab edh 'Drah, and might have joined the western shore near the ancient site of Masada. In *The Defender's Study Bible*, we read: "These 'slime pits' were so extensive that the Dead Sea was called the Asphalt Sea by early writers. They probably represented accumulations of organic debris from the flood, collecting in the unique basins of the Great Rift Valley which transverses the region."[4]

Strictly speaking, the La Brea Tar Pits are asphalt deposits. Asphalt is a bituminous derivative of petroleum containing varying proportions of organic and mineral materials. Others believe that the petroleum and gases found in the region were used by God to produce the fires that destroyed the cities of the plain.[5]

It is interesting that Noah in Genesis 6:14 was instructed to "pitch" [seal] the ark with "pitch." The Hebrew word for "pitch" in this verse is *zepheth,* which implies a tree resin. After the Flood the word for "slime" used as mortar or to seal ships' planking is *chemar,* as we have seen in the above scriptures, clearly referring to asphalt. The reader may wonder what all this has to do with the La Brea Tar Pits, but there is an important time factor involved. The reason that the La Brea animal skeletons are not considered more prominently in science books is that evolutionists have trouble explaining both the chronology and the animal types.

A common evolutionary explanation for fossil fuels, and particularly coal, is that they were formed within a time period of between 275 to 45 million years ago. The common theory concerning how fossil fuels developed is that they are the decayed matter of vegetation, fruits, and animals that possibly settled in water and gradually consolidated under pressure. Creation scientists like Dr. Edward Blick, Dr. Henry Morris, Dr. Walter Brown, and others, dispute this explanation, contending that fossil fuels

---

4. Henry M. Morris, *The Defender's Study Bible* (Grand Rapids: World, 1995), note on Genesis 14:10).

5. Charles Pfeiffer, *Baker's Bible Atlas,* rev. ed. (Grand Rapids: Baker, 1973), p. 57.

were the result of the compression of a vastly more luxuriant, earthly environment in a gigantic catastrophe, possibly the Noahic Flood, less than ten thousand years ago. The "slime pits" were the result of an after-upward flow of oil escaping under pressure. Again, it is interesting that during the past two thousand years asphalt ceased floating on the Dead Sea and the major slime pits around the world have mostly dried up. Even the La Brea Tar Pits have declined in size. Geologists and anthropologists who embrace the theory of evolution must place the La Brea Tar Pits' origin in the Later Quaternary Era, from forty thousand to ten thousand years ago, but others date them later, possibly forty-five hundred to four thousand years ago.[6] Having considered all the available evidence—scientific and biblical—we conclude that the animals whose remains are found in the La Brea Tar Pits were buried alive four millennia ago.

Although these animal skeleton remains are referred to as fossils, they are not fossils in the usual understanding. These remains are actual bones. Being referenced as fossils insinuates millions of years rather than just thousands of years.

Continental Separation

The La Brea asphalt deposits raise many interesting questions. For example, how do we account for the remains of the large cats resembling African lions? Is this phenomenon explained by Genesis 10:25, where we are told that in the days of Peleg "was the earth divided"? Many years ago Edward Bullard proposed the theory of an original "continental fit." The northwest bulge of Africa seems to fit into the Atlantic Coast of the United States; eastern South America seems to fit into the west coast of Africa. This might suggest the dividing of a single post-Flood continent into the different land areas of the present day. Does this, in some way, explain how and why many of the animals at La Brea became extinct?

The Edward Bullard presentation of the continental breakup, as shown on page 84 of *In the Beginning*, by Dr. Walt Brown, chief of science and technology studies at the Air War College, has some proportional

---

6. Harris and Jefferson, p. 1.

flaws. Nevertheless, it was an aggressive and bold effort to suggest how the earth's landmass was broken up. Other charts depicting the continental separation on the same page perhaps are more accurate. *Scientific American* has included several scientific studies on this subject in several editions since 1950. It is agreed by reputable geologists that the landmass of Earth was at one time one continent, but something happened to break up this one continent, and the various chunks were somehow separated and "floated" apart. It is fairly easy to think of the continents and islands as pieces of a jigsaw puzzle that can be fitted back together again. Most geologists espouse the theory of evolution, and they suggest that this continental separation occurred over millions of years.

A separation of the continents would, of course, result in a drastic change in the environment and ecology of the different landmasses. There are no dinosaurs in the La Brea Tar Pits, indicating that this separation might have occurred after the demise of the dinosaurs. However, there are dinosaur fossils in the western United States, which would suggest that the continental breakup might have occurred after the Genesis Flood. If the separation occurred in the far-distant past, then how could, as taught by the theory of evolution, African lions, camels, and zebras have evolved simultaneously on different continents, separated by thousands of miles of oceans, in different environments? It seems evident that perhaps fifty percent of the animals could not adjust to the changing environment and became extinct in certain areas, like the African lion in California. Other animals, like the mastodon and mammoth, became extinct worldwide.

We read in Genesis 10:25: "And unto Eber were born two sons: the name of one was Peleg; for in his days was the earth divided; and his brother's name was Joktan." The footnote in the *Pilgrim Study Bible*[7] reads: "'WAS THE EARTH DIVIDED': The word 'earth' in Hebrew means 'dry land.' From this verse, we believe that at one time all dry land was on one continent. Something, perhaps an earthquake, occurred to divide it into the continents and islands that we know today. . . ."

We read in Genesis 7:11 that even before the rain at the time the

---

7. *Pilgrim Study Bible* (New York: Oxford University Press, 1952).

Flood began the "fountains of the great deep" were broken up. Something evidently occurred to crack the surface of the Earth. Immanuel Velikovsky, in his book *Worlds In Collision*,[8] theorized that when the orbit of Mars was more elliptical, the planet came close to Earth, resulting in a major catastrophe. Velikovsky observes that the Babylonian name for Mars was Nergal, and that Nergal was feared for his violence. Shamash-shum-ukin, king of Babylonia and grandson of Sennacherib, wrote: "Nergal, the most violent among the gods."[9] God could have used this method to bring about the Flood, or, He could have only spoken a word. In any event, something happened to cause the continental separation and subsequent shift. According to the opinion of most geologists, the shift occurred over millions of years. According to the Bible, the shift occurred in the lifespan of one man, Peleg, or approximately in a period of two hundred years. Before the Flood, the biblical account describes men and women living to be eight and nine hundred years. After the Flood, the lifespan of man decreased seven or eight hundred years to approximately seventy years. The change in the upper atmosphere that allowed a more direct and harmful sunlight to reach the ground, plus a change in the oxygen content, may have accounted for the reduction in the number of years people lived after the Flood, as well as explain why there are no huge animals like the mastodons and mammoths around today.

How and Why?

Several books have been written about the ecology of Southern California, and adjacent areas in Arizona and Nevada, and present considerable evidence that this entire region was once replete with streams, lakes, and marshes. The vegetation would have been sufficient to provide food for herbivores, which in turn provided abundant food for the larger carnivores. But after the continental shift which, according to Dr. Walt

8. Immanuel Velikovsky, Worlds In Collision (Garden City, NY: Doubleday, 1950), pp. 362–368.

9. Ibid., pp. 241–242.

Brown,[10] probably occurred quite quickly, the ecology of the region began to change. Mountains rose higher, blocking off rain clouds from the Pacific Ocean. Slowly at first, the area began to dry up from the east, forcing many species of animal life closer to the ocean. In the summer months there was practically no rain, and the tar pits provided the only source of liquid, which was mainly poisonous water on top of an asphalt bed. This brought the animal life closer together. Some doubtless became bogged in the tar pits trying to find water, and meat eaters near the pits killed other herbivores. As far as we know, no mention is made by early Spanish explorers or early American settlers of seeing such animals in the area, although evidence of dung in caves indicates that some may have been alive at the time Columbus discovered America. Admittedly, carbon dating places the animals back in time. Bible chronology would seem to date the entrapment of the animals in the La Brea Tar Pits after 2500 B.C., probably over a period of four hundred years, even though some animal species may have survived on offshore Alaskan islands or remote areas in Canada until recent times.

What It Must Have Been Like

Gretchen Sibley, in her *La Brea Story,* takes us back in time and imaginatively describes what probably happened on a daily basis at the tar pits.

> The pits appear to be numerous pools of water, perhaps twenty scattered over an area of about twenty-five acres. Grasses spread to the water's edge. Tule reeds, tall hollow grasses, edge some of the pools.
>
> . . . The irregular banks of a nearby pool are blackened where the tar has soaked into the ground. Small bubbles rise and break and as we watch, a foot-wide bubble of asphalt gradually pushes above the water, releasing acrid gas into the air. The sun reveals the rainbow hues of the thin layer of oil on the water's surface. . . .
>
> This is the drama we have traveled so far to see and we move cau-

---

10. Walt Brown, *In the Beginning: Compelling Evidence for Creation and the Flood* (Phoenix: Center for Scientific Creation, 1995), pp. 78–90.

tiously toward the sounds. Coming on the scene we view the horror of an occurrence that repeats itself endlessly for centuries.

The pit is not large, perhaps twenty feet across. Near the edge, close to us, a large camel has become mired in the soft tar. His struggles have carried him into the pool and his hindquarters have sunk out of our sight. His front feet pull at the firm ground and drag through the tar frantically. His neck arches back and harsh cries wrench from his open mouth. His eyes are wild; he is fearful of sinking and of the predators. We too now see a crouching saber-toothed cat moving slowly through the grass and toward the pit. It stops at the edge and watches. . . .

It is suddenly silent and we wait—our eyes fastened on the crouching cat. Will it never spring? A yellow flash and a flying body strikes the camel. . . . He has captured his prey and rests on it—a small island in a sea of tar. The camel sinks a little deeper into the tar and the saber-toothed cat slowly slides down, still occupied with his catch. His hind foot touches water, dips into the tar beneath and is pulled out dripping with the black slime. He struggles but there is no footing. The instinct of the kill and his hunger fight against his endeavor to escape. . . .[11]

More About the Formation of the Pits

How did these tar pits form? It is believed that there were extensive natural reservoirs of the Salt Lake Oilfield in the area. Harris and Jefferson explain: "Crude oil seeped slowly upward along these cracks until it reached the ground surface. At the surface the lighter petroleum portion evaporated, leaving behind shallow sticky pools of natural asphalt. Numerous asphalt seeps were once visible at Rancho La Brea; a few can still be seen in Hancock Park today. It is in such asphalt deposits that the Rancho La Brea fossils were preserved."[12]

The Fossilization of Plants and Animals

The natural preservation of plant and animal remains occurs in a

11. Sibley, pp. 18–19.
12. Harris and Jefferson, p. 9.

variety of ways, but whatever method, there must be protection from the effects of rapid decay. The harder and more durable parts of animals—bones, teeth, and shells—tend to decay more slowly and are not so readily destroyed by predators and rodents. Because of the movement of the asphalt within a deposit, bones from one skeleton are often mixed with bones from another skeleton. Furthermore, bones that are moved around by the movement of the asphalt tend to rub against each other. Given a sufficiently long period of time this produces unusual grooves and holes in the bones known as "pit wear."[13]

Most of the bones found at Rancho La Brea are in an excellent state of preservation because they have been impregnated with asphalt, which also indicates hundreds or thousands of years rather than millions or billions of years. "Asphalt . . . protects those organic compounds in the fossils that might otherwise be leached out and carried away by ground water, or replaced during petrification. . . . As a result, the most delicate surface and internal structures of the fossils have survived. . . . Remains rarely found at other fossil sites are commonly preserved, including . . . thin-walled bones of birds, the flesh parts of leaves, and the iridescent coloration in beetle wing covers."[14]

What the Remains Tell Us About Life at La Brea

Some of the animals that lived in the La Brea area were quite large. In the book *Rancho La Brea: Treasures of the Tar Pits* we read:

> The imperial mammoth . . . was the largest of the elephants that lived in North America. Some individuals from Rancho La Brea stood over thirteen feet . . . tall. . . . Mammoths were closely related to the modern Indian and African elephants. . . . Mammoths differed from living elephants by having a greater number of enamel plates in each individual tooth. Mammoths and elephants also differ in the shape of the tusks.

---

13. Ibid., pp. 12–13.
14. Christopher A. Shaw, "How the Fossils Were Preserved," *Terra*, Fall 1991, p. 43.

Some mammoth species developed thick hairy coats to cope with cold arctic regions. The American mastodon . . . which stood slightly more than six feet . . . tall at the shoulder, was smaller than the imperial mammoth and also differed from it in a number of other features. Both possessed long elephant-like trunks, but mastodons had more teeth present in the jaw and instead of tall plates, these had low rounded cusps separated by V-shaped valleys. The shape of the tooth crown suggests that mastodons fed on leaves and twigs rather than on the grass that provided the main item in a mammoth's diet.[15]

The remains of three different kinds of bear were found. Evidently, from the number of fossils, the short-face bear, *Arctodus simus,* unique because of the absence of a long snout, had unusually long legs in proportion with the rest of the animal's body. It was even taller than the modern-day Alaskan Kodiak bear.[16]

The largest cat from the asphalt pits is the American lion, *Panthera atrox,* which strikingly resembles the modern African lion. Other large cats were the puma, the jaguar, and the bobcat.[17] In addition, there were two species of camels. The larger and more common form stood more than seven feet tall at the shoulder. Also represented by a few remains is an extinct llama, similar to the South American llama of today. A species of llama found at La Brea was about one-third larger than any living llama. Other large mammals were the ground sloths.

"Harlan's ground sloth . . . stood a little over six feet . . . tall and weighed about thirty-five hundred pounds. Its simple, flat grinding teeth indicated that it preferred a diet of grass, although it may have also fed on tubers, leaves, and twigs. These animals had nodules of bone, called dermal ossicles, embedded in the deeper layers of the skin of the neck and back. Those may have served as protection against attack by predators."[18]

15. Harris and Jefferson, pp. 267–27.
16. Ibid., p. 42.
17. Ibid., p. 44.
18. Ibid., p. 29.

The Extinction of Many Species

It has been estimated that almost forty percent of the larger species of mammals became extinct. No one is sure why this happened, though there are several possible reasons. If human settlers arrived in the area before most of these large mammals became extinct, as some maintain, it might be that these larger animals were wiped out because of hunting pressure. Some question this, however, on the basis that neither the human population was sufficiently large, nor the primitive hunting weapons available at that time were so effective as to cause animals to become extinct. Others have argued that climatic changes were so marked that the vegetation eaten by the larger herbivores disappeared, and this sparked the extinction of the large carnivores that preyed on them.[19] This, it would seem, is the better explanation. When the food supply of the herbivores was diminished that broke the food chain of the carnivores. This would be a sufficient explanation for the disappearance of certain species.

Plausible as this may be, there is another explanation for the extinction of many species that merits consideration, and that is the sudden disappearance of the vapor canopy. This disappearance produced what Joseph C. Dillow calls the "Catastrophic Freeze."[20] The water vapor canopy that encircled the antediluvian world (Genesis 1:6) created a "greenhouse effect" which is recognized by creation scientists. This assured a spring-like climate for the entire Earth, shielded the Earth from harmful radiation from space, and also retained and evenly distributed incoming solar heat. The canopy suddenly ceased to exist with the Flood and provided much of the water that fell on the Earth. This canopy and its disappearance would explain the remains of luxuriant tropical vegetation in the northern hemisphere. The Bereskova mammoth "was peacefully grazing in July, and suddenly within a half hour of ingestion of his last lunch he was overcome by temperatures colder than -150° F, and froze to death in

---

19. *Trapped In Time,* no page given. See also Harris and Jefferson, p. 76.
20. Joseph C. Dillow, *The Waters Above: Earth's Pre-Flood Vapor Canopy* (Chicago: Moody, 1981), pp. 397–420.

the middle of the summer."[21] The presence of flower petals preserved in the stomach of a frozen mammoth would require the sudden application of low temperatures that could not be explained as a seasonal weather change. Summer flora would be long gone before winter temperatures could prevail.

The degree of preservation of these animal remains is amazing. *TIME* magazine[22] reports on an eleven-foot-tall woolly mammoth found in Siberia. A trench has been dug around the mammoth, freeing it from the twenty-six tons of ice that contain the carcass. In the report we read the following interesting comment: "With tons of soft tissue on ice, geneticists have no shortage of mammoth DNA to play out their fantasy: tweeze a bit of it out, insert it into the ovum of an elephant—a close living cousin—and implant the embryo in the elephant's womb. Before long a woolly bundle should appear. Alternatively, scientists may try to harvest frozen sperm—provided the mammoth is indeed male—and fertilize a female elephant."

La Brea and Noah's Ark

A question that must surely come up in relation to the animals found in the La Brea Tar Pits is, how do they fit in with the Flood? Were there American lions, mammoths, mastodons, and sloths on Noah's ark, and did the Flood reach the La Brea area?

Before we can even attempt to answer these questions, we must affirm the Genesis account is historical, not allegorical. Unfortunately, Genesis chapters one through eleven are often separated from chapters twelve through fifty, the latter supposedly being historical, but the former supposedly not. However, chapters one through eleven are so closely integrated with what follows that if you affirm the historicity of chapters twelve through fifty, you must affirm the historicity of chapters one through eleven. The early chapters are presented as history. There is no indication that they constitute a parable or an allegory that is to be spiritualized.

21. Ibid., p. 396.
22. *TIME*, November 1, 1999, pp. 82–83.

The Genesis account of the Flood leaves no doubt that this was a worldwide flood of universal proportions. In Genesis 7:19 the inspired author implies that the waters covered the Ararat mountain range, and this is supported by Genesis 8:4 where we are told that "the ark rested in the seventh month, on the seventeenth day of the month, upon the mountains of Ararat." Surely, if the water covered mountains that were more than three miles in elevation, the waters were not confined to only one geographical region. Furthermore, God promises: "For yet seven days, and I will cause it to rain upon the earth forty days and forty nights; and every living substance that I have made will I destroy from off the face of the earth" (Genesis 7:4; see also 6:17). All of this suggests a universal flood which included the North American continent, a conclusion reinforced by the likelihood that at the time all the landmasses of the world formed one continent.

While it seems certain that the waters of the Flood reached the area that is now known as Los Angeles, the question concerning the presence of mammoths and mastodons on the ark is a little more complex. In Genesis 7:2 we read that God commanded Noah and said: "Of every clean beast thou shalt take to thee by sevens, the male and his female: and of beasts that are not clean by two, the male and his female."

From this it appears that whether or not mammoths and mastodons were "clean" animals, they could have been included in the ark since even unclean animals were taken aboard.

As already noted, subsequent to the Flood, with the disappearance of the water vapor canopy there were massive climatic changes all over the Earth. Significantly, these changes seem to have been indicated by the La Brea fossils. According to the *Study Guide to the Fossils of Rancho La Brea:*

> The fossils indicate that the climate and environment of Southern California have become warmer and drier over the past ten thousand years. . . . Some animals have become extinct. Other animals, like coyotes, most small mammal species, and many birds, have not changed. Some live in or near Los Angeles today. Some animals from Rancho La

Brea have since changed or evolved into modern forms. For example, the La Brea condor is the direct ancestor of the living California condor.

Though we would have to disagree with the dating and the evolutionary frame of reference, this quote is significant in that it corresponds with the biblical account in that the climate has become "warmer and drier." The vapor canopy and the resultant uniform temperatures of the antediluvian world all changed following the Flood.

Animals of the Pit

The La Brea Tar Pits are exceedingly valuable in that they are a depository of the remains of animals that lived in this specific area during a specific time. These same animals could have been prevalent in many areas of all five continents, but such tar pits and changing ecology are not common throughout the world. In our opinion, the fossil record refutes evolution rather than supporting it. The tar pits show no evidence of intermediate forms. Let us consider more closely some of the fossils of animals that are now extinct in the area and found in the tar pits:

The Mammoth and the Mastodon

The imperial mammoth (*Mammathus imperator*), and the smaller American mastodon, lived in North America, and especially in California in the Late Quaternary geological period. Fossils of the mammoth found in the La Brea Tar Pits reached a height of thirteen feet and weighed up to ten thousand pounds. According to information about this animal in the book *Treasures of the Tar Pits,* published by the Natural History Museum of Los Angeles County, it was only distantly related to the elephant, although the physical features appear very similar. Tusks on the mammoth reached up to ten or twelve feet in length. It was a huge animal and doubtless required hundreds of pounds of grass or tree leaves daily to survive, including ten to fifteen gallons of water. The mammoth, evidently requiring more food, water, and oxygen than a changing environment could supply, became extinct, not only in California, but also in all the world. The last stand of the mammoth possibly occurred at the La Brea Tar Pits ten thousand years ago according to paleontologists, though we believe that the date would be more approximately 2000 B.C.

Dr. Joseph C. Dillow, in his book *The Waters Above*,[23] states that the remains of the mammoths "are found all over the northern tundra in both Siberia and Alaska." Also, we read from the same account: "The first mention of the mammoth is found in Chinese ceremonial books of the fourth century B.C." This would mean that as late as twenty-five hundred years ago, mammoths were still alive in some parts of the world. Dr. Dillow continued to relate from documented sources that many of the hairy mammoths in northern regions were suddenly frozen so quickly that the grasses in their stomachs and buttercups in their mouths were frozen instantly. On page 315, Dillow reports that a Chinese ambassador going through Siberia to Russia noted: "The flesh of the animal is of a very refrigerating quality, and is eaten as a remedy in fevers." There are almost innumerable accounts of people in northern regions thawing the gigantic mammoths out of the ice and either eating the meat or feeding it to the dogs.

The Horse

The skeletons of many horses were found in the La Brea Tar Pits. This was surprising, as it had been previously thought that the first horses in North America were brought to the new world by the Spanish explorers. The explanation given in the book *The Treasures of the Tar Pits* is that the species of horse found in California was the Western horse, *Equus occidentalis,* which became extinct. This horse was slightly smaller in height, four feet, ten inches tall, but stockier than the thoroughbred or the Arabian. It seems strange that the horse would have become extinct. As evidenced by today's prolific Western wild horses, this animal has an amazing ability to adapt, and it could have outrun the carnivores of the area. This causes one to question if the horses of La Brea actually did become extinct, and that perhaps some of the mustang-type horses of the Western Plains Indians did not come from this particular stock.

23. Dillow, p. 314.

The Camel

The bones of two different types of camels were found in the tar pits of La Brea. The largest species, *Camelops hesternus,* was seven feet high at the shoulder, and with a hump would have been eight feet tall or more. This camel would have been larger than the camels of Africa and the Middle East. Another species of camel that lived in the area more closely resembled those used by desert caravans for transportation of cargo. That camels once roamed the Western Plains and forests supports the continental shift theory. To suppose that the camel migrated all the way from Africa, through Siberia and then Alaska, would raise insuperable difficulties.[24]

Bison

Two species of American bison, or buffalo, roamed the La Brea region. The smaller bison evidently adjusted to the changing ecology, and its descendants multiplied into the millions across the plains of North America. The larger La Brea bison was twice the size of the regular American buffalo. It had large horns with a spread of six feet. Fossilized bones of both species have been excavated from the La Brea pits, along with the bones of musk oxen.[25]

It is interesting that although hunters killed millions of bison in the nineteenth century for their hides, and also to deprive the Native Americans of food to force them onto reservations, few if any buffalo bones remain. Animal bones are biodegradable and will vanish within a few years unless fossilized. The La Brea Tar Pits provide a unique glimpse into the past because of the preservative action of the asphalt on animal remains.

Wolves and Coyotes

The most abundant animal remains from the Rancho La Brea deposits are representatives of the dog family (*Canidae*), and one of the most common predators found in the La Brea pits was the dire wolf. It is a relative of the gray wolf and the timber wolf which are still found in many areas of

---

24. Harris and Jefferson, p. 36.
25. Ibid., p. 38.

North America.[26] Wolves were evidently more numerous and ran in much larger packs at one time. When farmers and ranchers spread across the continent, the wolf was considered a threat to livestock. They were subsequently killed by the thousands and perhaps even millions. However, the wolf and the coyote have had little trouble surviving in a changing ecology during the past several thousand years. The ability to work together in large packs and to bring down large herbivores, or catch rodents on an individual basis, has made the wolf's survival possible.

Bears

The skeletons of three species of bears were found in the La Brea Tar Pits: the grizzly, the black, and the short-face. The grizzly and the black bears are omnivorous—their diet consists of both meat and vegetation—and this probably aided in their survival. However, it is thought by some that the short-face bear's diet was restricted to meat.[27] It has long legs in proportion to the rest of its body, ran faster than its two cousins, and, when mature, could reach as much as fourteen hundred pounds. It became extinct, however, possibly because it had a more limited diet and was not able to adapt in a changing environment. However, a nationwide nature TV production telecast in 1999 reported that a hunter on an offshore Alaskan island killed a short-face bear and skinned it. When he presented the skin to a wildlife reporting station for identification and credit, it was rejected on a technicality. At times, evidence that will contradict the evolutionary model will be rejected or disputed.

In his book *In the Beginning,* Dr. Walt Brown presents a full-color picture of a plesiosaur, caught in a net by Japanese fishermen off the coast of New Zealand in 1977.[28] According to the evolutionary timetable, the plesiosaur became extinct 66 million years ago.

Evolutionists speak about the coelacanth, a fish which is supposedly a missing link. It is said to have become extinct 75 million years ago, but

---

26. Ibid., pp. 40–41.
27. Ibid., p. 42.
28. Brown, p. 171.

recent reports indicate that they are being seen with increasing frequency in the ocean from Madagascar to Indonesia. Post-doctoral research fellow Dr. Mark Erdmann was on a honeymoon in September of 1997 when his wife spotted a strange fish being brought into the fish market. They excitedly took pictures of the fish because they recognized it as a long-extinct coelacanth. "The National Geographic Society, *Nature,* and the Smithsonian Institute jumped on the bandwagon decreeing a news embargo which kept the coelacanth research community in the dark for another year." On July 30, 1998, however, a live specimen was brought to Dr. Erdmann who tried to keep the fish alive by dragging it through the water, though the attempt failed.

In July of 1999 another TV presentation showed elephants on the border of Nepal and India that predated the extinct mammoths. This would lead one to rightly conclude that extinct animals may not have disappeared at the dates published.

African Lions

The largest of the cat family in the La Brea Tar Pits was much like male lions in Africa today, except it was approximately twenty-five percent larger. The female lions were much like their African counterparts. It appears that the area now known as Southern California was not only overrun with bears, wolves, mastodons, giant sloths, and many other animals, but it was also replete with many types of huge and vicious cats—lions, pumas, bobcats, cougars, and jaguars. The skeletons of all these ferocious felines were in the pits in large numbers. Of course, that African lions were roaming over Los Angeles, as well as other animals thought native only to Africa, adds to the mystery of the La Brea Tar Pits.

Tiger Cats (Saber-toothed Tigers)

Another member of the feline family that inhabited Southern California and the surrounding regions was the saber-toothed cat, also known as the saber-toothed tiger. Indeed, it approximated the tiger in size. There are so many skeletons of this animal in the tar pits that the last time we were at the George C. Page Museum, skulls of this animal, complete with teeth, could be purchased for two hundred dollars. Other than wolves, this awesome animal lived in greater numbers in this area than any other animal. The saber-toothed tiger must have had powerful jaw muscles in order to sink its foot-long teeth into its hapless victim. With all these hungry meat-eaters roaming the western part of North America, it would seem highly unlikely that human beings could exist. Yet, the record of the La Brea Tar Pits indicates that there were people living in this region, and this we shall discuss later in the chapter.

Ground Sloth

Fossils of three species of ground sloth have been found in the La Brea Tar Pits, the largest being the *Glossotherium harlani,* which stood six feet tall and weighed thirty-five hundred pounds.[29] In outward appearance this ground sloth is similar to the small tree sloth (which may weigh only ten to twenty pounds and lives in trees). The ground sloth ate plants and fruits, and was not suited to living on land. It apparently survived for a time after the Flood by using the giant redwood trees of northern California for its habitat. However, the number of huge trees for its home became limited, and it took to living in caves. The more common larger oak, elm, and trees of similar height, would not support a two-ton sloth, so the animal adjusted and was able to survive for a time. Fossil dung of this animal is still found in caves from California to Arizona and Nevada. Although huge in size, the land sloth was slow, and being forced to live closer to the ocean as the ecology changed, it fell prey to the vicious carnivores. Many ended up in the tar pits. It is interesting that the La Brea area confirms that the giant land sloth was alive and well in Southern California at least ten thousand years ago, and probably much later, yet evolutionists give the date of extinction at more than a million years ago. This is another example of how the proponents of evolution handle millions of years like politicians handle millions of tax dollars.

There were many other types of animals which fell into the tar pits: deer, antelope, tapirs, llamas, peccaries, rats, rabbits, zebras, snakes, several

29. Harris and Jefferson, p. 29.

dozen species of birds, and many different kinds of plants. Over one hundred thousand plant fossils have been recovered from the La Brea Tar Pits, and according to the Natural History Museum of Los Angeles, "some show evidence of being transported by flood."[30]

The Woman in the La Brea Tar Pits

The remains of only one human have been found in the Rancho La Brea Tar Pits. Known as the "La Brea Woman," studies from the fossil remains indicate that she was about four feet, ten inches in height, and about twenty to twenty-five years of age when she died. Her skull was broken in several places, and the bones of the facial area were separated from the bones of the brain case. How did her skeleton get in the tar pit and what were the circumstances of her demise? One theory is that she was murdered by a severe blow to the head and her body dumped in a shallow pool. It has also been suggested that her skeletal remains were deliberately buried as some sort of a religious ritual. Certain items found around the body suggest a ritual burial.[31] Information posted at the Page Museum suggests that the woman had Native American racial features and that she had possibly given birth to one child.

Though the remains of only one human being have been found, there are dozens of human artifacts that have been discovered. Seashells are the most common and were probably brought to the area for barter. Some of the seashells were evidently designed to serve as jewelry, but some of the shells were used as scoops. Other artifacts include scrapers made of elk horn (perhaps used for scraping hides), bone and wooden hairpins, wooden spear tips, and several *manos* (handheld grinding stones). In addition, several *atlatl* (a mechanical device for throwing spears) parts were also found.[32]

Some reports date the woman in the tar pits at nine thousand years ago. Yet a report dated September 22, 2010, announced the finding of ani-

30. Ibid., p. 67.
31. Ibid., p. 24.
32. George T. Jefferson, "People and the Brea," *Terra,* Fall 1992, p. 3.

mal bones of the same species in the La Brea Tar Pits at 1.4 million years. This again demonstrates the juggling of dates and times to accommodate the evolutionary theory.

And in the Middle East . . .

On the floor of the foundation of the Byzantine church on Mount Nebo, depicted in mosaic tile, are many of the animals indigent to the area in the fourth and fifth centuries A.D. Bears and lions that were evidently in Israel and Jordan at that time became extinct in the following centuries. In the book of Job written 2000 B.C., or perhaps earlier, we find animal names that cannot be identified with any certainty. These could be references to some of the animals whose remains are in the La Brea Tar Pits, or they could even refer to dinosaurs. On the walls of the ancient Assyrian palaces, the king was exalted through the killing of savage wild beasts. Genesis 10:9 tells us that the main qualifying characteristic of Nimrod was that "he was a mighty hunter."

After the Flood, the human race was divided into three main divisions: Japhetic, Hamitic, and Semitic. It appears that the woman in the tar pit at La Brea was Native American, which would probably make her Semitic, although one cannot be sure. Nevertheless, it would seem that the ferocious animals of this area would have posed a severe threat to human life. Yet, by the grace of God, in order to protect the small and fragile human population, after the Flood "the fear of you and the dread of you shall be upon every beast of the earth . . ." (Genesis 9:2). In the jungles of Africa man has been able to survive in spite of all kinds of wild beasts. Not only does man's intelligence help him to prevail over even the most savage of predatory animals, wild animals will generally flee from people, except on rare occasions.

The fact that the bones of mammoths found in the La Brea Tar Pits are related to frozen mammoths whose flesh is still fed to dogs and the DNA is also subject to reactivation also indicates a recent historical existence and not millions of years ago, as those who believe in evolution propose.

The fact that mixed in with the bones of these animals is the skeleton of a human female and weapons of humans who lived at the same time also refutes the theory of evolution. To quote the Apostle Paul:

> For the wrath of God is revealed from heaven against all ungodliness and unrighteousness of men, who hold the truth in unrighteousness; Because that which may be known of God is manifest in them; for God hath shewed it unto them. For the invisible things of him from the creation of the world are clearly seen, being understood by the things that are made, even his eternal power and Godhead; so that they are without excuse: Because that, when they knew God, they glorified him not as God, neither were thankful; but became vain in their imaginations, and their foolish heart was darkened.
>
> —Romans 1:18–21

While the La Brea Tar Pits have yielded up many of their mysteries—and many of them confirm biblical truth—many more mysteries yet remain.

Atlantis

A Mystery Continent

With the embodiment of the history, traditions, and activities of man, there are many marginal biblical mysteries. These mysteries may be based on sketchy and questionable historical accounts, legends, and myths. While these mysteries may not relate to basic Bible doctrine, the test of their authenticity, or even peripheral validity, is how they stand up in the light of the Scriptures.

Perhaps the most noted of the marginal mysteries to intrigue mankind for the past twenty-four hundred years is the story of the Lost Continent of Atlantis. Although one author counted over twenty thousand volumes written on this subject, all rest upon the validity of the original account written by the Greek philosopher Plato (427–347 B.C.) in his dialogues *Timaeus* and *Critias.* These dialogues are the written records of philosophical debates, the favorite pastime of the intellectuals of Athens. The stated thrust of the Greek philosophers was to discover truth and its merits. And since Plato was a philosopher and not a fiction writer, many believe that he recorded this story accurately as he heard it and that they believe it to be the truth. Others believe that the story was a parable devised to emphasize his moral concepts. However, true or not, he did not use the story to emphasize its historical value or vast riches, but to morally demonstrate the result when good decays into that which is evil. If that truly were his motive, then the need to embellish the story would have been reduced.

Today, this mystery continues to consume the entire lives of some individuals, not for its moral implications, but rather for its historical value and for the thrill of the hunt. Its location is the quest of both visionary and occultist alike. Atlantis has been suggested to be located in the Atlantic Ocean, the Mediterranean Sea, and even the Indian Ocean. The Incas, Polynesians, Native Americans, Egyptians, Asians, Indians, Greeks, and Semites are included in a partial list of possible descendants. Modern scientists have narrowed the list down to either the Bahamas or the Azores in the Atlantic, or Thera (modern Santorini) and Crete in the Mediterranean Sea. Following is a brief study of Atlantis and some of the possibilities of its existence and location.

According to the story about Atlantis, there was once a large and populous continent connecting the landmasses of the old and new worlds. This huge landmass was suddenly rocked by earthquakes and volcanic action, and it sank into the ocean in a matter of hours, or days at most. The *Encyclopaedia Britannica* provides the following account:

> Atlantis, a legendary island in the Atlantic Ocean. Plato in *Timaeus* describes how Egyptian priests, in conversation with Solon, represented the island as a country larger than Asia Minor with Libya, situated just beyond the Pillars of Hercules. Beyond it lay an archipelago of lesser islands. Atlantis had been a powerful kingdom nine thousand years before the birth of Solon, and its armies had overrun the Mediterranean lands, when Athens alone had resisted. . . . It is impossible to decide how far this legend is due to Plato's invention, and how far it is based on facts of which no record remains. Mediaeval writers, receiving the tale from Arabian geographers, believed it true. . . . Even in the seventeenth and eighteenth centuries the credibility of the legend was seriously debated, and sometimes admitted, even by Montaigne, Buffon, and Voltaire.

The account in the *Encyclopaedia Britannica* continues to list the various islands and peoples where the story of Atlantis prevails, and the islands and lands that were discovered by explorers looking for the remains of the sunken continent. It appears that Plato's story about Atlantis, as told by Solon to Critias, is the basis for all subsequent theories concerning the lost continent. Plato's theme is a discussion between Socrates and Critias during the Panathenaic festival in Athens in 421 B.C. It was originally told to Socrates when he was ten years old by his great-grandfather who was ninety years old at the time. Quoted below is a brief portion of the story as given in *Timaeus*.

Listen, then, Socrates, to a story which, though strange, is entirely true as Solon, wisest of the Seven, once affirmed. . . . There were great and admirable exploits performed by our own city long ago, which have been forgotten through the lapse of time and destruction of human life. . . . In Egypt, said Critias, at the apex of the Delta, where the stream of the Nile divides, there is a province called the Saitic. . . . Solon said that, when he traveled thither. . . . There have been, and will be hereafter, many and diverse destructions of mankind, the greatest by fire and water, though other lesser ones are due to countless other causes. . . . To begin with, you people remember only one deluge, though there were many earlier; and moreover you do not know that the bravest and noblest race in the world once lived in your country. From a small remnant of their seed you and all your fellow-citizens are derived; but you know nothing of it because the survivors for many generations died leaving no word in writing. Once Solon, before the greatest of all destruction by water, which is now the city of the Athenians, was the most valiant in war. . . . Many great exploits of your city are here recorded for the admiration of all; but one surpasses the rest in greatness and valour. The records tell how great a power your city once brought to an end when it insolently advanced against all Europe and Asia, starting from the Atlantic Ocean outside. For in those days that ocean could be crossed, since there was an island in it in front of the strait which your countrymen tell me you call the Pillars of Hercules. The island was larger than Libya and Asia put together; and from its voyagers of those days could reach the other islands, and from these islands the whole of the opposite continent bounding that ocean. . . . Now on this Atlantic island there had grown up an extraordinary power under kings who ruled not only the whole island but many of the other islands and parts of the continents. . . . They were the lords of Libya so far as Egypt, and of Europe to the borders of Tyrrhenia. All this power, gathered into one, attempted at one swoop to enslave your country and all the region within the strait. Then it was, Solon, that the power of your city was made manifest to all mankind. . . . Afterward there was a time of inordinate earthquakes and floods, and there came one terrible day and night, in which all your men of war were swallowed bodily by the earth, and the island of Atlantis also sank beneath the sea and vanished. Hence to this day that outer ocean cannot be crossed or explored. . . . Now Socrates, I have given you a brief account of the story told by the old Critias as he heard it from Solon.

One will notice that in this quoted portion of Plato's story, the philosopher indicated that the fabled continent suffered a catastrophic judgment before the Great Deluge. This would indicate that the Greeks, Egyptians, and other nations of the Mediterranean accepted the Flood of Noah's day as fact. In the story, Plato also stated that before the Great Deluge there were other floods and judgments. One will have great difficulty substantiating such pre-Flood catastrophes from the Scriptures.

From the book *Ancient Astronauts—Cosmic Collisions* by William H. Stiebing, Jr., one finds a resumé of the entire Atlantis legend. Quoting in part, Stiebing says:

Critias describes how, more than nine thousand years before Solon's time (which is given for the date for the destruction of Atlantis), gods divided up the earth with Hephaestus and Athena receiving Athens as their portion. They created wise and courageous people to live there. . . . Poseidon took Atlantis as his share, dividing the island into ten parts, one for each of his sons. The largest and most fertile part of the island went to Poseidon's oldest son, Atlas, who reigned as king over his brothers who, in turn, were princes controlling large territories and populations. . . : The island contained deposits of every kind of metal. . . . There were forests to supply wood, all types of wild animals and domesticated animals (including elephants), and a variety of grains, spices, fruits, canes, vegetables, olives, and grapes. . . . The capital city was located in a large plain (about three hundred forty-five miles long and two hundred thirty miles wide) surrounded by high mountains. The mountains contained many villages which supplied enough men to field a military force of one hundred twenty thousand heavily-armed soldiers, a like number of both archers and slingers, two hundred forty thousand light-armed troops, ten thousand chariots and twelve hundred warships. Every one of the other nine sections of Atlantis had similar wealth and manpower. . . . For many generations, the kings ruled wisely and in obedience to Poseidon's laws. But as their divine strain became increasingly diluted by marriage to mortals, they grew greedy and power-hungry. When Zeus saw this, he called a council of the gods to decide how to discipline them. Here the account ends in mid-sentence as Zeus begins addressing his fellow gods.

In the story told by Plato, it is related that the inhabitants of Atlantis were the descendants of the gods mentioned in Grecian mythology. These gods were still worshipped by the Greeks in the early Christian era. On visiting Pergamos, one of the seven cities of the churches listed in Revelation, we saw the base where the temple of Zeus stood. Many believe this site is referenced in Revelation 2:13: "I know thy works, and where thou dwellest, even where Satan's seat is: and thou holdest fast my name, and hast not denied my faith, even in those days wherein Antipas was my faithful martyr, who was slain among you, where Satan dwelleth."

Plato also stated that the inhabitants of Atlantis were gradually weakened over the centuries when they married mortal women. This part of the legend somewhat coincides with Genesis 6:1–4:

And it came to pass, when men began to multiply on the face of the earth, and daughters were born unto them, That the sons of God saw the daughters of men that they were fair; and they took them wives of all which they chose. And the LORD said, My spirit shall not always strive with man, for that he also is flesh: yet his days shall be an hundred and twenty years. There were giants in the earth in those days; and also after that, when the sons of God came in unto the daughters of men, and they bare children to them, the same became mighty men which were of old, men of renown.

The footnote in the *Pilgrim Bible* reads: "The feats of these giants may well have been the basis for the ancient stories about mythical Atlas, Hercules, and many gods and goddesses." The Hebrew text clearly indicates that the sons of God were angelic beings, the angels who left their first estate to follow Satan, as described by Peter and Jude. If there were such a place as Atlantis, it is of interest to again point out that there is no scriptural reference to its destruction before the Flood. This does not mean it could not have happened; there is simply no biblical account.

There are other historians who give credence to the possibility that the names of these mythical gods or demons could be based on fact and not fiction. One of these is Edward Gibbons, who some believe to be the greatest historian outside Scripture. In *The History of the Decline and Fall of the Roman Empire* (Vol. II, pp. 89–90), Gibbons also considers the possibility that demons could be the gods of antiquity. Here he expresses the sentiments of the primitive church as he quotes Justin Martyr as saying: "It was the universal sentiment both of the Church and of heretics that the demons were the authors, the patrons, and the objects of idolatry." Gibbons then adds:

Those rebellious spirits who had been degraded from the rank of angels and cast down into the infernal pit were still permitted to roam upon earth to torment the bodies and to seduce the minds of sinful men. The demons soon discovered and abused the natural propensity of the human heart toward devotion, and artfully withdrawing the adoration of mankind from their Creator, they usurped the place and honors of the Supreme Deity. By the success of their malicious contrivances they at once gratified their own vanity and revenge, and obtained the only comfort of which they were yet susceptible—the hope of involving the human species in the participation of their guilt and misery. It was confessed, or at least it was imagined, that they had distributed among themselves the most important characters of polytheism.

He then quotes Tertullian as saying: "One demon assuming the name and attributes of Jupiter; another of Aesculapios; a third, of Venus; and a fourth, perhaps of Apollo." Based upon these assumptions, it would be plausible that these ancient gods were named after actual demons.

Ignatius Donnelly, a Republican congressman from Minnesota, wrote what is considered by wrote what avid Atlantis researchers consider the definitive work on Atlantis, titled *Atlantis: The Antediluvian World*. Donnelly lists thirteen propositions concerning the existence of Atlantis based upon his understanding of Plato's account. These are as follows:

1. That there once existed in the Atlantic Ocean, opposite the mouth of the Mediterranean Sea, a large island, which was the remnant of an Atlantic continent, and known to the ancient world as Atlantis.
2. That the description of this island given by Plato is not, as has been long supposed, fable, but veritable history.
3. That Atlantis was the region where man first rose from a state of barbarism to civilization.
4. That it became, in the course of ages, a populous and mighty nation, from whose overflowings the shores of the Gulf of Mexico, the Mississippi River, the Amazon, the Pacific coast of South America, the Mediterranean, the west coast of Europe and Africa, the Baltic, the Black Sea, and the Caspian were populated by civilized nations.
5. That it was the true antediluvian world; the Garden of Eden; the Garden of the Hesperides—where the Atlantides lived on the River Ocean in the west; the Elysian fields—grandson of Poseidon and

son of Nausithour, king of Phaeacians of the island of Scheria; the Mesomphalos—or Navel of the Earth, a name given to the Temple at Delphi, which was situated in the crater of an extinct volcano; Mount Olympus—of the Greeks; the Asgard—of the Eddas; the focus of the traditions of the ancient nations; representing a universal memory of a great land, where early mankind dwelt for ages in peace and happiness.

6. That the gods and goddess of the ancient Greeks, the Phoenicians, the Hindus, and the Scandinavians were simply the kings, queens, and heroes of Atlantis; and the acts attributed to them in mythology, a confused recollection of real historical events.

7. That the mythologies of Egypt and Peru represented the original religion of Atlantis, which was sun worship.

8. That the oldest colony formed by the Atlanteans was probably in Egypt, whose civilization was a reproduction of that of the Atlantic island.

9. That the implements of the Bronze Age of Europe were derived from Atlantis. The Atlanteans were also the first manufacturers of iron.

10. That the Phoenician alphabet, parent of all the European alphabets, was derived from an Atlantis alphabet, which was also conveyed from Atlantis to the Mayas of Central America.

11. That Atlantis was the original seat of the Aryan or Indo-European family of nations, as well as the Semitic peoples, and possibly also of the Turanian races.

12. That Atlantis perished in a terrible convulsion of nature, in which the whole island was submerged by the ocean, with nearly all its inhabitants.

13. That a few persons escaped in ships and on rafts, and carried to the nations east and west the tidings of the appalling catastrophe, which has survived to our own time in the Flood and Deluge legends of the different nations of the Old and New worlds.

He continues:

If these propositions can be proved, they will solve many problems which now perplex mankind; they will confirm in many respects the statements in the opening chapters of Genesis; they will widen the area of human history; they will explain the remarkable resemblances which exist between the ancient civilizations found upon the opposite shores of the Atlantic Ocean, in the old and new worlds.

Donnelly is not discouraged by the fact that Atlantis was considered as fable by educated skeptics. He states:

The people nearest to the past are not always those who are best informed concerning the past. For a thousand years it was believed that the legend of the buried cities of Pompeii and Herculaneum were myths: they were spoken of as "the fabulous cities."

Also, until one hundred years ago scholars believed that the existence of the cities of Troy and Mycenae was only a fictional part of Homer's epic poem *The Iliad,* and that they were based on nothing more than legend. But a German named Heinrich Schliemann (1822–90), armed with no more than *The Iliad* and his adventurous nature, proved that it was based on fact when he discovered the legendary city of Troy. Homer was born in the modern city of Izmir, Turkey, about two hundred miles south of the ruins of the city of Troy. Being almost a neighbor, he would have most certainly been privy to the information needed to write the poem. Troy is near the Aegean Sea just south of Canakkale, in western Turkey. On occasion, our tours have allowed us to visit these ruins and climb into their replica of the Trojan horse.

Today, we know that these cities were indeed not myths but were ancient accounts of real places and have been, in recent times, proven to exist. This gives new hope for those that look for Atlantis. Donnelly's point is well taken that since those cities that were thought to be myths really existed, it is also reasonable to believe that Atlantis and the kings or gods that ruled them also existed. In his proposition number five, we notice that he points out his belief that Atlantis existed as the pre-Flood world and its kings were the same as the "sons of God" in Genesis. In his proposition number six, Donnelly implies that the gods of Genesis and Atlantis are one and the same. Although we can agree that the names of demons or angels and the names of idols and Grecian gods may be the same, we cannot accept them as being identical with the "sons of God" of Genesis 6 because of the date discrepancy. However, if the names are the same, it would prove that Atlantis existed after Noah's Flood, which is more in line with accepted biblical chronology.

During the time of the Spanish exploration of the new world, the bishop of Yucatan brought back to Madrid a book of Mayan history and culture. In the book, we read the following account:

> The year six Kan, on the eleventh of Muluc, in the month of Zac, there occurred terrible earthquakes, which continued without intermission until the thirteenth of Chuen. The country of hills of mud, the "Land of Mu," was sacrificed. Being twice upheaved, it suddenly disappeared during the night, the basin being continually shaken with volcanic forces. Being confined, these caused the land to sink and rise several times and in various places. At last the surface gave way, and the ten countries were torn asunder and scattered in fragments; unable to withstand the force of seismic convulsions, they sank with their sixty-four million inhabitants, eight thousand and sixty years before the writing of this book.

The account of the destruction of the land of Mu by the Mayan historian, and that of the demise of Atlantis by Plato, correspond in almost every detail. Both legends agree that the continent, or large island, was destroyed by volcanic action. Both agree that this land was divided into ten nations, and they also agree that it happened approximately 9000 B.C. Both accounts agree with the Scriptures that before the Flood all mass was connected, but there is a discrepancy with the Bible as to the time the Earth was separated into continents and divided by oceans. According to

Genesis 10:25, the division of the landmass occurred about 2200 B.C., not 10,000 B.C. Science now accepts as fact that all the land was on one continent. It was broken up and floated apart, and the continents and islands can be pieced together like a jigsaw puzzle. The difference in the biblical record, the Atlantis legend, and modern science, is the time factor.

It is obvious that when the Earth broke up there were tremendous earthquakes and catastrophic volcanic action. We read that it was at this time that the Babel builders attempted to erect a tower that would reach into heaven and thus escape from these severe calamities, which they must have thought would kill everyone in the world.

Now we read in the Mayan records that in the destruction of the continent of Mu, which probably was the same as Atlantis, that 64 million people died. One wonders why such a figure was chosen, when at the time of the Mayan civilization there was probably not over 10 million souls on the entire planet, and the Mayans could have known of only a few hundred thousand at most. It is obvious they could have gotten these statistics only from an ancient source. And, according to the Bible, before the Flood man increased over the face of the Earth. With Earth's citizens living to almost a thousand years of age, over a thousand-year span, the population could have easily reached 3 to 4 billion. As far as the date given by Plato and the Mayans for the destruction of Atlantis, there seems to be a consensus among scientists that a major catastrophe did occur about ten thousand years ago. Again, if such is the case, then either Ussher's chronology is off by several thousand years, or this calamity occurred in a previous civilization, and the creation in Genesis 1:1–2 is a second generation. This second generation theory is one to which many Bible scholars subscribe.

Another possible explanation for Atlantis is the eruption that occurred at Thera about 1450 B.C. In the previous one hundred years, several eruptions had occurred on this beautiful island chain. Finally, the big one came, and it left nothing of Thera (or modern Santorini) but a huge crater in the ocean and an outer ring totaling about fifteen square miles. To sail into Santorini and into the huge crater and look up at the cliffs caused by the explosion is an awesome sight. To the south of Santorini is the island of Crete, settled by the Minoans at about the time Abraham was at Ur, 2000 B.C. By 1500 B.C. the Minoan civilization had reached its peak. The capital city, Knossos, was by far above any other of the time. The palace alone had hundreds of rooms, complete with planned air circulation that kept the temperature cool. The bathrooms and restrooms were complete with tile plumbing as well as hot and cold running water. But a catastrophe also struck Minoa and the capital city, Knossos. It is suggested by some that the tremors and tidal wave from the Santorini eruption resulted in thousands of deaths on Crete and caused such havoc that Minoa never recovered.

Those believing Atlantis is located in the Atlantic because of Plato's description may be relying on false information. Some modern translators now believe that Plato's words, "the island was larger than Libya and Asia put together," would be better translated "between Libya and Asia." This would make Santorini the prime location, for it is between Libya and Asia on the southern tip of Greece. This would also mean that either the Pillars of Hercules are not the Straits of Gibraltar, that Plato misunderstood the directions, or that he added this for clarification and was himself mistaken. Therefore, the Azores and Bahamas are for the most part no longer considered a viable location for one reason or another. In 1956, Greek seismologist Angelos Galanopoulos proposed that Atlantis was located north of Crete on what was the island of Thera in 1450 B.C., today's Santorini. Another translation error may solve the problems of size and date.

> Galanopoulos offered a fascinating bit of mathematical speculation in support of his contention that Thera was Atlantis. Plato had described the dimensions of an Atlantean plain as three hundred forty by two hundred thirty miles, an area larger than all of Greece. And he placed the time of its destruction at nine thousand years before the rise of Athens—an impossibly early date for such an advanced civilization. Since the legend had come from the Egyptians, Galanopoulos suspected a translation error. He found that dividing Plato's dimensions by ten yielded an area the size of Thera. Similarly, if nine thousand years was

read as nine hundred, the annihilation of Atlantis as related by Plato coincided almost precisely with the time of Thera's eruption.

—Time-Life: *Planet Earth,* 1982

Another reason some believe that Galanopoulos may be on the right track is the belief considered by some that the volcanic eruption of Thera may coincide and have actually contributed to the plagues of Egypt (1447 B.C.) that led to the Exodus of the Hebrews. One of the plagues was darkness that could be felt: "And Moses stretched forth his hand toward heaven; and there was a thick darkness in all the land of Egypt three days" (Exodus 10:22). Both took place within the same time frame. Most translators believe that the word translated "thick" actually means that the darkness could be felt. Therefore, some believe that this could actually mean that this darkness was a result of ash spewed out of an enormous volcanic eruption such as the one described in the story of Atlantis.

In his book *The Long Day of Joshua,* Donald W. Patten attributes many of the accounts of biblical catastrophes to volcanic action as a result of the nearness of the fly-bys of the planet Mars. These ancient near-misses happened when Mars, within its cyclical orbit, would pass near or through the Earth-moon system. According to Patten, these ancient cycles happened every fifty-four years. Near fly-bys include: the Noachian Flood about 2500 B.C.; the destruction of Sodom and Gomorrah in 1877 B.C.; the Exodus catastrophe in 1447 B.C.; the long day of Joshua in 1404 B.C.; the greater Davidic catastrophe in 972 B.C.; the Joel-Amos catastrophe in 756 B.C.; and the Isaiahic catastrophe in 701 B.C. Although much scientific evidence is given for all the above, we are only concerned with the Exodus catastrophe here.

Of Atlantis and the Exodus, Patten writes:

The Thera-Atlantis disaster cannot be understood fully without its correlation to ancient cosmology and the fly-by of Mars in March 1447 B.C., a fly-by which we estimate was perilously close. In the broadest panorama of thought, the Atlantis-Exodus-Thera scene is best understood in terms of the cyclic nature of catastrophes of that millennium, and of the entire area from 250 B.C. to 701 B.C. The Atlantis-Exodus-Thera event is to be understood in the same cosmic context as is the Long Day of Joshua, or the Isaiahic Catastrophe, or the Tower of Babel Catastrophe.

Although Patten contends that all the plagues of the Exodus are a natural result of the volcanic explosion of Thera, we are not particularly interested in just one here, the *darkness* that could be felt. Patten reasons that the *darkness* was a result of the volcanic ash thrust into the air at Thera. There are many examples of volcanic explosions written in historical records. One such is the description of the Krakatoa explosion as he quotes J.V. Luce:

> A pall of darkness spread rapidly outward as the great central column of dust and vapour began to descend. By 10:30 a.m. it had become so dark in Lampong Bay that the Gouverneur-General Loudon had to anchor. An hour later complete darkness had spread to Batavia 160 km. [100 miles] away, and a heavy dust-rain went on till 3 p.m. Eventually the darkness extended to Bandung nearly 240 km. [150 miles distant and 2,400 feet above sea level] east of Krakatoa.
>
> —pg. 244

In comparing Thera to Krakatoa, a smaller model, Patten quotes James W. Mavor:

> The caldera of Thera has a surface area of thirty-two square miles and is some thirteen hundred feet deep, with a volume about five times that of the Krakatoa caldera. Based on the volume of collapsed land, a Hungarian scientist, P. Hedervaris, has estimated that the heat energy released during the Thera eruption must have been four and one-half times that of Krakatoa. The total energy unleashed during the Krakatoa eruption has been estimated as four hundred thirty times more powerful than the explosion of an Eniwetok H-bomb.
>
> —p. 245

If these calculations are correct, it would mean that the explosive force of Thera was five times greater than Krakatoa. Some scientists believe that an explosive force of an estimated five hundred to one thousand atomic bombs which created waves of three hundred feet or higher could be responsible for the sudden disappearance of the ancient Minoan civilization in Crete. It would seem reasonable, based on a comparison of the size and scope of these two explosions, for the volcanic ash from Thera to have reached Egypt at the time of the Exodus. Whether this was the case or not, we do know that God uses natural forces to accomplish His plan and purpose.

After the final battle of Atlantis, in the last paragraph of *Timaeus,* Plato records these curious words:

> But afterward there occurred violent earthquakes and floods, and in a single day and night of rain all your warlike men in a body sank into the earth, and the island of Atlantis in like manner disappeared beneath the sea. And that is the reason why the sea in those parts is impassible and impenetrable, because there is such a quantity of shallow mud in the way; and this was caused by the subsidence of the island.

In other words, the remains of most of the island had turned into mud. It could be that it being shallow, the mud was just under the surface of the water, or that a thin layer of mud was floating on top of the water. The extent of the dispersal of ashes and volcanic rock from Thera was carried as far as 435 miles to the southeast over more than 100,000 square miles. Oceanographers have found these sediments as far as 87 miles from the volcano at a depth of 9,850 feet in a layer approximately seven feet thick. One report of another like explosion says that the floating ashes made it impassable for boats. This could possibly be the shallow mud reported by Plato (*The World's Last Mysteries,* Reader's Digest, 1978).

It is not an uncommon belief that the remains of Santorini and the other islands that made up the kingdom of Thera were actually the Atlantis that Plato spoke about. Perched high on the almost perpendicular cliffs of Santorini is the capital, Thera. Upon disembarking from the ship and ascending over a thousand feet by mule, we entered this beautiful and charming little city. One of the first buildings that caught our eye was the Hotel Atlantis. It is a common belief by the people on the island that Santorini was the center of the fabled island kingdom of Atlantis. However, as stated before, the volcanic holocaust that occurred at ancient Thera does not agree with Plato and others concerning the demise of Atlantis in size, date, and population. In fact, there has been to this date no marine geological explorations or archaeological evidence of the sudden destruction of a continent the size of Plato's Atlantis. Some recent marine geological explorations have taken place at Santorini which have produced exciting artifacts that suggest that it is the location of Atlantis. However, the Greek government continues to refuse permission for a full exploration. Maybe in the future this location may provide the real answer concerning the existence and location of this great marginal mystery.

Although it is possible that the story told by Plato in the fourth or fifth century B.C. may be based on a fictional account and the name Atlantis may be a figment of his imagination, underwater cities do exist. When these cities were consumed by the oceans is pure conjecture in most cases. However, the quest for the site of Atlantis was the catalyst that has led to the discovery of many ancient underground formations, and the list of discoveries continues to grow.

In January of 2011, marine scientists in India discovered an underwater city 120 feet under water in the Gulf of Cambay. It carbon dated from about 7,500 B.C., pre-dating the Genesis account over 1,500 years. In the Caribbean Sea off the coast of Alexandria, the ruins of what is believed to be the quarters of Cleopatra have been found. They believe it to be a result of an earthquake over 1,500 years ago. More recently a Thai temple was discovered in Lake Phayao that has been submerged some 500 years. Another is the find by a scientist who discovered what is called megalithic ruins in the Yucatan Channel near Cuba. Several years ago a tremendous discovery near Japan revealed mysterious pyramids and foundational processes thought unavailable in ancient Japan.

According to an aolnews.com report from March 13, 2011, Richard Freund, a University of Hartford professor, believes he and his research team have found the legendary island-city. Using satellite photography, ground-penetrating radar, and underwater technology, he said his team pinpointed the city in a vast marsh in southern Spain that dries out one month a year. The search began in 2008 with a space satellite photograph showing what looked to be a submerged city in Spain's Doña Ana Park. The discovery was clinched with the later find of "standing stones" and a series of memorial cities in central Spain built in the image of Atlantis. Freund believes the memorial sites are significant because refugees from the lost city would have built smaller-scale versions in tribute. A Spanish scientist led him to ancient sites surrounded by concentric moats—and a museum featuring standing stones with a symbol similar to Plato's drawing of Atlantis. More excavations are planned at the Spanish site, but Freund said his current findings would not put an end to the debate.

These discoveries beg the question, when were they built and who lived in them? Is it possible that these cities—including Atlantis—were built prior to Noah's Flood and were destroyed because of the Flood? Could Plato's story have been repeated down through the millennia, beginning with Noah and his family when they came off the ark? The Bible verifies the fact that there were cities built before the Flood. For example, Genesis 4:17 tells of a city built by Cain after his expulsion, "And Cain knew his wife; and she conceived, and bare Enoch: and he builded a city, and called the name of the city, after the name of his son, Enoch." That city and its occupants were buried with water because of the Flood and could be submerged and still exist today. Could Atlantis be one of those cities?

Aristotle, famous student of Plato, doubted that there ever was an Atlantis, while Crantor, a noted contemporary, believed the story. Other ancient historians, such as Judaeus, Tertullian, and Marcellinus, also agreed with Crantor. Others who disputed its existence were Origen, Amelius, and Longimus. Pliny and Plutarch simply considered the evidence without expressing an opinion. And on down through history, from the time of Plato and Socrates, historians, explorers, geologists, and others have debated among themselves on this matter—some have believed Atlantis a fact, while others have concluded it was only myth. As far as biblical truth is concerned, some scriptures appear to support its existence, while others appear to preclude the possibility of such a place in time or space. In any event, Atlantis is one of those marginal mysteries that may never be fully explained or understood, at least in this present age.

The Mystery of the Bermuda Triangle

Does the Devil Stir These Waters?

Down through the corridors of human history, the sea has been regarded with both fear and awe. Nothing can be more frightening than to be on the high seas in a storm, when huge waves and high winds threaten even the largest of ships. On the other hand, the depth of the waters and the fact that they hide what is unseen, coupled with their incessant restlessness, evidenced in the perpetual motion of the ocean, are characteristics of the sea that have moved both poet and bard. The Bible adds another dimension, however. It gives us God's perspective on the sea and shows how Divine revelation unveils both the mysteries of God and the mysteries of the natural world.

What kinds of statements are found in the Bible concerning the sea? Job 26:5 seems simple enough: "Dead things are formed from under the waters, and the inhabitants thereof." Some may suggest that statements such as this are just the opinion of man and reflect views conditioned by ancient culture; yet we must not forget that verse seven speaks about the Lord hanging the Earth on nothing, and is often used to show how the Bible is compatible with discoveries of modern science. It is far better to regard scriptural statements about the sea as true and factual, indicating something the Lord would have us to believe for our own spiritual betterment.

There is much about the sea in the Bible. It has been used by God as an instrument of judgment (Jonah 1:4). In the Tribulation God will vent His fury on the sea and destroy a good source of the Earth's bounty (Revelation 16:3). Isaiah seems to equate the destruction of Leviathan "in that day" with a future eschatological victory: "In that day the LORD with his sore and great and strong sword shall punish leviathan the piercing serpent, even leviathan that crooked serpent; and he shall slay the dragon that is in the sea" (Isaiah 27:1).

Many have perished at sea—both in the past and in the present—but the day is coming when the sea will give up her dead (Revelation 20:13). The Apostle John goes on to state: "And I saw a new heaven and a new earth: for the first heaven and the first earth were passed away; and there was no more sea" (Revelation 21:1).

Christopher Columbus and Sea Lights

Columbus and his crew were on the *Santa Maria* sailing through an area that is now known as "the Bermuda Triangle" when they saw a strange sight. On October 11, 1492, about two hours after sunset, they saw lights so bright and real that the crew thought that they were approaching some large city on the shore of some distant continent. It was no city, however, and the lights shortly disappeared.

Earlier that year—on September 15, 1492—Columbus and his crew observed a huge bolt of fire streak across the heavens. A few days later the early explorers were also filled with dread as something affected the ship's compass so that it behaved in a very erratic manner. Interestingly, the astronauts above *Apollo 12* noted that there were "luminous streaks or flumes in the water as the last lights visible to them from the earth."[1] Biblical references to the sea monster Leviathan make mention of strange fires and lights, as we see from the following scriptural quotations:

By his neesings [sneezings] a light doth shine, and his eyes are like the

---

1. Charles Berlitz, *The Bermuda Triangle: An Incredible Saga of Unexplained Disappearances* (Garden City, NY: Doubleday and Co., 1974), p. 62.

eyelids of the morning. Out of his mouth go burning lamps, and sparks of fire leap out. Out of his nostrils goeth smoke, as out of a seething pot or caldron. . . . He maketh the deep to boil like a pot: he maketh the sea like a pot of ointment.

—Job 41:18–20, 31

Praise the LORD from the earth, ye dragons, and all deeps: Fire, and hail; snow, and vapours; stormy wind fulfilling his word.

—Psalms 148:7–8

When the Triangle Became Famous

The Bermuda Triangle received national acclaim on December 5, 1945, when five Navy Avenger torpedo bombers mysteriously vanished, along with a Mariner rescue plane that went out to look for the Avengers—a total of six aircraft and twenty-seven men. World War II had been over for some three months. This was a routine training mission. No one knew how unusual a flight it would be.[2]

The pilots were studying advanced navigational methods and low-level bombing techniques. Each aircraft carried enough fuel to enable it to cruise for five and a half hours, even though the anticipated time in the air was just two hours. The short, stubby planes started taking off at two in the afternoon. Ten minutes later all five planes were aloft and were flying east over the Atlantic. After target practice, they began their navigational exercises. Their course would take them east 160 miles, north 40 miles, then west-southwest and back to their base in Fort Lauderdale.

Around 3:15 p.m. the radio operator at the Fort Lauderdale Naval Air Station received what seemed to be an unusual communication from Lt. C. C. Taylor, commander of the four other pilots and pilot of his own plane. He announced that his compasses were not reading properly. He transmitted this message: "This is an emergency. We seem to be off course. We cannot see land. . . . Repeat. . . . We cannot see land."

The tower responded by asking Lt. Taylor for his position. Taylor re-

2. www.parascope.com

plied: "We are not sure of our position. We cannot be sure just where we are. . . . We seem to be lost. . . ."

Assuming that the planes were over the Atlantic, the tower gave Taylor instructions to assume a bearing due west. Taylor's response was startling: "We don't know which way is west. Everything is wrong. . . . Strange. . . . We can't be sure of any direction—even the ocean doesn't look as it should."

The tower operators were surprised, as the weather was balmy with clear skies. Surface winds were twenty knots (about twenty-three miles per hour) with gusts up to thirty knots, but this should not have been a problem for the Avengers, which were sturdily built and equipped with powerful engines.

Evidently, Taylor and his pilots were becoming more alarmed at their inability to know precisely where they were—a frightening situation in which to be, especially when flying over the ocean and not being able to see any clearly discernible landmarks.

Taylor spoke with the tower again. This time he sounded frantic: "Both my compasses are out. . . ." In spite of the increasing static, the operators felt sure that Taylor had said something about being over the Florida Keys. At about 4:45 p.m. Taylor announced that somehow the flight had gotten lost and they were flying over the Gulf of Mexico, far off course. At about that time a storm front hit the area, bringing forty-knot winds, wind-driven sheets of rain, and twelve- to fourteen-foot waves whose crests were whipped into a foam by the driving wind and rain. At 6:02 p.m. one of the Avengers announced, "We may have to ditch any minute."[3]

Some feel that there is really no mystery here and that there is sufficient data to give a logical explanation to the Avenger tragedy. They have asserted that the patrol leader, Lt. Taylor, was suffering from a hangover and was flying simply because he could not pass off this flight duty to someone else. It is argued that Taylor was having compass problems, but

---

3. Norman Gaffron, *The Bermuda Triangle: Opposing Viewpoints* (San Diego: Greenhaven Press, 1995), pp. 10–13.

chose to fly by dead reckoning. He thought the islands below were the Florida Keys and, since he lived in the Keys, felt confident that he could guide his flight home even without the compass. However, the storm decreased visibility and Taylor lost his way. Thinking that they were over the Gulf of Mexico, Taylor led the flight east—toward what he thought was the Florida mainland. In reality, they were over the Atlantic. Taylor's miscalculation caused him and his trainees to head out to the open ocean.

A search party was dispatched which included a huge Martin Mariner with capabilities for landing on the sea. It, too, disappeared and has been listed as a casualty of the same mysterious forces that did despair to the Avengers. This has been challenged. While it is true that the Mariner never returned to base, it was probably because of an explosion on board. Martin Mariners were equipped to stay aloft for twenty-four hours and had a huge supply of fuel on board. They were known as "flying gas tanks." The plane, however, was notorious for gasoline seepage and fumes. It was common for pilots to search for crew members before each flight to make sure no one had any matches or cigarette lighters. The Mariner had such a notorious reputation that they were grounded after the Mariner that was sent to "rescue" Flight 19 disappeared.[4]

On May 27, 1991, both *Newsweek* and *TIME* magazines announced that the lost patrol, also known as Flight 19, may have been found just ten miles off the coast of Florida by a research vessel. It was forty-six years after their disappearance. Many were jubilant. Perhaps the sea was at last yielding its lost squadron and the "mystery" would be explained to everyone's satisfaction. The *Deep See,* a sixty-foot research and exploration vessel, had lowered their underwater camera and saw what was thought to be the image of one of the Navy Avengers. The aircraft had star roundels on the wings, and the distinctive rear gun turret marked it as the type of plane lost nearly half a century before. Other planes were found. One bore the marking "FT," which was the designation for the Fort Lauderdale base. Another plane had the number "28" on it, which was the number of Lt. Taylor's plane. The nation waited to see what the verdict would be. While

4. www.history.navy.mil

everyone waited, a legal battle developed between the owners of the *Deep See* and the United States Navy. Who had legal rights to the wreckage?

No matter how the legal battle turned out, everyone expected a positive identification, but on June 17, 1991, *TIME* followed up on its story. One of the writers announced that "in a surprise about-face last week, high-tech salvagers who found the Avengers announced they were not the lost squadron after all. They appeared to be five separate aircraft that had crashed within one mile of each other on individual training mission."[5]

Some Other Strange Occurrences

The disappearance of the Avengers is by no means the only occurrence of such strange and seemingly unexplainable happenings. Though space and time do not allow us to present every case, we have selected a few that we feel might create a better understanding of the Bermuda Triangle phenomena.

The Mary Celeste

In 1892 the Mary Celeste was found abandoned on the high seas about four hundred miles off its intended course on its voyage from New York to Genoa. Though the crew of ten was missing, it is quite possible that they had, for some reason, abandoned ship since the ship's only lifeboat was missing. Why did the ship's crew abandon ship? Was there some kind of infectious disease on board? Had the crew gone insane? Were they facing a storm that they felt the ship could not survive? This is a view that has been offered, but it seems illogical. If a ship couldn't make it through the storm, how could a mere lifeboat? When sailors from the rescue ship *Dei Gratia* boarded the ship they found that three barrels of its crude alcohol had burst open. Had the captain ordered everyone into the lifeboat fearing some kind of a sudden explosion? And yet debunkers point out that whatever the reason, the "mystery" of the Mary Celeste cannot be called

---

5. Gaffron, p. 94.

a Bermuda Triangle "mystery" because the ship was off the coast of Portugal, several thousand miles from the Triangle.[6]

The USS Cyclops *and the* USS Scorpion

New information regarding the loss of the *Cyclops* and the nuclear submarine *Scorpion* has raised questions about whether or not these are Bermuda Triangle "mysteries." The *Cyclops* disappeared in March of 1918, but the captain was rather eccentric and was reportedly fond of pacing the quarterdeck wearing a hat, twirling a cane, and dressed only in his underwear. Prior to the ship's disappearance there had been a small mutiny which was put down by the captain, and which raises a good possibility that something other than the mysterious tentacles of a giant octopus—as had been reported—had caused the ship to disappear.

Regarding the disappearance of the *Scorpion,* that too cannot be considered a Triangle "mystery." It was found by oceanographic ship *Mizar* about four hundred miles southwest of the Azores, nowhere near the Bermuda Triangle.[7]

The SS Marine Sulphur Queen

In February of 1963 the *SS Marine Sulphur Queen* disappeared without a trace, along with thirty-nine people who were on board while traveling from Beaumont, Texas, to Norfolk, Virginia. The tanker was last heard from on February 3 when she routinely radioed her position, which was in the Florida Straits near Key West. Three days later the Coast Guard found a solitary life jacket in a calm sea forty miles southwest of the tanker's last known position. Was this a mystery or is there some logical explanation?

Howard L. Rosenberg, writing for the Navy Historical Center,[8] offers a credible explanation. For one thing, the disappearance of thirty-nine men may be explained by the fact that the waters are infested with bar-

---

6. www.parascope.com. See also Colin Wilson, *The Unexplained Mysteries of the Universe* (New York: DK Publishing, 1997), p. 25.

7. www.history.navy.mil

8. Ibid.

racuda and sharks. As for the tanker itself, it was carrying a highly volatile cargo—fifteen thousand long tons of *molten sulphur* kept in four metal tanks heated to 275 degrees Fahrenheit by a network of coils connected to the two boilers. No one can be sure if the ship exploded, but that is a distinct possibility. "If gas escaped from the tanks and poisoned the crew, the radio officer may not have had time to send a distress call before being overcome. The slightest spark could have set the leaking sulphur afire in an instant." Perhaps significantly, the officers on a banana boat bearing a Honduran flag reported to the Coast Guard "that their freighter ran into a 'strong odor' fifteen miles off Cape San Antonio, the western tip of Cuba, just before dawn on February 3. The odor was acrid." Of further significance is that T-2 class tankers, to which category the *Sulphur Queen* belonged, had a record of splitting in half.

The Wild Goose

Several years ago, the 65-foot boat *Wild Goose* was be towed by the 104-foot *Caicos Trader.* The weather was clear. Captain Talley, skipper of the *Wild Goose,* was asleep in his bunk below deck. Suddenly, Talley was awakened by a flood of water washing over him with great force. Talley instinctively grabbed a life jacket and struggled through an open porthole. He encountered a line and pulled himself to the surface of the ocean, later reckoned to be a distance of 50 to 80 feet. Apparently, the *Wild Goose* had been pulled under the surface by some sudden, unexplained force.

When Talley bobbed to the surface, the *Caicos Trader* was continuing to sail away without Talley. He later found out that the sudden force that had pulled the *Wild Goose* under the surface was also threatening to capsize the *Caicos Trader* because of the connecting towline. The crew of the *Caicos Trader* severed the towline in a desperate act of self-preservation. About half an hour later *Caicos Trader* returned to the area and rescued Talley.[9]

Several later incidents have occurred:

---

9. Berlitz, pp. 66–67.

» October 1976—*Sylvia L. Ossa*, a 590-foot vessel operated under Panamanian registry, disappeared approximately 140 miles west of Bermuda with a crew of 37.

» August 1991—An American Airlines airbus makes an emergency landing in Bermuda after an air pocket sent the aircraft plunging 1,000 feet. About 30 passengers were injured.

» March 1993—*Charley's Crab*, a 40-foot ketch, disappeared in 30-foot seas with winds of 70 miles per hour between the Bahamas and Florida. This was later called "the storm of the century."

» November 1994—On another American Airlines airbus more than 40 people were injured, six seriously, when the aircraft ran into unexpected turbulence over the Caribbean. The turbulence was in clear air and was not created by a storm.

» June 1995—On Continental Airlines Flight 207 twenty-two passengers were injured when the aircraft was battered by clear air turbulence. The plane was on a flight to Puerto Rico.

» October 1996—*Intrepid,* a 65-foot yacht, goes missing thirty miles off Fort Pierce, Florida, after issuing a quick distress call.

» April 1999—*Miss Fernandina,* an 85-foot shrimp trawler, and her four-member crew disappeared off the Florida coast in the area of Port Canaveral.

» June 1999—A Cessna 210 disappeared from radar three miles north of Great Harbor Cay, in the Bahamas. There were two people aboard. The aircraft had six life jackets.

» July 1999—Continental Airlines Flight 800, a Boeing 737, was forced to make an emergency landing in Bermuda due to severe turbulence over the Atlantic

» March 2001—Comair Flight 5054, an aircraft with 25 passengers on board, rolled from side to side and dived steeply after the crew reported a buildup of ice on the aircraft. The plane was flying at 18,000 feet when ice covered the plane's windshield.[10]

---

10. www.byerly.org/bt5.htm

Some Facts About the Triangle

There are some unusual features relative to the Bermuda Triangle that no one doubts. It is, for example, one of the few areas on Earth where the magnetic compass points to true north instead of magnetic north. This phenomenon produces what is known as "compass variation." "The amount of variation changes by as much as twenty degrees as one circumnavigates the Earth," which could get a navigator into deep trouble if proper allowances in navigation are not made. Furthermore, an area called the "Devil's Sea" by Japanese and Filipino seamen is located off the east coast of Japan. It exhibits the same magnetic characteristics as the "Devil's Triangle," which is another name for the Bermuda Triangle.[11]

The Bermuda Triangle is located in a larger area of the Atlantic known as the Sargasso Sea. Aristotle (384–322 B.C.) was the first individual known to investigate the strange phenomena associated with the breeding of eels. They were known to leave their ponds, lakes, streams, and small rivers that empty into the sea, but where do they go from there? Do they head for the Triangle?

In later years, Danish scientist Dr. Johannes Schmidt has shed much light on this question. It is now known that eels swim on into the Atlantic where they join millions of other eels to swim *westward* for some four months until they reach the Sargasso Sea where they spawn at considerable depths. There the adult eels die, but the newly-born eels start their long trip back to Europe, which takes about two years. The pattern of North American eels is similar, except they swim *eastward* into the Sargasso Sea. Both North American and European eels spawn in the same area, yet they somehow know enough to return to their ancestral homes. Newly-born European eels swim to Europe and newly-born North American eels swim to North America. This remarkable behavior of eels to be able to find their ancestral place of origin (*nostophylia*) has given rise to some interesting theories. One that keeps cropping up is the theory that the eels' original spawning ground was an ancient river that once flowed through

---

11. www.history.navy.mil

a continent that is now thousands of feet under the sea. Some who hold this theory even maintain that the Sargassum—the weeks of the Sargasso Sea—are actually evolved underwater remnants of the vegetation of a vanished Atlantic continent that sank with great rapidity. Such is highly theoretical and speculative, but it is a fact that eels spawn in the Sargasso Sea.[12]

The Area's Unique Environmental Features

Is there a mysterious place where ships and planes are swallowed up by the sea? Even the debunkers would say "yes"—provided that the area of the Bermuda Triangle is described as a place where ships and planes can be suddenly and unexpectedly overcome by "the forces of nature."

Many scientists are willing to state that the disappearances and other unusual occurrences are most likely resulting from natural reasons. The United States Coast Guard, for example, states in one of its official documents: "The majority of disappearances can be attributed to the area's unique environmental features. These include raging storms, strong currents, waterspouts, and mysterious forces yet to be understood."[13] What are some of these mysterious forces?

Hurricanes

These storms rage in this area between June and September. Hurricanes usually form when the sun is directly overhead and the surface of the sea is warm. Water evaporates rapidly from a warm patch of ocean, causing the moisture-laden air to rise. Cooler, denser air swirls in to replace the rising air, but this cool air is warmed and also rises. Often when this process begins, a spiral is created that can grow to monumental proportions, leading to the birth of a full-blown hurricane.

A small hurricane can grow rather rapidly and can virtually escape detection because of the speed with which they are sometimes formed. Satellites cannot detect small, violent tropical storms if they are too small, or if they occur while the satellite is not over that area. "There is a twelve-

---

12. Berlitz, p. 63.
13. Gaffron, p. 32.

hour gap between the time the satellite passes over a specific part of the globe until it passes again," observes Howard L. Rosenberg. "During these twelve hours, any number of brief, violent storms could occur."[14]

Balls of Fire

Hurricanes produce a tremendous amount of energy, but many of the Triangle vanishings have occurred in generally clear weather. However, there is a phenomenon that can catch mariners and aviators by surprise, and that is "ball lightning." It is a self-contained bright light that is usually round, but sometimes is pear-shaped at the edges and appears in a variety of colors. It bounces and moves erratically and may scorch the objects with which it comes in contact.

Another unusual phenomenon is a brilliant electrical discharge known as "St. Elmo's fire." It looks like a flame and sometimes is seen on the prominent parts of a ship, such as the top of the mast. It can create a terrifying experience but appears to be harmless. However, we must observe that the accounts of the mysterious losses in the Triangle do not seem to describe any unusual phenomena of this nature. Many of the accounts begin with the words "the sky was clear and blue, and the sea was calm," indicating that there were no spectacular warnings that something unusual was about to happen.

Deep Water Eddies

Most of us have seen tiny whirlpools in small streams and along the curb of a city street during and after a summer downpour. But ocean whirlpools, known as "eddies," are much more powerful and can suck a small ship underwater. Scientists know that such eddies occur on or near the ocean's surface, but other eddies occur at various depths beneath the surface.

Waterspouts

While eddies are whirlpools in the sea, a waterspout is a whirlpool in

---

14. www.history.navy.mil

the air above the sea. Known as "wet tornadoes," waterspouts are rapidly rotating air funnels filled with mist and water. The winds in the vortices of waterspouts can reach up to one hundred miles per hour—certainly nowhere near as powerful as a land-based tornado—and can devastate a small ship or plane.

Gas Leaks

Deposits of gas are trapped beneath the bottom of the sea, and some researchers believe that gas leaks may be a possible explanation for the Bermuda Triangle mystery. Some have suggested that violent plumes of gas escaping at high pressure from natural gas pools under the sea floor may pose a threat to ships and planes. "Enormous pressures and low temperatures at the sea bottom shape water and gas molecules into gas hydrates, unique structures that resemble ice."[15] Supposedly, if the domelike seal over an undersea reservoir of gas were ruptured by seismic activity, offshore drilling, or a sudden rise in temperature, an enormous volume of gas could escape. As the gas neared the surface, it would dissipate into smaller and smaller bubbles. Ships sailing in gaseous frothy seas lighter than the surrounding water might suddenly lose their buoyancy and sink. Low-flying aircraft flying into a "gas bubble" could experience engine failure or be in the midst of an actual explosion as the highly flammable bubble of gas enveloped it.

Magnetic Irregularities

A magnetic field surrounds the Earth, but the strength of the field is not constant, shows varieties and changes, and differs in intensity at different points of the Earth's surface. The Earth itself is a giant magnet, and the source of the Earth's magnetism can be thought of as "a giant bar magnet at the core of the planet."[16] The ends of the magnet are located approximately at the north and south poles, but the magnetic poles of the Earth are not perfectly aligned with the geographical poles, nor do the

15. Gaffron, pp. 46–47.
16. Ibid., p. 51.

geographical poles control the compasses used on ships and planes. It is for this reason that compass needles point to magnetic and not true north.

Compass irregularities are problems that occur when a marine or aviation compass does not behave in a normal manner. Such irregularities have been reported in the Triangle area. Charles Lindbergh, the first pilot to make a solo nonstop flight across the Atlantic, flew over the ocean southeast of Florida one year after his historic flight. On this later flight in 1928 Lindbergh noted that both of his compasses malfunctioned and could not be trusted.[17]

Suggested Solutions

Not everyone believes that the mystery of the Bermuda Triangle is a mystery. Triangle debunker Larry Kusche, in his book *The Bermuda Triangle Mystery Solved,* tells the following story in making his point.

In 1975 National Airlines Flight 120 was flying from Fort Lauderdale in a northerly direction at thirty-three thousand feet when one engine suddenly quit. Shortly after that another engine quit, and then the third did likewise. Totally without power, but still one hundred miles from the coast, which was to the west, the plane was surely doomed. Hoping for the best, the pilot turned the plane toward the west, put the plane in a glide, and watched the plane slowly descend. Then, suddenly and mysteriously, the engines, one by one, started up. The pilot landed in Jacksonville without a mishap. But perhaps an even bigger mystery was that the airliner was carefully examined to find out what caused the malfunction, but all of the equipment was found to be in perfect condition!

One of the well-known writers of that time speculated that it had something to do with the "mysterious forces of the Bermuda Triangle." He said that the engines restarted when the plane left the affected area.

A few weeks later, however, a "logical explanation" for the "mystery"

---

17. Ibid., pp. 51–52.

was announced. The plane had several fuel tanks spread throughout the wing area. The flight engineer is responsible to regularly switch the tanks from which the engines draw fuel in order to keep fuel weight evenly distributed. However, when switching to a new tank it is necessary to turn on a booster pump to get the fuel flow started. The engineer had forgotten to turn on the pump and had inadvertently "killed" the first engine. When he panicked, he "killed" the remaining two engines in the same way. After a short while, the engineer realized what he had done and got the pumps going again. The engines restarted, and the plane flew safely to Jacksonville. Kusche concludes by stating: "Let's suppose now that the airline had not had so much altitude when the engines died, that the plane had crashed, and that the crew had perished. The real answer might never have been learned, and the 'mysterious Triangle' would have claimed another victim."[18]

A number of interesting, and perhaps bizarre, explanations have been offered. Some have even suggested that clairvoyants be brought in. Kusche believes that none of that is necessary.\

> My research, which began as an attempt to find as much information as possible about the Bermuda Triangle, had an unexpected result. After examining all the evidence I have reached the following conclusion: *There is no theory that solves the mystery.* It is no more logical to try to find a common cause for all the disappearances in the Triangle than, for example, to try to find one cause for all automobile accidents in Arizona. By abandoning the search for an overall theory and investigating each incident independently, the mystery began to unravel.[19]

Kusche argues that there is a rational explanation for all the strange happenings that supposedly occurred in the Bermuda Triangle. Those mishaps that remain unsolved "are those for which no information can be

---

18. Larry Kusche, *The Bermuda Triangle Mystery Solved* (Amherst, NY: Prometheus Books, 1995), pp. x–xi.

19. Ibid., p. 275.

found."[20] There have been "mysterious" disappearances of ships and planes all over the world, and not just in the Bermuda Triangle, argues Kusche. Many mishaps that were claimed to have occurred in the Bermuda Triangle actually occurred many miles outside the Triangle area, as was true in the case of the nuclear submarine *Scorpion.* Either the oceans of the entire world are in some manner "cursed" or the waters of the Bermuda Triangle are no different from ocean waters elsewhere, argues Kusche.[21]

As is true with any unusual phenomenon, there will be debunkers. However, in 2003 Gian Quasar published a book entitled *Into the Bermuda Triangle: Pursuing the Truth Behind the World's Greatest Mystery.* The back cover states: "Still unsolved, still baffling, still claiming new victims. The author debunks 'debunkery' and focuses his attention, in particular on the 1975 reprint of Larry Kusche's *The Bermuda Triangle Mystery—Solved.*"

What Are We To Think?

Debunkers are quick to point out that whenever man is unable to explain the forces of nature or the events of the natural world, it has been characteristic to resort to mythological explanations. Some tragedy, disaster, or natural calamity is explained as being caused by the gods, demons, monsters, and, more recently, by extraterrestrial invaders. No doubt, this is true. A pre-scientific people often resort to pre-scientific explanations, and such explanations are often religious. Unexplainable and terrifying phenomena are traced to the world of "the gods." However, while this is a valid observation, it shouldn't be pushed too far. Such argumentation could very well explain away biblical miracles, demonic spirits, and the very existence of God.

Atheists, materialists, and communist leaders have tried to explain the biblical faith in psychological terms. Because religion is allegedly "the opiate of the people," belief in God is no more valid than a chemically-induced experience. While we must appreciate careful investigation of Bermuda Triangle phenomena, UFOs, and other "mysteries," it is wise to

---

20. Ibid.
21. Ibid., p. 276.

keep an open mind, knowing that there may be more involved than can be explained rationally.

Some writers, such as Johnson and Tanner, connect the Bermuda Triangle with "the gates of hell." They notice from the Bible that Jesus spoke of "the gates of hell" (Matthew 16:18) and that Isaiah 38:10 speaks of "the gates of the grave." Does this imply some kind of an entrance to and egress from the nether world? Understandably this may sound farfetched, but it is interesting that if we were to bore a hole in the vicinity of the Triangle and went straight into the Earth, we would emerge in the area of the Devil's Sea in the Far East. "Could the disturbances in the Bermuda Triangle and the Devil's Sea have some connection with the entrances to the biblical Sheol–Hades?" ask Johnson and Tanner. "Are its gates being bombarded by internal and external spiritual forces, releasing tremendous physical forces in nature?"[22]

Though it is easy to become entangled in wild flights of fancy, one cannot ignore the language of the Bible in that it speaks of "the depths" as being the entrance to the nether world. In Luke 8:31 it is recorded that the demons asked our Lord "that he would not command them to go out into the deep," literally "the abyss," the domain of evil spirits. Revelation 9:1 adds to our understanding of the scriptural teaching on this point: "And the fifth angel sounded, and I saw a star fall from heaven unto the earth: and to *him* was given the key of the bottomless pit," literally "the pit of the abyss." Henry M. Morris makes a relevant comment:

> Since Hades is also revealed to be a great pit in the heart of the earth, it is probable that the pit of the abyss is either the same as Hades or at least connected directly with it. It seems clear that there are a number of different prisons in Hades. Tartarus, where the twice-fallen angels are confined, is one of these. Before the cross, the spirits of the lost and the spirits of the saved were separated by "a great gulf" (Luke 16:26). The "pit of the abyss" is possibly still another compartment of Hades,

---

22. George Johnson and Don Tanner, *The Bible and the Bermuda Triangle* (Plainfield, NJ: Logos, 1976), p. 91.

in which have been stored a horde of fearsome creatures waiting to be unleashed. The legion of demons allowed by Christ to enter the herd of swine had urged Him not to send them into the abyss (Luke 8:31). Possibly these demonic beings could even be the fallen angels of Genesis 6 and Jude 6, bitterly resenting their confinement and chafing to take vengeance on men, whom they regard as proximate causes of their unhappy circumstances.[23]

Also interesting in this regard are the passages that speak of the place of the departed as being under the seas, or being connected in some way with the seas. The word *tehom* ("the deep") occurs more than thirty-five times in the Old Testament and is pictured as the entranceway to the realm of the spirits. "Hast thou entered into the springs of the sea? or hast thou walked in the search of the depth? Have *the gates of death* been opened unto thee? or hast thou seen the doors of the shadow of death?" (Job 38:16–17). *Sheol* is even presented in the Bible in parallel with the sea, as in Amos 9:2–3: "Though they dig into hell [*sheol*], thence shall mine hand take them; . . . and though they be hid from my sight *in the bottom of the sea,* thence will I command the serpent, and he shall bite them."

In the Bible, the depths of the sea are interesting places with interesting creatures. "Praise the LORD from the earth" we read in Psalm 148:7, "ye dragons [sea monsters], and all deeps." The depths are not impersonal, but are personified and call to one another: "Deep calleth unto deep at the noise of thy waterspouts . . ." (Psalms 42:7).

---

23. Henry M. Morris, *The Revelation Record* (Wheaton, IL: Tyndale, 1993), p. 156.

Biblical Giants

Hybrid Monsters, or Monstrous Hype?

There are a number of imponderables in the first ten chapters of Genesis over which theologians have debated: When was the beginning of Genesis 1:1? Was there a gap between Genesis 1:1 and Genesis 1:2? Were the days of creation ages, or were they literal twenty-four–hour days? Whom did Cain marry? Was the antediluvian Flood a regional or a worldwide judgment?

There are many other questions presented in the first few chapters of Genesis that could be added to the above list, but perhaps one of the areas of frequent disagreement among Bible scholars has to do with the identity of the sons of God in Genesis 6. Who are "the sons of God"? Genesis 6:1–4 relates the following:

> And it came to pass, when men began to multiply on the face of the earth, and daughters were born unto them, That the sons of God saw the daughters of men that they were fair; and they took them wives of all which they chose. And the LORD said, My spirit shall not always strive with man, for that he also is flesh: yet his days shall be an hundred and twenty years. There were *giants* in the earth in those days; and also after that, when the sons of God came in unto the daughters of men, and they bare children to them, the same became mighty men which were of old, men of renown.

Several views have emerged regarding the meaning and interpretation of this passage. In this section, we shall present these views and representative arguments.

First of all, there is the view of antiquity. For example, **the ancient Greek translations of the Old Testament,** completed by the fourth century A.D. and known as the Septuagint, reads: "... *the angels of God* saw the daughters of men ..." (Genesis 6:2).

The first century A.D. **Jewish historian Josephus** wrote:

> Many angels of God accompanied with women, and begat sons that proved unjust, and despisers of all that was good, on account of their own strength....These men did what resembled the acts of those whom the Grecians called giants.... There was till then left the race of giants, who had bodies so large, and countenances so entirely different from other men, that they were surprising to the sight, and terrible to the hearing. The bones of these men are still shown to this day.[1]

In commenting on Genesis 6:2, the **Ante-Nicene Fathers** wrote that the angels fell "into impure love of virgins, and were subjugated by the flesh.... Of these lovers of virgins therefore, were begotten those who are called giants."[2]

Justin Martyr, who lived between A.D. 110 and 165, commented on the conditions before the Flood as based on a portion of the Septuagint: "... the angels transgressed and were captivated by love of women and begat children."[3]

Methodius, who lived between A.D. 260 and 312, said: "The devil was insolent ... as also those [angels] who were enamored of fleshly charms, and had illicit intercourse with the daughters of men."[4]

Martin Luther, and other contemporary ministers of the Reforma-

---

1. Josephus, *Antiquities of the Jews,* Book I, chapter 3; Book V, chapter 2.
2. *The Ante-Nicene Fathers,* Volume II, p. 90; Volume VII, pp. 85, 273.
3. Justin Martyr, Volume II, p. 190.
4. Methodius, Volume VI, p. 370.

tion Era, also taught that the Scriptures clearly indicated that before the Flood, the angels who left their created order committed fornication with women and produced a race of giants.

The fact that there was at one time a race of giants on the Earth is without controversy. Josephus wrote that some of the bones of the ancient giants were still in evidence in his day, or about A.D. 80. Josephus was commissioned by the Roman government to write the history of the Jews; therefore, he would not have recorded that something was in evidence in his day if it could not be substantiated. Also, the footprints of giants eighteen to twenty-two inches long can be found in the rock bed of the Paluxy River near Glen Rose, Texas. So much for the view of antiquity.

Secondly, there is the view of modernity, which is that "the sons of God" were men from the godly line of Seth and the "daughters of men" were from the line of Cain. This is based on the reasoning of Bible commentators, rather than on the Word of God.

Matthew Henry's *Commentary* interprets Genesis 6:2 in the following way: "The sons of Seth (that is the professors of religion) married the daughters of men, that is, those that were profane, and strangers to God and godliness. The posterity of Seth did not keep by themselves, as they ought to have done, they intermingled themselves with the excommunicated race of Cain."

This, of course, is simply the conclusion of Matthew Henry. Nowhere in the Bible does it even infer that the "sons of God" were men from the line of Seth or that the "daughters of men" were women from the line of Cain. All were destroyed in the Flood with the exception of Noah and his household—both the lineage of Seth and the lineage of Cain were judged equally by God.

The footnote in the *Scofield Bible* on Genesis 6, perhaps more than any other commentary, has promoted the understanding that the "sons of God" were men from the line of Seth. Dr. Scofield was, without doubt, an excellent scholar, and the King James Version of the Bible with the Scofield footnotes has been used of God, but only the scriptural text in the Bible is inerrant. Dr. Scofield was fallible, just like everyone else. The Scofield footnote on Genesis 6:2 says:

> Some hold that these "sons of God" were the "angels which kept not their first estate" (Jude 6). It is asserted that the title is in the Old Testament exclusively used of angels. But this is an error (see Isaiah 43:6). Angels are spoken of in a sexless way. No female angels are mentioned in Scripture, and we are expressly told that marriage is unknown among angels (Matthew 22:30). The uniform Hebrew and Christian interpretation has been that verse two marks the breaking down of the separation between the godly line of Seth and the godless line of Cain.

We believe that the footnote in the *Scofield Bible* contains three statements that are open to serious question.

First, the statement that the title "sons of God" used within the context of the Old Testament has reference to both men and angels is highly questionable. The reference given is Isaiah 43:6, which reads: "I will say to the north, Give up; and to the south, Keep not back: bring my sons from far, and my daughters from the ends of the earth." This scripture is a prophecy. It looks forward to the time when the Messiah comes, Israel looks upon the One whom they have pierced, and they believe in Jesus Christ as Lord and Savior. Then the remnant of Israel will be called "the sons of God," just as Christians are today sons of God by adoption through the New Birth.

Second, the statement that angels are spoken of in a sexless way in the Bible is debatable. Angels are often called men in the Scriptures. The reason they are called men is because they have male characteristics. The reason the men of Sodom shunned Lot's daughters to get at the angels is because they were masculine specimens. The reference given by Dr. Scofield is Matthew 22:30: ". . . in the resurrection they neither marry, nor are given in marriage, but are as the *angels of God in heaven.*" Jesus was speaking here of the angels of God in Heaven who had not followed Satan, and who had not left their first estate, or created order (Jude 6). No one that we know of has medically examined an angel, and until this is done, we believe we must accept the biblical description of angels in the masculine gender. It is rather obvious that the angels of God in Heaven do not marry because there are no female angels.

Dake's Annotated Reference Bible has an interesting observation on this point:

> There are two classes of fallen angels—those with Satan who will be cast down to earth during the future tribulation (Revelation 12:7–12), and those who are now bound in hell for committing fornication (2 Peter 2:4; Jude 6–7). Had the ones in hell not committed the additional sin of fornication, they would still be loose, with the others, to help Satan in the future. Their present confinement proves they committed a sin besides that of original rebellion with Satan. That it was a sex sin is clear from Second Peter 2:4 and Jude 6–7, which fact identifies the class of fallen angel as the sons of God of Genesis 6:4.

Third, the statement in the Scofield footnote that the uniform Hebrew and Christian interpretation has always been that "the sons of God" in Genesis 6:2 were the descendants of Seth does not hold up in light of the research that we have done. In fact, we could not find a single reference before the fifth century that presented the explanation offered in the *Scofield Bible*. Besides the sources we have previously given, Philo, the Talmud, and many other ancient sources indicate the belief that the "sons of God" of Genesis 6 were angels. We must at least give Josephus, and others, the credit for knowing their own language.

We would consider that the Scofield edition of the Bible is a good one. We would probably agree with ninety-five percent of the footnotes. But we feel that the explanation of Genesis 6:2 was a forced matter, for the same men who worked on the *Scofield Bible* also wrote the footnotes for the *Pilgrim Bible,* and the primary explanation in the *Pilgrim Bible* is that the "sons of God" were fallen angels. This brings us to the all-important question: **Who are the "sons of God"?**

A "son of God" is a direct creation of God. Adam was created a son of God, because God made him. The first man had no human father. We read in Luke 3:38: ". . . Adam, which was the son of God." But in the genealogy of the human race, there is no son of God mentioned between Adam and Jesus Christ. We read in 1 John 3:9: "Whosoever is born of God doth not commit sin; for his seed remaineth in him: and he cannot sin, because he is born of God." Adam was created by God, and Adam sinned. The angels were created by God and many of them sinned. The virgin Mary was enabled to conceive by the Holy Spirit, and Jesus Christ was born of God.

After Adam sinned, all men were born in sin, and no man between Adam and Jesus Christ could claim a son relationship with God. Therefore, all references in the Old Testament to "sons of God," except two or three scriptures where the redemption of Israel is prophesied when the Messiah comes, refer to angels. We read in Job 1:6: "Now there was a day when the sons of God came to present themselves before the LORD, and Satan came also among them." It is obvious that the meaning here is the angelic host. The angels are also called "the sons of God" in Job 38:7. Besides the reference in Isaiah 43:6 that we have already noted, the one other place in the Old Testament where the phrase "sons of the living God" is found is Hosea 1:10: "Yet the number of the children of Israel shall be as the sand of the sea, . . . and it shall come to pass, that in the place where it was said unto them, Ye are not my people, there it shall be said unto them, Ye are the sons of the living God." This reference again is prophetic, looking forward to the regathering of Israel after they have been born again by receiving Jesus Christ as their Redeemer at the beginning of the Messianic Age (Romans 11:25–26).

The restoration of fallen man to a sonship relation with God was first given to Israel, but because Israel as a nation rejected the promised Redeemer, the invitation was extended to the gentiles. We read in John 1:11–12: "He came unto his own, and his own received him not. But as many as received him, to them gave he power to become the sons of God, even to them that believe on his name." As explained in the third chapter of the Gospel of John, through faith in Jesus Christ who died for the sins of all men, anyone can become a son of God through the New Birth. It is through the New Birth that a believer in Jesus Christ is constituted a new creation (2 Corinthians 5:17).

The words of the beloved apostle in 1 John 3:1–2 were a revelation that was first proclaimed by Jesus Christ, later preached by the Apostle Paul, and then by John: "Behold, what manner of love the Father hath bestowed upon us, that we should be called the sons of God: therefore the world knoweth us not, because it knew him not. Beloved, now are we the sons of God, and it doth not yet appear what we shall be: but we know that, when he shall appear, we shall be like him; for we shall see him as he is."

If the "sons of God" mentioned in Genesis 6:2 were men, why did Jesus Christ have to die on the cross? If salvation could come by conscience, by law, or by good works of men, then as we read in Galatians 2:21, Christ died in vain. But as Jesus Himself said, now anyone, regardless of his sins, can by faith in Him as the One who died for sin, receive a New Birth and become a son of God. This invitation is to "whosoever believeth" (John 3:16).

The Giants of Old and Mythical Deities

Not only does context and word usage indicate that the "sons of God" were angels who left their created order, but this evidence is substantiated by archaeology and the writings of the Greeks. This conclusion is not only supported by Josephus, but the very words of the Hebrew text and the Septuagint indicate this to be the correct interpretation. We submit, for substantiation purposes, the interpretations of two recognized authorities.

The Pilgrim Bible footnote reads:

It is thought by many scholars that these "sons of God" were fallen angels who fell with Satan. These scholars say: 1) The phrase "sons of God" in the Bible always stands for being directly created by God, as Adam, angels, or born-again believers in Christ (these last according to 2 Corinthians 5:17 and John 1:13). The only beings at the time of Genesis 6 directly created by God were angels. 2) Here the phrase "sons of God" is in contrast to the phrase "daughters of men." 3) The Hebrew word translated "giants" means fallen ones. Jude 6 may refer to them.

Clarence Larkin says:

If the sons of Seth and the daughters of Cain were meant, why did not Moses, who wrote the Pentateuch, say so? It is not sufficient to say that the men of Moses' time knew what he meant. The Scriptures are supposed to mean what they say. . . . Four names are used in Genesis 6:1–4. "Bne-Ha-Elohim," rendered "sons of God"; "Benoth-Ha-Ad-am," "daughters of men"; "Hans-Nephilim," "giants"; "Hog-Gibborim," "mighty men." The title "Bne-Ha-Elohim," "sons of God," has not the same meaning in the Old Testament that it has in the New. In the New Testament it applies to those who have become the "sons of God" by the New Birth (John 1:12; Romans 8:14–16; Galatians 4:6; 1 John 3:1–2). In the Old Testament it applies exclusively to the angels, and is so used five times. Twice in Genesis (6:2–4), and three times in Job, where Satan, an angelic being, is classed with the "sons of God" (Job 1:6; 2:1; 38:7). A "son of God" denotes a being brought into existence by a creative act of God. Such were the angels, and such was Adam, and he is so called in Luke 3:38. Adam's natural descendants are not the special creation of God. Adam was created in the "likeness of God" (Genesis 5:1), but his descendants were born in his likeness, for we read in Genesis 5:3 that Adam "begat a son *in his own likeness, after his image."* Therefore all men born of Adam and his descendants by natural generation are the *"sons of men,"* and it is only by being *"born again"* (John 3:3–7), which is a *"new creation,"* that they can become the *"sons of God"* in the New Testament sense. That the "sons of God" of Genesis 6:1–4 were *angels* was main-tained by the Jewish synagogue, by Hellenistic Jews at, and before, the time of Christ, and by the Christian church until the fourth century.[5]

---

5. Clarence Larkin, *The Spirit World,* p. 26.

In Genesis 6:4 Moses shows the result of the union of the "sons of God" with the "daughters of men"—"There were giants in the earth in those days; and also after that, when the sons of God came in unto the daughters of men, and they bare children to them, the same became mighty men which were of old. . . ."

Men of Renown

Those who hold to the viewpoint that the "sons of God" were the sons of Seth have yet to explain how children born to believers and unbelievers produced men of renown, or men of great reputation, any more than children born to marriages where both are believers, or where both are unbelievers. The footnote in the *Pilgrim Bible* gives the following explanation: "MIGHTY MEN. The feats of these giants may well have been the basis for the ancient stories about mythical Atlas, Hercules, and many gods and goddesses."

Josephus wrote in *Antiquities of the Jews,* Book I, chapter 3: ". . . Many angels of God accompanied with women, and begat sons that proved unjust and despisers of all that was good, on account of the confidence they had in their own strength, for the tradition is that these men did what resembled the acts of those whom the Grecians called giants."

Dake's Annotated Reference Bible states:

> The revelation we have of giants, in Scripture, gives us a true picture of what Greek mythology tries in vain to give. Ours is an accurate account because Divinely inspired. Mythology is the outgrowth of traditions, memories, and legends telling of the acts of the supernatural fathers and the offspring—the perversions and corruptions in transmission of actual facts concerning these mighty beings. The fact that giants were partly of supernatural origin made it easy for men to regard them as gods.[6]

Most historians agree that mythology is based on ancient traditions that have at least a historical base. The hideous creatures and gods worshipped

6. *Dake's Annotated Reference Bible,* p. 62.

by the Greeks could have had their beginning in the "men of renown" mentioned in Genesis 6:4.

One of the questions that theologians have wrestled with is why God chose one man, Noah, out of the millions that were on Earth at the time of the Flood to be saved. We read that Noah was "perfect in his generations" (Genesis 6:9), yet he needed the grace of God to be saved.

In What Sense Was Noah "Perfect"?

The Bible is plain that Noah was a just man who found favor with God in an age of worldwide moral corruption. However, we do not believe the inspired text indicates that he was "perfect" in the sense of being sinless.

The Companion Bible has the following footnote to Genesis 6:9:

> The Hebrew word *tamin* means "without blemish," and is the technical word for bodily and physical perfection, and not moral perfection. Hence it is used of animals and of sacrificial purity. It is rendered "without blemish" in Exodus 12:5; 29:1; Leviticus 1:3 (and a host of scriptures too numerous to mention). . . . This shows that Genesis 6:9 does not speak of Noah's moral perfection, but tells us that he . . . alone had preserved their pedigree and kept it pure, in spite of prevailing corruption brought on by fallen angels.

It seems conclusive that Noah's bloodline had remained free from the genetic contamination that had been brought about by the fallen angels, and that physically he was without blemish in the midst of a corrupted human race. This was evidently a massive attempt by Satan to corrupt mankind and prevent the coming of the promised Seed of the woman who would bruise his head (Genesis 3:15; Romans 16:20).

We read of the judgment of God upon the corrupted generation in Genesis 6:12–13: "And God looked upon the earth, and, behold, it was corrupt; for all *flesh* had corrupted his way upon the earth. And God said unto Noah, The end of all *flesh* is come before me; for the earth is filled with violence through *them;* and, behold, I will destroy them with the earth."

The subject of these two verses of scripture is "flesh," which would require a singular pronoun as the object. However, the pronoun "them" is plural, and would refer to a plural noun. The plural noun, as evidence would seem to indicate, is the giants, or men of renown, mentioned in the fourth verse. "All flesh," meaning the entire human race, was corrupted through "them," meaning the giants, with the exception of Noah. We do not believe this to be forcing the meaning at all when the scope of the downfall of the antediluvian civilization is read within a single context, as it should be studied.

Giants After the Flood

The Scriptures declare that this same profane condition occurred after the Flood, as we note in Genesis 6:4: "There were giants in the earth in those days; *and also after that,* when the sons of God came in unto the daughters of men. . . ."

Concerning the next appearance of giants on the Earth, after the Flood, we quote from the *Companion Bible,* Appendix 25:

> . . . We read of Nephilim (fallen ones) again in Numbers 13:33, "there we saw the Nephilim, the sons of Anak, which come of the Nephilim." How, it may be asked, could this be, if they were destroyed in the Flood? The answer is contained in Genesis 6:4. . . . So after that, meaning after the Flood, there was a second eruption of these fallen angels, evidently small in number and more limited in area, for they were for the most part confined to Canaan, and were in fact known as "the nations of Canaan." It was for the destruction of these that the sword of Israel was necessary, as the Flood had been before. As to the date of this second eruption, it was evidently soon after it became known that the Seed was to come through Abraham; for when he came out from Haran (Genesis 12:6) and entered Canaan, the significant fact is stated: "The Canaanite was then in the land." And in Genesis 14:5 they were already as

"Rephaims" and "Emims," and had established themselves at Ashtoroth Karnaim and Shaveh Kiriathaim....As Rephaim they were well known, and are often mentioned; but, unfortunately, instead of this, their proper name ...it is variously translated as "dead,""deceased," or "giants."These "Rephaim" are to have no resurrection.This fact is stated in Isaiah 26:14 (where the proper name is rendered "deceased" and verse 19, where it is rendered "the dead").... It is certain that the second eruption took place before Genesis 14, for there the Rephaim were mixed up with five nations or people, which included Sodom and Gomorrah.

The commentary notes in *Dake's Annotated Bible* agree with those in the *Companion Bible* that the Hebrew Bible indicates quite plainly that the "giants" or offspring of the union between fallen angels and women on Earth have no resurrection.There are other reliable sources that could also be quoted.This is why some Bible authorities present the possibility that demons are the spirits of the "giants" that perished in the Flood, and afterward in Canaan.That there were giants afterward in Canaan is obvious from the report of the spies of Israel who complained that the inhabitants of the land made them look like grasshoppers (Numbers 13:28, 33).

The Anakim were a people great and tall in body (Deuteronomy 1:28).The land of Ammon was a land of giants (Deuteronomy 2:19–20). The valley of the giants is mentioned in Joshua 15:8 and 18:16.And these giants in several scriptures are also referred to as the "fallen ones" in the Hebrew text. In Genesis 6, Moses wrote that there were giants in the world before the Flood, the result of the union of the "sons of God" (or "angels" as stated in the Septuagint) and women. If, as some believe, these giants were the result of the daughters of Cain marrying the sons of Seth, where did the giants of Canaan come from? Moses said the same conditions produced both races of giants, and it would be difficult to prove, to say the least, that there were any righteous men or women in the land of Canaan. In fact, God would not have destroyed Sodom, Gomorrah, and the surrounding cities if there had been ten righteous people in the entire land.

The Pattern of Angelic Fornication

In Noah's Day

In *Antiquities of the Jews,* Book I, chapter 3, Josephus declares that for seven generations Seth, his sons, and his grandsons regarded the Name of the Lord, but from the seventh generation a moral decay ensued, and men began to blaspheme the Name of God and worship other gods. It was in this falling away and iniquity that many angels who rebelled against God were able to infiltrate the human race and begin abominable relationships with women.

Most ancient Jewish commentators inform us that they began to worship "their own gods," suggesting they called the stars and idols their gods, and worshipped them. Paul wrote of the antediluvians: "Professing themselves to be wise, they became fools, And changed the glory of the uncorruptible God into an image made like to corruptible man, and to birds, and fourfooted beasts, and creeping things" (Romans 1:22–23). Forsaking the fact of true astronomy—in which "the Gospel is written in the stars"—they instituted astrology with its idolatrous system of false gods.

Another hallmark of Noah's day was homosexuality, as Paul brings out in Romans 1:26–27: "... even their women did change the natural use into that which is against nature: And likewise also the men, leaving the natural use of the woman, burned in their lust one toward another. . . ." These immoral and abominable conditions drew these wicked angels like slop draws flies.

The Canaanite Corruption

God destroyed Sodom, Gomorrah, and the cities thereabouts for the same reason that He destroyed the antediluvians in the Flood—apostasy and sexual abominations. Then, over four hundred years later, when the descendants of Abraham through Isaac returned, the Canaanites were worshipping false gods, committing every type of filthiness of the flesh, and evidently were having sexual associations again with fallen angels, because giants filled the land. God used Israel as His agent to destroy the Canaanites lest all human flesh become again corrupted through them.

The Last Days

Jesus said in Matthew 24:37: "But as the days of Noe were, so shall also the coming of the Son of man be." The spiritual state of the world in general does parallel the work of Noah. Before the rise of Antichrist, we read in 2 Thessalonians 2:7 that the mystery of iniquity will sweep the world. In 2 Timothy 3:1–5, the last days are prophetically marked with divorce, juvenile delinquency, crime, and homosexuality. Also, as it was in the days of Noah, Satanism, and astrology are very much in evidence. Within the setting of the wicked abominations that would come upon the Earth in the last days, Paul wrote in 1 Timothy 4:1: "Now the Spirit speaketh expressly, that in the latter times some shall depart from the faith, giving heed to seducing spirits, and doctrines of devils." The Scriptures contain many verses concerning angelic invasion during the Tribulation, a period that will be climaxed with the casting down of all the angels of the devil to the Earth (Revelation 12:7–12), and we read this warning in verse 12: "...Woe to the inhabiters of the earth and of the sea!...."

There is an old saying: "Coming events cast their shadows before." The pattern of past spiritual conditions on Earth that resulted in the satanic corruption of mankind indicates the world is again on the threshold of a like abomination, and even this is prophesied in Scripture. But Christians who are alert and grounded in the Bible need have no fear, because we are comforted and strengthened by the promise in Ephesians 6:10–13:

> Finally, my brethren, be strong in the Lord, and in the power of his might. Put on the whole armour of God, that ye may be able to stand against the wiles of the devil. For we wrestle not against flesh and blood, but against principalities, against powers, against the rulers of the darkness of this world, against spiritual wickedness in high places. Wherefore take unto you the whole armour of God, that ye may be able to withstand in the evil day, and having done all, to stand.

Supporting Evidence

We have already given several quotations from ancient sources, as well as from modern students of the Word. But in view of the fact that many good Christians consider our interpretation of Genesis 6:1–4 to be bizarre, farfetched, and outlandish, we believe that it is only right that we devote this section to quotes from a large number of the best Bible students on this subject. These individuals are highly respected in the best Christian circles, and their judgment should be properly evaluated. We believe it is of great importance to recognize the angelic invasion before the Flood as we now face the demonic explosion for the end times.

Two New Testament Passages

For if God spared not the angels that sinned, but cast them down to hell, and delivered them into chains of darkness, to be reserved unto judgment; And spared not the old world, but saved Noah the eighth person, a preacher of righteousness, bringing in the flood upon the world of the ungodly.

—2 Peter 2:4–5

And the angels which kept not their first estate, but left their own habitation, he hath reserved in everlasting chains under darkness unto the judgment of the great day. Even as Sodom and Gomorrha, and the cities about them in like manner, giving themselves over to fornication, and going after strange flesh, are set forth for an example, suffering the vengeance of eternal fire.

—Jude 6–7

Arno C. Gaebelein, in *Gaebelein's Concise Commentary on the Whole Bible,* says:

The question is who are the sons of God who took the daughters of men. . . . "Sons of God" is the term applied in the Old Testament to supernatural beings, both good and evil. Angels good and fallen are termed sons of God in the Old Testament. Satan himself is reckoned among the sons of God in Job 1:6 and 2:1. The term sons of God must mean here supernatural evil beings. These evil beings came down out of the air and began to take possession of the daughters of men as they chose.

William Kelly, in *Lectures Introductory to the Old Testament,* relates:

The true key to this account is supplied in the Epistles to Jude. It is hardly so commonplace and ordinary a matter as many suppose. When understood, it is really awful in itself and its results. But the Holy Spirit has veiled such a fact in the only manner that became God and was proper for man. . . . "The sons of God," in my judgment, mean the same beings in Genesis as they do in Job. This point will suffice to indicate their chief guilt in thus traversing the boundaries which God had appointed for His creatures. No wonder that total ruin speedily ensues. It is really the basis of fact for not a few tales of mythology which men have made up. Anyone who is acquainted with the chief writings of the old idolatrous world, of the Greeks and Romans especially, will see that what God has veiled in this brief statement, which passes calmly over that of which more had better not be spoken, is what they have amplified into the Titans and the giants and their greater deities. I do not of course enter into details, but here is the inspired account, which shines in the midst of the horrors of that dark scene which fabulists portrayed. But there is enough in man's amplification to point to what is stated here in a few simple words of truth.

W. R. Newell says in *Studies in the Pentateuch:*

There is no possible explanation of these verses except the fact of an invasion of human beings, by beings of another order (. . . who were, alas, fallen angels that "kept not their own principality, but left their proper habitation"). . . . The warning of these verses is needed in these days, when . . . spiritualism or "spiritism," with its hidden communion with fallen spirits, demons, is gaining ground on every hand. . . . The condition of things in verse 1–4 exists today. . . . The author met, many years ago, a woman who claimed to be married to a spirit. She refused, with contempt, marriage to a *human being!* . . . Genesis 6 is startling. . . . The Flood is coming: wickedness has ripened. The terrible leaven of sin has worked in both lines of the race. . . .

C. A. Coates, in *An Outline of the Book of Genesis,* states:

There is a somewhat corresponding state now, but it will be developed to its full height in a coming day. . . . Men became associated with spiritual powers greater than themselves. . . . The result was a terrible state of things. . . . What happened before the Flood was a foreshadowing of that outbreak of spiritual wickedness which will give character to the apostasy of the last days. Men will get an unnatural, or perhaps one might say a supernatural, greatness in the days of apostasy. The beast and the antichrist will be indeed men of renown, heroes in man's eyes. But I believe the source of their power will be outside man; wicked spirits who have been in the heavenlies—fallen angels—will endow them with their wonderful powers. It is terrible to think of this combination between two distinct orders of fallen beings—an order superior to man joining with man in apostasy, and giving man powers that he would never have had naturally. We know that even now there is a spiritual power of wickedness in the heavenlies; wicked spirits—real beings— who are the source of influences opposed to God and to Christ, and against which saints are now called upon to wage holy warfare. But in a coming day under supernatural influence men will be lifted up against God in a way the thought of which might well fill us with terror. And I think we can see the beginnings of this kind of thing even now. Men are already talking about the superman, and they are coming more and more under the power of supernatural beings. There is a great deal of evil commerce today with the unseen world. Superstitious religions are coming in from the east. . . . And the result will be that men will appear on earth who will be "men of renown" energized by Satan; they will be heroes in man's eye, and people will give themselves up to hero worship.

It will be a state of things which will necessitate the intervention of God in judgment; it cannot be allowed to continue any more than the antediluvian state of things could be suffered to continue.

It is of interest to note that this profound statement by Mr. Coates was made over ninety years ago in 1919.

James M. Gray, in *Spiritism and the Fallen Angels,* says:

We find that "sons of God" is used everywhere in the Old Testament to designate angels, and why should it not be so used here? Moreover if it were so used, it would carry with it a confounding of two distinct orders of creatures and the production of a mixed race, partly human, partly superhuman, which would be just such a derangement of the Divine plan as to warrant that which occurred, namely, the almost total extermination of all who were upon the earth.... This was the prevailing view of the passage in the ancient synagogue of the Jews and among Christian theologians for the first three or four centuries of the Church.... The "sons of God" who took to themselves wives of the "daughters of men," were evil angels, who entered upon that intercourse the offsprings of which were the "Nephilim," "the fallen ones," the mighty heroes of antiquity. These in their turn, presumably, furnished the ground for the stories of the loves of the gods and demigods of classic lore.

John Milton, the famous poet, in his earlier book *Paradise Lost,* took the position that the "sons of God" were of the line of Seth. But upon more mature reflection, he reversed this position. The following quatrain from *Paradise Regained, Book II,* will reveal that he saw fallen angels in the Genesis 6 passage:

Before the flood, thou with thy lusty crew,
False titled sons of God, roaming the earth,
Cast wanton eyes on the daughters of men,
And coupled with them, and begot a race.

F. C. Jennings points out in *Satan,* that "the sons of God" in Job are, beyond any serious question, angels. Then, he states:

> Genesis 6:2 is no exception; there may be physiological difficulties; but we know so little of the possibilities of angelic existence that we may well leave this. That angels should eat and drink; feed on meat and bread; might certainly involve equal difficulties, but it is equally stated in Genesis 18 and 19. Thus they appear to have either a power of materializing, and of assuming the functions of a human body; or, indeed, they may have a kind of spiritual body adapted to them as spirits, as some claim.

Erich Sauer states in *The Dawn of World Redemption:*

> If by the "sons of God" fallen angels are meant, then occultism and spiritism are likewise a distinct principle of the Cainite civilization. This explanation is upheld by the majority, e.g., Philo, Josephus, most of the rabbis, the Septuagint, Kurtz, Delitzsch, Gunkel, Konig, Pember.

Kyle M. Yates, Sr., in *The Wycliffe Bible Commentary,* writes:

> The reference to the marriage of the *bne Elohim* ["sons of God"] to the daughters of men has been dealt with in many ways. To translate it literally would make the passage say that members of the Heavenly company selected choice women from the earth and set up marriage relationships with them, literally and actually. . . . In the light of the facts and the accurate rendering of the words of the text, we conclude that some men of the heavenly group (angels or messengers) actually took wives of earthly women. They used superior force to overpower them, to make the conquest complete. The "sons of God" were irresistible.

In *Unger's Commentary on the Old Testament,* **Merrill F. Unger** relates:

> This was the co-mingling of "divine beings" (literally, "sons of God" . . .

with "daughters of men," a Hebraism meaning simply "human daughters")....The sample sin plumbs the depths of pre-Flood wickedness. It was far more serious than mixed marriages between believers and unbelievers. It was a "catastrophic outburst of occultism" such as will precipitate the return of the days of Noah at the end of the present age at the glorious advent of Christ (Matthew 24:24, 37–39). The awful invasion from the realm of evil supernaturalism by the fallen angels precipitated "incubi" and "succubae" phenomena of satanism and extreme spiritistic cults. . . . The Nephilim, "fallen ones" . . . were the spirit-human, angelic-demon offspring of the sons of God (angels) and the daughters of men (human females)....The thought is of spirit beings (fallen angels, demonic powers) cohabiting with women of the human race producing what later became known in pagan mythologies as demigods, partly human and partly superhuman. This is not mythology but the truth of the intermixture of the human race with the angelic creation from which later mythology developed "the titans" (giants, partly superhuman). Greek mythology (Hesiod, Pseudo-Apollodorus) recall such beings. Zeus, one of the great gods, had to battle with a group of giants known as Titans. Phoenician lore (earlier than the Greek) also echoes a similar tradition. Hittite texts containing Hurrian myths have been discovered that carried the idea back even earlier to the source of all this in the revealed facts given in [Genesis] 6:1–4. Gilgamesh, the hero of the Babylonian flood story, was himself a demigod, partly human, partly divine, or superhuman. . . . Occult literature is replete with such superhuman phenomena illustrating the general lawlessness of occultism, here seen in the perversion of God's ordained order of creation and the laws that govern sex in the human order.

Frederick A. Tatford, in *Satan: The Prince of Darkness,* says:

It was Satan's purpose . . . to contaminate the whole of Adamic womanhood and thereby to prevent the advent of the promised Seed. . . . Angelic beings voluntarily left their aerial habitation and surrendered their dignities and responsibilities in order to commit the impious outrage of cohabiting with Adam's descendants. Using their inherent power of materialization, they entered into incongruous union with women on earth, the offspring of these unnatural marriages being "the heroes who were of old, men of renown." Mythology is full of incidents reflecting the scriptural story. Hercules, the powerful giant of antiquity, for example, was alleged to have been born of the illicit union of Zeus and Alcmena. Aztec traditions tell of a race of wicked antediluvian giants of supernatural origin; the Persian sacred books refer to the corruption of the world by Ahriman and the punishment of the people's iniquity by a rainstorm. The apocryphal book of Enoch says that certain angels, divinely set as guards of the earth, were perverted by the beauty of women, whom they taught sorcery, and being banished from heaven, had sons three thousand cubits high, thus originating a celestial and terrestrial race of demons. Similar traditions are found in North America, Egypt, India, and China. It seems clear then that, at the direction of their leader (but also willingly, since their depraved desires had already been fixed upon the women of the earth), a number of angels descended to earth to enter into union with human beings. It has sometimes been thought that the origin of the demons, whose habitat is the air, but who so earnestly yearn for embodiment, is to be found in these unnatural marriages.

Tatford continues on the preaching of spirits in prison as recorded in 1 Peter 3:18–20:

One fact emerges clearly, viz., that our Lord actually took a journey involving movement from one place to another, for this is what is specifically signified by the word used. C. F. Hogg writes: "This journey was undertaken at a time defined by the context, namely after His resurrection, and as the Word indicates, it had a beginning, a course, and an end. Moreover it was He, Himself, who undertook the journey. There is no hint that He went by deputy of any kind. The words seem plainly to imply a personal journey here as they certainly do in verse 22, "having gone into heaven." In both cases, there was a local motion; as in Ephesians 4:9–10, the ascent involved a descent.

If the journey was undertaken by our Lord, the preaching was also undertaken by Him and not by Noah acting in His name and by His Spirit. But to whom did He preach? It was clearly to beings who were in existence in antediluvian days and whose disobedience and unbelief were manifested in those days. It is plain that it was their disobedience—and not the preaching—which occurred in the days of Noah. Moreover, the imprisoned spirits, to whom the message came, were evidently spirits at the time of their disobedience and there is, in fact, no evidence in the context that they were at any time anything other than spirits. The verse refers only to "spirits" and not to "spirits of men."

What message could be brought to such? It could not have been the New Testament evangel, since that is solely for mankind (e.g. John 3:16). But the message preached by Old Testament prophets at times was one of denunciation and judgment and not of mercy and forgiveness. The preaching referred to in Acts 15:21, for example, was of the law and not of grace. Satanically inspired spirits had committed a crime of such enormity in the eyes of God that they had been plunged down to the depths. To those thus incarcerated, came the Lord Jesus Christ, now risen from the dead, but not to proclaim the possibility of salvation or deliverance from wrath because of His atoning work: There could be no expiation of the guilt of these spirits and no ground of redemption for them. The only message He could bring was of man's victory and of Satan's condemnation. The Redeemer had come; Satan's plans had been frustrated; the scheming of the centuries had failed; and mankind was now to be reconciled to God. He could proclaim that victory and could declare the inevitability of judgment for the forces of evil, but no other message could He bring for rebels such as these. It was to this limited company in that dread abode that the message came. Whether He, at the same time, liberated the spirits of the believing dead and triumphed over the prisoners in this very act, we do not know. One there was who must have realized the full implications and the great adversary must have been more than ever conscious of the failure of his age-long machinations.

In *Earth's Earliest Ages,* **G. H. Pember** writes:

> Through a misapprehension of the Septuagint . . . the English version renders *Nephilim* by "giants." But the form of the Hebrew word indicates a verbal adjective of noun, of passive or neuter signification, from *nephal,* "to fall" hence it must mean "the fallen ones," that is, probably the fallen angels. Afterward, however, the term seems to have been transferred to their offspring, as we may gather from the only other passage in which it occurs. In the evil report which the ten spies give of the land of Canaan, we find them saying: "All the people which we saw in it were men of great stature. And there we saw the Nephilim, the sons of Anak, descended from the Nephilim: and we seemed to ourselves as grasshoppers, and so we did to them" (Numbers 13:32–33).
>
> It was doubtless the mention of the great stature of these men, together with the Septuagint rendering (*gigantes*) that suggested our translation "giants." The roots of the Greek (*gigas*) have, however, no reference to great stature, but point to something very different. The word is merely another form of *geegenes:* it signifies "earth-born," and was used of the Titans, or sons of Heaven and Earth—Coelus and Terra—because, though superior to the human race, they were of partly terrestrial origin. The meaning of "giants" in our sense of the term, is altogether secondary and arose from the fact that these beings of mixed birth were said to have displayed a monstrous growth and strength of body.

As we have demonstrated, the view that "sons of God" refers to angels has been a common view, both in the past and in the present. It is a view that is solidly supported by the biblical text. To teach that "the sons of God" is a reference to the godly line of Seth, and that what is described in Genesis 6 is the godly sons of Seth cohabiting with the daughters of Cain does not stand the test of scrutiny. As **Chuck Missler and Mark Eastman** write in their book *Alien Encounters:* "There is no evidence, stated or implied, that the line of Seth was godly. Only one person was translated from judgment to come (Enoch) and only eight were given the protection of the ark. No one beyond Noah's immediate family was accounted worthy to be saved. . . ."

It Is Not Reasonable, But . . .

We believe that the evidence is overwhelming for the position that we have advanced. To be sure, it is not reasonable that alien angels would co-habit with women and sire children. But it is also not reasonable that God would create all things out of nothing. It is not reasonable that prophets of old could perfectly predict the future. It is not reasonable that a virgin could conceive a child. It is not reasonable that Jesus Christ could rise from the grave, ascend to Heaven, and return to this Earth. If we measure the sixty-six books of the Bible by reason, they would be discarded as foolishness. The Bible is not to be appraised by reason, because as the Word of Special Creator it is to be received as Divine revelation. Revelation does not contradict reason, but rather transcends it. Geology evidences revelation; archaeology evidences revelation; history evidences revelation; conscience, intellect, the mental faculties, and, last but not least, moral and spiritual verities evidence revelation. Through biblical revelation, it is evident that an invasion of rebellious angels so corrupted mankind that only eight souls were saved through a great flood that destroyed the remainder of mankind. This revelation is a warning to the present generation to be prepared for another catastrophic judgment at the end of the age.

UFOs

The Marginal Mystery That Is Becoming a Major Issue

Have you seen any UFOs lately? Don't laugh at the question. An increasing number of individuals worldwide—including military pilots and radar operators—have reported seeing objects flying through the sky that have never been identified. And Russian nuclear submarine crews have reported USOs—Unidentified Swimming Objects.

Who, or what, are UFOs? Does the Bible address this issue? Are UFOs spacecraft occupied by beings from other planets, or are they realities from another dimension? How does the UFO phenomenon tie in with end-time events prophesied in Scripture?

In this chapter, we will investigate these and other issues. Whatever the reader concludes about UFOs, we think one thing is clear: the UFO phenomenon is the marginal mystery that is becoming a major issue, an issue that could have far-reaching consequences for life on planet Earth.

UFOs have been seen by a number of high-ranking people, including President Jimmy Carter. In the first edition of *Marginal Mysteries,* Noah Hutchings writes of his own sighting:

> I would like to say at the beginning that while serving as a radar operator in the South Pacific in World War II, I never picked up anything on the radarscope that I could not explain. Besides airplanes, both friendly

and enemy, there were weather fronts, thunder clouds, electrical disturbances, and on one occasion we even tracked a pelican that had swallowed a piece of tin foil from a ship's garbage. However, in 1935, one
evening about dusk, I did see three UFOs that I could not explain then
or since. Three objects, orange, white, and blue, arose in the sky from
the east at considerable speed. They stopped motionless in the sky and
remained stationary for about an hour. Then they sped off to the south
as rapidly as they appeared. Their maneuverability was unlike any aircraft
I have ever seen or heard of. In 1935, at the age of twelve, I had never
heard of a UFO, but since then, literally millions of sightings of strange
objects in the sky have been reported.[1]

The Beginning of the Modern UFO Era

June 25, 1947, marks the beginning of the modern UFO era. On that date
Seattle businessman Kenneth Arnold was flying his small plane at approximately five thousand feet over the Cascade Mountains. He suddenly saw
a bluish-white flash and nine large disk-shaped objects flying at what Arnold estimated to be sixteen hundred miles per hour. Arnold claimed that
they skipped through the air as a saucer would if it were skipped across
water; hence, the coining of the term "flying saucer." Arnold's report was
repeatedly ridiculed by the media and military. Arnold later stated that he
now hesitates to report even "a flying ten-story building."[2]

A few weeks later, on July 8, 1947, there was an alleged recovery
of a crashed flying saucer near Roswell, New Mexico. Initial newspaper
reports indicated that the government had recovered the craft, but by the
next day military officials were claiming that it was just a weather instrument of some sort. This fueled speculation that there was some kind of a
massive military coverup. Some asserted that the government had actual
proof that there were space beings in the crashed spacecraft, but wanted to

---

1. Noah Hutchings, *Marginal Mysteries* (Oklahoma City: Southwest Radio Church, 1985),
   p. 33
2. Chuck Missler and Mark Eastman, *Alien Encounters: The Secret Behind the UFO Phenomenon* (Coeur d'Alene, ID: Koinonia House, 1997), p. 55.

hide that information lest it create a panic among the general population. Others believed that the government was covering up the existence of a secret Russian weapon that put the American public at great peril. Some news reporters and fiction writers linked the Roswell incident with the nuclear devices that had been recently detonated. By 1947 the United States had produced nuclear explosions at Alamogordo, New Mexico, and Hiroshima and Nagasaki, Japan. Was it possible that alien civilizations who were keeping watch on planet Earth had become alarmed that mankind now had terrible weapons of mass destruction and needed to be watched ever more closely, hence the sudden rash of UFO sightings?

In assessing this view, we should note that a "UFO crash" in the Roswell area fits in with this hypothesis. In 1947 the 509th bomb group was stationed at Roswell and was the only flight group to have nuclear weapons in its arsenal. Is it possible that the "space brothers," as they were being called, were greatly concerned about the destructive capabilities of the 509th and were flying low when their craft developed mechanical difficulties? A quick glance at a map of New Mexico will show that the nuclear weapons facility at Alamogordo and the Roswell crash site are all in the southeastern corner of the state. Moreover, the White Sands Missile Test Range is in the same general area. In 1947 newspapers were reporting that rockets from the White Sands facility were "probing the mysteries of the cosmos at heights above one hundred miles."[3]

Sightings Involving the Military

Many who scoff at the idea of UFOs believe that they have only been reported by a few hysterical individuals who didn't know the difference between a balloon, a flight of geese, and a real UFO. They would, however, give the whole UFO issue more weight if there were only reports of UFOs from reputable military observers. Well, such individuals must leave their skepticism behind because there have been numerous sightings by military observers.

One of the earliest involved the so-called "Battle for Los Angeles."

---

3. *Chronicles of America* (New York: DK Publishing, 1997), p. 732.

On February 25, 1942, just a few months after the attack on Pearl Harbor, several unidentified "aircraft" were sighted over Los Angeles, California. The sirens went off, and anti-aircraft batteries went into operation, firing 1,430 rounds at the craft. It was reported by gunners that one very large UFO hung motionless over the batteries as the shells exploded on or near the UFO, though it suffered no apparent damage. There could be little doubt that there was "something up there in the sky." The firing went on for about an hour, causing considerable damage to several homes and public buildings. The city was littered with pieces of metal from exploded ordnance. "At least six civilians died as a result of automobile accidents and heart attacks. . . ."[4]

More recently, in the summer of 1961, UFOs destroyed Russian guided missiles over Rybinsk, located about ninety miles from Moscow. Tension between East and West had been mounting, and the Russians had recently installed a new defensive missile shield around Moscow. When a "very large discoidal UFO" appeared at an altitude of twelve miles, along with several smaller UFOs, the Russian military launched several missiles. None of the missiles reached the target. They all exploded two miles short. As the Russians were preparing to launch more missiles, the smaller UFOs approached the launch site and were evidently responsible for causing a massive malfunction so that no further missiles could be launched. When the small UFOs finally left the area, the equipment resumed functioning.[5] A similar incident was recorded in the U.S. An Atlas F missile was launched from Vandenberg Air Force Base in California and tracked by a television camera attached to a telescope. A UFO began to follow the missile. As it approached, the UFO emitted several brilliant flashes of light. Shortly thereafter, the missile went out of control at an altitude of approximately sixty miles.[6]

One of the most unusual encounters involving military personnel

---

4. Jim Marrs, *Alien Agenda: Investigating the Extraterrestrial Presence Among Us* (New York: Harper Collins, 1997), p. 162. See also David Ritchie, *UFO: The Definitive Guide to Unidentified Flying Objects and Related Phenomena* (New York: Facts on File, 1994), p. 25.

5. Ritchie, p. 179.

6. Ibid., p. 18.

occurred when a UFO apparently injured a reservist in the Cuban army in June of 1968. The 42-year-old reservist, Isidro Puentes Ventura, was ordered to stand guard at a particular location in Cuba. Ventura was on duty between the hours of 6:30 in the evening and 2:45 in the morning, the hour when he was supposed to turn in his weapon at the end of his watch. At five minutes after midnight, machine gun fire was heard from Ventura's location. Several patrols went out to look for him. At dawn he was found in a comatose condition and was transported to the provincial hospital in Pinar del Río where he remained in a withdrawn condition, unable to speak. He was examined by Cuban medical experts who found no brain damage, but concluded that he had gone through some horrifying experience.

Cuban intelligence contacted Soviet UFO investigators. They found forty-eight machine gun cases and fourteen bullets that had been flattened by impact against some hard, unyielding surface. A depression was visible in the soil, with a central hole three feet in diameter and three small depressions around it. The soil had been exposed to a high degree of heat. Cuban radar operators reported that they had detected an unidentified flying object that suddenly vanished amid a lot of "electronic noise." Thirteen days after the incident, Ventura came out of his coma. He reported that he had seen a white light behind some trees. When he went to investigate, he found a strange round object with several antennas on top. He concluded that the craft was some kind of American military helicopter and opened fire. Ventura knew his bullets were having no effect. After firing about forty rounds Ventura stated that the object became orange and emitted a loud whistling sound. That was the last thing that he remembers.[7]

The Hudson Valley Sightings

One of the most unusual series of UFO sightings—lasting over a period of several years—occurred in the Westchester County area, just north of New York City. J. Allen Hynek and his associates investigated a total of

7. Jacques Vallee, *UFO Chronicles of the Soviet Union* (New York: Ballantine, 1992), pp. 82–86.

7,046 Hudson Valley UFO sightings that occurred from 1982 to 1995. Hynek began as a skeptic, but became thoroughly convinced that UFOs are real.

Hynek's work cannot be discredited on the grounds that he is an amateur science buff with an overactive imagination. He was a professional astronomer and for twenty years was the scientific consultant to the U.S. Air Force in its investigation of UFO phenomena. Prior to his death, Hynek served as the director of the Lindheimer Astronomical Research Center at Northwestern University and was chairman of Northwestern's astronomy department. Hynek found that most of the reports in the Hudson Valley sightings describe the UFO as a triangle, boomerang, or V-shaped object. There were a variety of estimates regarding the size of these "giant, glowing boomerangs with lights," but remember that it is nearly impossible to estimate the size of an object at night without first knowing the object's altitude. All the reports, however, agree that the UFOs were of great size, some of the estimates claiming that the objects were several hundred feet in length. Nearly seventy percent of the witnesses said that the craft displayed lights of many colors, although other witnesses said that they saw only one or two colors. Fifty-five percent of the witnesses claim that they heard a humming sound and compared it to a finely-tuned electric motor, but barely audible. Even a formation of low-flying Cessna-type aircraft would make considerable noise, so it seems illogical to conclude that these UFOs were a formation of aircraft.[8]

The Hudson Valley sightings were remarkable not only because of the size of the UFOs and the number of sightings, but because of the very large number of different people from varied backgrounds who were willing to publicly affirm what they saw. Hynek states: "The caliber of the people who were willing to go on record as having seen this UFO was remarkable. Many of these people were professionals who had nothing to gain, and much to lose by reporting they had seen a UFO—scientists, engineers, doctors, lawyers, pilots, police officers, and many other people

---

8. J. Allen Hynek, *Night Siege: The Hudson Valley UFO Sightings,* Second Edition (St. Paul: Llewellyn, 1998), pp. 229–243.

who are stable, respected residents of the area. If these people could not tell the difference between a UFO and a bunch of planes or a blimp, who could?"[9]

But surely, the skeptic thinks, *there must be some other explanation!* Hynek answers that by saying, "Usually, a UFO that is seen over a long period of time has a logical explanation. In this case, we found none."[10] The FAA, however, disagrees. The "official" FAA explanation for the Hudson Valley sightings is a natural one: "The entire series of sightings was caused by planes in formation flown by stunt flyers from some unknown airport, possibly Stormville." Hynek gives twelve reasons why this cannot be. We will condense his reasons in three points:

1. The UFOs do not show the characteristics of a plane. Many of the witnesses saw planes at the same time as the UFOs and had no trouble distinguishing the two. UFOs move as one solid piece, often very slowly, and sometimes hover—something that is not usually possible for an airplane. Helicopters hover and fly slowly, but they are very noisy.
2. Specific UFOs were seen on evenings when it was definitely established that there were no planes in the air from the Stormville airport.
3. No one claimed the thousand dollar reward offered by Peter Gersten for information leading to an explanation of the UFO reports.[11]

Unusual Sightings in Russia

Another credible UFO researcher is Jacques Vallee, former principal investigator on Department of Defense networking projects. Author of several highly acclaimed books on UFOs, Vallee was born in France where he was trained in astrophysics. In 1962 he moved to the U.S. and in 1967 received his Ph.D. in computer science. He has worked closely with J. Allen Hynek. Vallee's research has taken him to many parts of the world, and he has

---

9. Ibid., p. 53.
10. Ibid., p. 244.
11. Ibid., pp, 244–253

done extensive research into Russian UFO phenomena.

The Voronezh Sightings

On October 8, 1989, Vallee received a phone call from an editor of the *Wall Street Journal* who revealed that in September of 1989 the Russian newspaper *Tass* reported that "scientists have confirmed that an unidentified flying object recently landed in the Russian city of Voronezh.... The scientists have also explored the landing site and found traces of aliens who made a short promenade about the park."[12] The *New York Times* ran a story on October 9, 1989, but Vallee stated that the *Times* report was loaded with factual errors and "ridiculed the story instead of researching it."[13]

No doubt, the Soviet media may itself have contributed to the confusion. Drunken with the newfound freedom inspired by *glasnost* [openness], Soviet reporters seemed to have adopted a tabloid style that introduced more than a glimmer of sensationalism into the otherwise dreary Russian lifestyle. Vallee determined to go to Voronezh. Following a wave of additional UFO sightings in the Soviet Union, Vallee and Martine Castello, a science reporter for the prestigious French newspaper *Le Figaro* went to the Soviet Union in January 1990 and met with the major Soviet researchers of UFO phenomena.

The city of Voronezh, located about three hundred miles south of Moscow, became famous for its highly-publicized UFO sightings in the fall of 1989. Local news reported that several teenagers who were playing soccer in the park encountered extraterrestrials. The teenagers reported seeing a UFO land, and a tall humanoid, about ten feet tall and wearing a silver coverall and boots of a bronze hue, emerge from the craft. More reports from Voronezh appeared in the media, some of them indicating that human observers actually disappeared as they were approached by the humanoids, only to appear shortly thereafter. The landing sites were investigated by biolocation, a technique practiced in Russia similar to dowsing

---

12. Vallee, *Soviet Union,* p. 4.
13. Ibid., p. 5.

for water.[14] It is used for the detection of hidden mineral water, or living entities by paranormal means and involves the use of a pendulum, rod, or stock.[15]

The Russians have tried to approach their UFO problem scientifically. Russian aviation engineer and UFO researcher Alexander Mosolov investigated many of the sightings involving children. Mosolov discussed his methodology with Vallee. "We began with the schoolchildren," stated Mosolov. "We separated them. We found out that many of them did not know the others. We had them make separate drawings." The children's reports were also collated with the reports of adult witnesses, plus physical evidence left by the UFOs, such as an increase in radiation in the area of the sighting.[16]

Russia's leading ufologist is Professor Vladimir Azhazha. At their first meeting Vallee and Azhazha discussed the latter's experiences in UFO research. Azhazha verified that he had been a longtime skeptic and thought that all the sightings were hoaxes. When Vallee asked him, "What made you change your mind?" Azhazha related how he, as a former submarine officer in the Soviet navy, "was asked to perform certain hydrospheric studies.... I was asked to serve as the scientific director of a group studying underwater UFOs." The Soviets have taken the whole matter of "USOs" very seriously. Vallee reports Azhazha's explanation:

"We had to [take them seriously]. There were too many incidents that could not be denied. It all began when we tried to understand the nature of certain underwater objects that followed our submarines. At times they even anticipated our maneuvers! Initially, we thought they were American devices," added Azhazha, raising a hand to his forehead as he recalled what must have been a difficult research project. "One day such an object came to the surface in a rather spectacular fashion. One of our icebreakers was working its way in the Arctic Ocean when

14. Ritchie, pp. 229–230.
15. Vallee, *Soviet Union*, p. 5.
16. Ibid., p. 54.

a brilliant spherical craft suddenly broke through the ice and flew up vertically, showering the vessel with fragments of ice. All the officers on the bridge saw it. And it was hard to deny the hole in the ice!"

"Could it have been a missile test?"

Our interpreter quickly translated the question and obtained the following answer: "You don't shoot a missile that way. You have to break the ice first. Furthermore, the object was a bright sphere. We knew what nuclear missiles looked like!"[17]

Azhazha reported that such sightings were not limited to the Arctic, but that Russian ships in the Pacific have "also reported flying objects, vertical cylinders." On October 7, 1977, Azhazha reported, the submarine repair ship *Volga* while at sea was circled by nine disk-shaped objects. As the objects drew near, the radio, the onboard communications system, and all electronic systems malfunctioned. This lasted for about eighteen minutes.[18] These sightings from the *Volga* were witnessed by several people. They were, it would seem, by virtue of their military and technical training, reputable witnesses. Other sightings in Russia were likewise witnessed by large numbers of people. Azhazha, for example, told Vallee of a UFO sighted on February 13, 1989, between nine and ten o'clock in the evening, that was "seen by thousands of people—truck drivers, people in cars. *It was a huge cylindrical object that was estimated at about fifteen hundred feet in length.*"[19]

UFOs in Russia, as well as in other parts of the world, are polymorphous and "can change shape dynamically in flight." Vallee believes that this is an important indicator that they are *not* extraterrestrial in origin. The fact that UFOs materialize suddenly and then disappear just as suddenly has convinced him that they have "a multidimensional origin rather than a simple spatial or interplanetary origin. . . ."[20] Azhazha, with whom

17. Ibid., pp. 28–29.
18. Ibid.
19. Ibid., p. 32.
20. Ibid., p. 33.

Vallee is in agreement, maintains that ufology is a complex domain that demands knowledge of biotechnology, space physics, psychology, and sociology. "We need a multidisciplinary approach," states Azhazha. "Historians and folklore experts should get involved. We need physics and we need physicists. We even need philosophers."[21]

Soviet Alien Abductions

Alien abductions have been reported around the world, but Soviet ufologists such as Vladimir Azhazha have done some careful studies and have sought to explain "the abduction mechanism." One mechanism identified by Azhazha has been called *Dialego* because abductions often begin with a verbal exchange between the alien abductor and the human abductee. One incident cited by Vallee was investigated by Alexander F. Pugach, a Russian who holds a Ph.D. in physics and mathematics.

The incident involved the attempted abduction of Vera Prokofiyevna, a retired factory worker, her friend Alexandra Stepanovna, an engineer, and Alexandra's six-year-old daughter. As they were strolling in a park near the city of Kiev on July 4, 1989, they saw what appeared to them to be a boat with three humanoids on board. The humanoids were very pale, had absolutely the same features, and therefore looked like identical triplets. They were wearing collarless silver shirts resembling nightgowns and had long blond hair and large eyes. The humanoids approached the terrified women and told them that they came from another planet. "Our planet is so far that your mind cannot fathom that," they said. "When you become like us, you will know. Every day we take one person from Earth to our world. We will take you. Our ship is nearby. We will show it to you." Prokofiyevna said they spoke good Russian but had an archaic accent.

The women were, of course, terrified, and the little girl began to cry. The women begged the humanoids not to take them away because they had families. The women saw their craft. It was silvery in hue like their clothing, and looked like a gigantic barrel with a circular antenna on top. The beings responded to their fear of being taken away. "Well," they said,

---

21. Ibid., p. 39.

"we won't take you. We will find others." They went inside their craft by using a ladder with three steps. The ladder was withdrawn, the door closed, and the craft left the ground without disturbing the sand beneath it.

Pugach believes that the sighting was genuine in that the women experienced a real phenomenon. Pugach believes that some force intruded itself into their minds. Vallee states: "In other words, his position is close to the views of those, like myself, who believe that UFOs are from a different dimension or another reality—although in my opinion, this does not exclude a material, physical presence at the time of the sighting."[22]

The reader will perhaps remember the account of Balaam, the donkey, and the angel who was invisible to Balaam but quite visible to the donkey; and also the account of Elisha's servant who did not see what was really there:

Then the LORD opened the eyes of Balaam, and he saw the angel of the LORD standing in the way, and his sword drawn in his hand: and he bowed down his head, and fell flat on his face. And the angel of the LORD said unto him, Wherefore hast thou smitten thine ass these three times? behold, I went out to withstand thee, because thy way is perverse before me: And the ass saw me, and turned from me these three times: unless she had turned from me, surely now also I had slain thee, and saved her alive.

—Numbers 22:31–33

And when the servant of the man of God was risen early, and gone forth, behold, an host compassed the city both with horses and chariots. And his servant said unto him, Alas, my master! how shall we do? And he answered, Fear not: for they that be with us are more than they that be with them. And Elisha prayed, and said, LORD, I pray thee, open his eyes, that he may see. And the LORD opened the eyes of the young man;

22. Ibid.

and he saw: and, behold, the mountain was full of horses and chariots of fire round about Elisha.

—2 Kings 6:15–17

Biblical teaching about angels and demons and the unseen powers that Scripture declares to be real, seem to be replicated in some of the UFO reports. If they are from another dimension, might they be from the dimension of darkness?

The Catastrophe at Tunguska

On June 30, 1908, at seven o'clock in the morning, there was an explosion of tremendous magnitude that rocked Siberia. As blinding flash was observed followed by a fiery column ascending into the sky. Then followed the sound of a large explosion that reverberated several times. It was heard 750 miles away, and even at that distance chandeliers swung from the ceiling. Men who were on horseback 200 miles distant were knocked to the ground. Windows facing the explosion were shattered in houses that were 150 miles away. Earth tremors were recorded in Jena, Germany. Within sixteen miles of the blast all trees were uprooted and blown over to face the same direction. Within ten miles of the explosion they were burned, yet, at the very place of the explosion—ground zero—they were unharmed.

Russian scientist Alexis Zolotov observed that "if a foreign body had actually hit the earth at a speed of about three miles per second, i.e., over ten thousand miles per hour, there would have been a sudden heating of the soil which could have risen to thousands of degrees." It would have created a huge crater, such as the Meteor Crater in Arizona. "But where is the Tunguska crater?" Zolotov asks. "It does not exist. Nothing actually hit the ground there."[23] S. B. Semenov, a farmer living forty miles away from the site of the explosion, described what happened to him: "I was sitting on my porch facing north when suddenly, to the northwest, there appeared a great flash of light. There was so much heat that . . . my

23. Ibid., pp. 66–67.

shirt was almost burned off my back. I saw a huge fireball that covered an enormous part of the sky. . . . Afterward it became dark and at the same time I felt an explosion that threw me several feet from my porch. I lost consciousness."[24]

There have been a variety of hypotheses offered to explain what happened at Tunguska. In the early 1930s the comet hypothesis was first proposed, though there are no telltale traces, metals, minerals, or a crater that would support that view. However, there are signs of radiation damage, damage that is seen in the form of diseases in local reindeer herds and the genetic changes in plants growing in the area. Moreover, radioactive cesium 137 was found in abnormal quantities in the 1908 tree ring of nearby trees.

Some Russian writers, notably Alexander Kazantsev, believe that the explosion was due to antimatter. That theory has been discredited, however, because scientists claim that if that were the case, the explosion would have taken place as soon as the antimatter came into contact with the stratosphere which would have been at a much higher altitude than actually occurred.

The hypothesis that is gaining increasing favor, especially in view of the innumerable UFO sightings in Russia and elsewhere, is that the explosion was caused by a reactor on a UFO. One Russian scientist who supports this view reports that eyewitnesses claim to have seen a bright object in the sky that suddenly reversed its course just prior to the explosion. In 1989 Japanese scientists who traveled to the site stated that their research clearly indicated that the catastrophe at Tunguska had been due to a nuclear reactor explosion, probably aboard a nuclear-powered spacecraft. They erected the first monument commemorating what is believed to be a UFO crash.[25]

Categories

UFO encounters are not all the same and fall into several broad areas of

---

24. Ibid., p. 68.
25. Ibid., pp. 68–73.

categorization. The following categories are generally accepted, though different UFO researchers give some variations.

Close Encounters of the First Kind are those encounters in which there is no interaction between the UFO and the witnesses and environment. It is an encounter in which the UFO is simply observed.

Close Encounters of the Second Kind are those encounters in which a visible record of the UFO has been left. Such physical effects may include marks on the ground that remain visible for some time. There are a variety of marks and signs such as the scorching of plant life, discomfort to animals shown in their nervousness, and even physical effects on the human observer such as temporary paralysis, a feeling of heat or cold, or other sensation.

Encounters in which there is the presence of alien creatures are known as *Close Encounters of the Third Kind*. These may be humanoids, occupants of UFOs, "ufonauts," and even "ufosapiens."[26]

Jacques Vallee believes that these three categories are insufficient and has added two more. *CE4* are those encounters where there is a "reality transformation in the life of the percipient." The encounter is not simply shocking, but leads to a change in the witnesses' values or view of things. CE5 describes an encounter in which there is a lasting injury—physical or emotion—to the individual.[27]

Effects of the Encounters

Fear

To say the least, an encounter with a UFO and its occupants can be a devastating experience, especially when the aliens seem indestructible. In Kentucky, two men, one armed with a .22 caliber rifle and the other with a shotgun, fired at an alien that was about twenty feet away. The alien did a quick flip and disappeared into the darkness. The men retreated to their

26. J. Allen Hynek, *The UFO Experience: A Scientific Inquiry* (Chicago: Regnery, 1972), pp. 88, 110, 138.
27. Jacques Vallee, *Confrontation: A Scientific Search for Alien Contact* (New York: Ballantine, 1990), p. 239.

home, but in a short while they noticed the alien watching them through the window. They promptly fired at "it" and the alien disappeared. Had they scored a hit? The men went outside to check. As they were making their way to the rear of the house, a claw-like hand reached down from the roof and touched one of the men on the head. The men opened fire at whatever was on the roof, and at another alien that appeared in a nearby tree. The latter was apparently hit, or so they thought, but seemed to float to the ground and then ran off. Hynek observes that "nothing seems to unnerve the Kentucky countryman as much as the ineffectiveness of guns, and soon the entire family was confined within the house behind bolted doors."[28]

Are They Dangerous?

This raises the question as to whether or not the aliens are hostile. Indeed, humans have been hurt in an encounter, but that does not necessarily prove that the aliens are hostile. No doubt, they may appear to be hostile for a variety of reasons, but "when a child puts two fingers into an electrical socket . . . one should not infer from the result, alarming as it is, that the utility company is hostile."[29]

The fact, however, that the aliens seem invincible and that they seem to have abilities and powers that humans do not is sufficient to be intimidating. UFOs have been seen on radar traveling at speeds far in excess of what is capable to man at the present state of our knowledge and technology. In northern Minnesota, for example, a UFO that was hovering silently above a radar station suddenly shot up more than 200 miles in an instant before disappearing from radar screens. On another occasion a U.S. Navy destroyer tracked a UFO moving at 3,000 miles per hour from a point 155 miles southeast of Cape May, New Jersey, up to Massachusetts. When it reached the area off Nantucket Island, the UFO shot straight up and was lost after moving 100 miles into space.[30]

---

28. Hynek, *UFO Experience,* p. 151.

29. Vallee, *Confrontations,* pp. 228–229.

30. Hynek, *Night Siege,* p. 252.

Emotional Devastation for Mankind

Would society be able to keep its sanity and coexist with aliens? *How would you feel if you knew for sure that there were creatures that have landed on planet Earth that are far stronger and more intelligent than any human being?*

Therefore, the expectation of the arrival of extraterrestrials could be emotionally devastating. "As we reach the Millennium," writes Vallee, "the belief in the imminent arrival of extraterrestrials in our midst is a fantasy that is as powerful as any drug, as revolutionary as any delusion that marked the last millennium, as poisonous as any of the great irrational upheavals of history."[31] The realization that "we are not alone" will affect every field of human endeavor. Contact with superior beings that look something like us could be shattering.

This suggests a positive motive for a government coverup—if indeed that is what is happening. Government leaders may try to prevent the very thing that has destroyed almost every indigenous culture that has come up against Western technology, such as the Plains Indians with their primitive weapons facing fur traders armed with Henry repeating rifles. Of course, not telling us does not remove the danger. It only delays the panic.

At any rate, some have suggested that the reason the government has suppressed "the truth" about the existence of aliens is for the good of the population. An admission by the president of the United States and military officials that aliens are real would have catastrophic emotional and psychological effects. Civilization as we know it might topple. In support of this view, Jim Marrs cites a Brookings Institute report that states: "Anthropological files contain many examples of societies sure of their place in the universe, which have disintegrated when they had to associate with previously unfamiliar societies espousing different ideas and different life ways. . . ." This warning was picked up by the *New York Times,* which carried a headline stating, "Brookings Institution Report Says Earth's Civilizations Might Topple If Faced by a Race of Superior Beings."[32]

---

31. Jacques Vallee, *Revelations: Alien Contact and Human Deception* (New York: Ballantine, 1991), p. 228.
32. Marrs, p. 22.

If there ever came a time when there was a world consensus regarding the existence of aliens, that realization could cause the entire fabric of civilization to unravel. Is it possible, then, that there is a deliberate suppression of information concerning UFOs in the belief that such is being done in the public interest?

An Encouragement to Evolutionists

In a sense, however, some feel that the discovery of highly developed extraterrestrials coming from outer space would probably make evolutionists happy. If man evolved, and is in the process of evolving, it is conceivable to the evolutionist that there could be some beings in other places in the universe more highly evolved than the humans found on planet Earth. Those who believe that man evolved here on planet Earth find it completely compatible with their evolutionary view to think that evolution happened elsewhere. For them, as man on Earth has evolved far beyond the earthworm, these space beings from other galaxies have evolved far beyond man. The discovery of extraterrestrials, some believe, would support the evolutionary hypothesis.

Fostering World Unity

Some dramatic and cataclysmic changes will have to occur in the last days to so motivate people to put aside their differences and to unite into a one-world arrangement. If earthlings were convinced that there was a major threat from alien forces equipped with high-tech weaponry, that perceived threat could drive all mankind—irrespective of race, religion, and political ideology—into a common union for mutual support and encouragement. All national distinctions could very well disappear almost immediately. Significantly, this is what is happening. The search for extraterrestrials is already having a unifying effect.,

Karen Brandon, writing in the August 30, 1999, edition of the *Chicago Tribune* writes that a special all-volunteer effort, known as the Search for Extraterrestrial Intelligence at Home (SETI@home), "is a novel worldwide project made possible by the Internet's global reach, a programmer's

feat." Since May of 1999 more than one million volunteers have partici-
pated by downloading software from the Internet. This produces a special screensaver that has the capacity to analyze sounds from outer space.
Participants simply leave the computers on overnight and the next morning they can check their computer to see whether they have picked up
anything from outer space that would indicate the existence of intelligent
life forms. But why would anyone even want to participate in such a program? The reasons given in the computer program are forty-three pages
in length and many of the reasons have to do with global unity and the
bringing together of all peoples everywhere by the common knowledge
that "we are not alone." One participant in SETI@home stated: "People
in every country are united by a vision of something bigger than they are,
something that transcends nationalism, and makes it irrelevant. The idea
is captivating."

Captivating, indeed, but maybe even more captivating is the idea expressed by President Jimmy Carter in 1977. The *Voyager* spacecraft carried
a message on a gold record that was affixed to the exterior of the craft. The
message was signed by Carter, and reads as follows:

> This *Voyager* spacecraft was constructed by the United States of Ameri-
> ca. We are a community of 240 million human beings among the more
> than 4 billion who inhabit the planet Earth. We human beings are still
> divided into nation states, but these states are rapidly becoming a single
> global civilization.
>
> We cast this message into the cosmos. It is likely to survive a billion
> years into our future, when our civilization is profoundly altered and
> the surface of the Earth may be vastly changed. Of the 200 billion stars
> in the Milky Way galaxy, some—perhaps many—may have inhabited
> planets and spacefaring civilizations. If one such civilization intercepts
> *Voyager* and can understand these recorded contents, here is our message:
>
> This is a present from a small distant world, a token of our sounds,
> our science, our images, our music, our thoughts, and our feelings. We
> are attempting to survive our time so we may live into yours. We hope

someday, having solved the problems we face, to join a community of galactic civilizations. This record represents our hope and our determination, and our good will in a vast and awesome universe.

—(signed) Jimmy Carter, President of the United States of America, The White House, June 16, 1977[33]

A Government Coverup?

One does not have to look very far in UFO literature to find that reputable UFO researchers believe that the government is not telling us the truth. Jacques Vallee, certainly a careful and reputable researcher, believes that there are multiple coverups. The inside jacket of Vallee's book *Revelations* summarizes his views:

. . . Dr. Vallee presents startling evidence that well-constructed hoaxes and media manipulations have misled UFO researchers, diverting them from the real issues at hand in the UFO phenomenon. Focusing in-depth on cases reported in the United States and throughout the world in recent decades, Dr. Vallee here analyzes the full gamut of sensational UFO "incidents," from the alleged history of saucer "crashes" and the retrieval of aliens by the U.S. government, to reports of a subterranean community of hostile humanoids in the American Southwest. In the process, he reveals that some of the most remarkable sightings are actually complete hoaxes that have been carefully engineered. Moreover, the witnesses are merely the victims and instruments rather than the authors of the hoaxes.

Who is perpetrating such deliberate fabrications, and what is their goal? Dr. Vallee suggests that in some instances this is the work of private groups with fantastic delusions and a compulsion to spread them to a larger segment of the public. Other cases have been crafted by government agencies engaged in psychological warfare, in an attempt to draw attention away from the actual UFO phenomenon.

---

33. Dave Hunt, *The Occult Invasion: The Subtle Seduction of the World and Church* (Eugene, OR: Harvest House, 1998), p. 363.

The result, according to Dr. Vallee, is that too many false reports of alien contact are accepted as real, while far too many actual cases have gone overlooked or have been misreported. And none of these supposed "revelations" provide the shadow of an answer to the global UFO mystery—an answer that can only arise from diligent scientific research.

J. Allen Hynek, another credible scientist who has devoted his life to UFO research, also expresses similar views. In the foreword of his book *Night Siege,* he writes:

> Something truly astonishing is happening, but those who are responsible for protecting us—the law enforcement agencies, state and federal government, and the military—are deliberately ignoring it.
>
> Hundreds of people living within commuting distance of one of the world's largest cities [New York] were astonished and frightened by what they could only regard as a very bizarre event. Yet the Federal Aviation Administration, which monitors the air lanes where the boomerang-shaped object was sighted, persists in denying its existence.

This was Hynek's response to what was basically a media blackout after the "Westchester County Boomerang" was sighted. "It moved slowly and silently and was easily as big as a football field—some witnesses said as big as three football fields." This UFO was close to the ground and hundreds saw it, many who were educated professionals representing a variety of disciplines. "This was a flying city . . . it was huge," one witness said.[34]

Hynek worked with the Air Force on Project Blue Book, the Air Force's official investigation of UFO phenomena that was carried on from 1952 to 1969. Blue Book explained most of the sightings as hoaxes, hallucinations, or misidentifications. Hynek became increasingly critical of the Air Force's methodology and conclusions. On September 4, 1968, a letter was sent to Hynek from Colonel Raymond S. Sleeper, Commander, Headquarters Foreign Technology Division at Wright-Patterson Air Force

---

34. Hynek, *Night Siege,* xi.

Base in Ohio, making the following three points, and we quote from Colonel Sleeper's letter:

1. During the past few years you have publicly criticized Project Blue Book for their lack of scientific evaluations of some unidentified flying object reports.
2. I would like you to address your efforts, during the next thirty days, towards defining those areas of scientific weakness which presently exist in the Project Blue Book office. Please confine your paper to scientific methodology which should be used and do not concern yourself with Air Force policy or history.
3. Your recommendations should be precise, detailed, and practical. Your report should reach my offer no later than October 1, 1968.[35]

Hynek gave a lengthy reply to Sleeper. Among other things, Hynek took issue with the Air Force's determination that UFOs have no hostile intent against the United States:

> . . . The only logical basis on which it can be stated that UFOs do not constitute a possible threat to the United States is that so far nothing has happened to the United States from that source. . . . Many reports are not investigated until weeks or even months after they are made; clearly if hostility were ever intended, it would occur long before the report was investigated. (This is akin to having the Pearl Harbor radar warnings [which went unheeded] investigated three weeks after Pearl Harbor.)[36]

The statistical analyses performed by the Air Force were also faulted by Hynek who labeled them "a travesty on the branch of mathematics known as statistics." He also stated that "Blue Book is a closed system. It has, so to speak, fallen victim to the closed loop type of operation, to its own propaganda."[37]

---

35. Hynek, *UFO Experience,* p. 167
36. Ibid., p. 36.
37. Ibid., pp. 255–256.

Another slant on the government coverup view is that the UFOs are some kind of secret weapon being developed by the United States, or perhaps by other governments in concert with the United States. Judging from some of the injuries witnesses have received—burns, dizziness, faintings, comas, and amnesia—it is sometimes asserted that these are the effects of high-tech experimental weapons.

To be sure, the major powers of the world have experimented with microwave technology, known under the acronym HPM (high power microwave). Such technology has many military applications such as jamming or burning the electronic software of enemy missiles, aircraft, or tank systems. Furthermore, microwaves have been shown to have an adverse effect on living tissue by heating and possibly burning tissue. Brain temperature increases of only a few degrees can cause convulsions, unconsciousness, and even death. Relatively weak microwave pulses can disturb cell membranes and affect an individual's ability to function.

UFOs and NASA

Generally speaking, U.S. astronauts have denied that they have any verifiable evidence of UFO encounters. Jim Marrs, however, thinks this is part of the plan, a concerted effort to hide the truth about UFOs. In fact, Marrs argues that NASA means "Never A Straight Answer,"[38] and points out that there are at least two astronauts who have departed from the NASA "party line." They are Edgar Mitchell and Gordon Cooper.

On an "Oprah Winfrey" show aired on July 19, 1991, Mitchell stated: "I do believe that there is a lot more known about extraterrestrial investigation than is available to the public right now. . . . It's a long, long story. It goes back to World War II when all of that happened, and is highly classified stuff."

Mitchell was even more candid on a 1996 "Dateline NBC" broadcast: "I have no firsthand experience, but I have had the opportunity to meet with people from three countries who in the course of their official duties claim to have had personal firsthand encounter experiences . . . with ex-

---

38. Marrs, p. 18.

traterrestrials." When asked whether he thought that extraterrestrials have already visited planet Earth Mitchell said: "From what I now understand and have experienced and seen the evidence for, I think the evidence is very strong, and large portions of it are classified . . . by governments."

Gordon Cooper explained that astronauts are generally reluctant to divulge what they know about UFOs "due to the great numbers of people who have indiscriminately sold fake stories and forged documents abusing their names and reputations without hesitation."[39]

In a chapter entitled "Never A Straight Answer," Whitley Strieber reports on what he believes is a NASA coverup of an incident that happened on September 15, 1991. At a time when large numbers of UFO sightings were being photographed and videotaped in Mexico, a video aboard the space shuttle *Discovery* shows approximately a dozen objects moving through the sky at a high rate of speed. One of the objects, which has come to be known as the "target," appears near the horizon. The objects suddenly stop. Shortly thereafter there is a bright flash, and the objects move off at high speed. Two seconds later two streaks come up from below, moving through the area previously occupied by the "target." A hypothesis that has been gaining surprising support is that the streaks are pulses of energy from an advanced beam weapon.

NASA responded to congressional inquiries by stating that "the objects seen are orbiter generated debris illuminated by the sun. The flicker of light is the result of firing of the attitude thrusters on the orbiter, and the abrupt motions of the particles result from the impact of gas jets from the thrusters."[40]

Congress, the scientific community, and the American public have generally believed the NASA explanation. Two men, however, have not. Dr. Jack Kasher, a physicist, and Dr. Mark J. Carlotto, an imaging specialist, have dismissed the NASA explanation. But what explanation have they come up with? Dr. Kasher states: "One possible explanation is that

---

39. Ibid., pp. 18–19.
40. Whitley Strieber, *Confirmation: The Hard Evidence of Aliens Among Us* (New York: St. Martin's Press, 1998), pp. 54–55.

we were firing at them." If such is true, it would mean that we possess defensive wounds of a technological level of development far in advance of what is publicly known and that we are currently engaged in hostilities against whom or what those dots represent. That, of course, would explain why the intelligence community, NASA, and the Air Force are tight-lipped about UFOs. After analyzing the data Strieber gives this possible explanation:

> A group of unknown objects are approaching the orbiter. They are targeted. But they detect the targeting process. They stop, presumably in order to determine the intended trajectory of some sort of incoming fire. A flash of light takes place, which must have revealed this information, because they then move off at high speed on new trajectories of their own. . . . A second later, two pulses of light come up from below, moving through the area where the "target" object was previously maneuvering.[41]

At the time of this incident the shuttle was near the west coast of Australia. There is a large, top-secret American installation at Pine Gap near Alice Springs in central Australia. The facility is managed by the supersecret U.S. National Reconnaissance Office, an organization loosely connected to the U.S. Air Force, but reporting to the CIA. Local residents have reported UFO sightings and strange flashes of light in the area.[42] For those who are inclined to be trusting of the government and to wince at the words "government cover-up," Jim Marrs has a word of advice:

> The truly skeptical must evaluate experts—particularly government experts—in the same manner they would any individual: Has this source proven trustworthy in the past? Unfortunately, the government's track record in veracity is shameful. U.N. ambassador Adlai Stevenson, based on information given him by government sources, assured the world

41. Ibid., p. 59.
42. Ibid.

that the United States had absolutely no connection with the ill-fated Bay of Pigs invasion in 1961. The public was told there was "light at the end of the tunnel" in Vietnam just prior to the 1968 Tet offensive. President Richard Nixon said he was not a crook just before he resigned to avoid impeachment. In 1975, the public was told there was a serious shortage of gasoline, yet storage tanks in Texas were filled to the brim. In 1980, President Ronald Reagan gained office by promising to balance the federal budget, then ran up a two trillion dollar deficit. President Clinton admitted he smoked marijuana but declared he never inhaled. The list is endless. If the U.S. government were an individual, no one would have anything to do with him.[43]

But Are They Space Brothers or Demon Spirits?

It is common to old that UFOs are space vehicles manned by extra-terrestrial beings from other planets. This view is very ancient. Zecharia Sitchen, a Russian-born linguistics expert who is one of the few people able to read the ancient Sumerian language, states that ancient Babylon and Sumerian sources claim that man's early history was shaped by visitors from a twelfth planet in our solar system which is called "Nibiru" by the Sumerians and "Marduk" by the Babylonians. The planet is "only a thirty-degree inclined orbit to the parallax of our solar system" which leads it far into space. It comes close to the Earth every thirty-six hundred years and is due back between the year 2060 and 2065. The ancients believed that the aliens from Nibiru wanted to return to their home planet but realized that to do so would cause a disastrous flood on planet Earth. Agreeing not to share their secret knowledge with anyone so that the flood-catastrophe would decimate the human population of planet Earth, they returned to their planet. One of their members, however, broke their agreement and warned the human Noah of a coming flood.[44]

Many in modern times have argued in similar fashion that aliens are simply inhabitants of other planets, and that they are physical beings just

43. Marrs, xiii.
44. Ibid., pp. 56–57.

like we are. Several voices, however, have been sounding a different note. Are these aliens perhaps from another dimension of existence?

The Multidimensional View

Several notable ufologists are arguing for just such a hypothesis. Vallee argues that there may be a form "of life and consciousness that operates on properties of space-time we have not yet discovered." And one need not think that this form of life has to come from outer space. "It could certainly come from another solar system in our galaxy, or from another galaxy. But it could also coexist with us and remain undetected. The entities could be multidimensional beyond space-time itself."[45]

Hynek shares similar views. If UFOs are physical phenomena subject to the laws of physics "we must still explain how such tangible hardware can change shape before our eyes, [and] vanish in a Cheshire cat manner. . . . We must wonder, too, where UFOs are 'hiding' when not manifesting themselves to human eyes."[46]

Ritchie likewise argues against identifying aliens as "corporeal beings from other planets and star systems, traveling in material spacecraft." This "extraterrestrial hypothesis," he argues, "strikes me as mere fancy . . . at the very least, it is unsupported by evidence." The fact that UFOs make phenomenal maneuvers at unbelievably high speeds proves to Ritchie that they are not material spacecraft because they perform contrary "to the known laws of motion." This does not mean, however, that Ritchie doubts that UFOs are real. He writes:

> The UFO phenomenon is essentially occult in character. Involvement in occultism precedes or accompanies close encounters in many individual cases, and various aspects of the UFO phenomenon—such as "channeling" of extraterrestrial entities—are virtually identical to occult practices outside the realm of UFO studies. Also, one finds numerous

45. Vallee, *Revelations,* p. 237.
46. Taken from Missler and Eastman, p. 53.

links between certain prominent "contactees" and practitioners of occultism.[47]

This would suggest that UFOs are a spiritual phenomenon tying in somehow with the struggle between the forces of good and evil. This is becoming apparent to some investigators because they seem to exercise control on human values and beliefs.

. . . Certain elements of belief appear so frequently in UFO contact reports that one must suspect that they form part of a belief system or systems that the UFO phenomenon is engineered (if one may use that word) to encourage. Those elements include collectivism; the unification of human society into some kind of global regime; veneration, bordering on worship, of nature and of natural objects; faith in occult principles and practices, such as mediumism or "channeling"; discouragement of traditional Judeo-Christian religious beliefs, such as the doctrine of the divinity, crucifixion, and resurrection of Christ; and a syncretistic set of religious beliefs with identifiable parallels in Buddhism, Hinduism, and shamanism. These elements also are all part and parcel of the so-called New Age movement, and one may view the modern UFO phenomenon as a companion to that movement.[48]

The occultic connection with UFOs must be taken seriously. In fact, many of the features and characteristics of UFO abduction accounts bear strong parallels with occultic literature, a conclusion Vallee has developed in many of his works. In *Invisible College,* Vallee shows "that the structure of abduction stories was identical to that of occult initiation rituals." In *Passport to Magonia,* Vallee concludes that "contact with ufonauts was only a modern extension of the age-old tradition of contact with nonhuman consciousness in the form of angels, demons, elves, and sylphs." Though sounding bizarre, Vallee maintains that "such contact includes abduction,

---

47. Ritchie, v.
48. Ibid., vi.

ordeal (including surgical operations), and sexual intercourse with the aliens."[49]

There are numerous other points of contact between the occultic phenomena and UFO sightings. For example, "in a small but significant number of UFO encounter reports, witnesses may report seeing a large black dog in the company of alleged extraterrestrials." Ritchie observes that "this element of UFO lore constitutes a close parallel with reports of such dogs in the literature on the supernatural." In Great Britain there is a legend about "Black Shuck," a large dog with glowing eyes. Supposedly, anyone who sees Black Shuck will die within a year after the experience. Interestingly, the sensation of a feeling of deathly cold, or deep chill, is common to Black Shuck encounters as well as encounters with UFOs and their occupants.[50]

Other connections with the occult and UFOs can be seen in the life of the Russian occultist Helena Petrovna Blavatsky whose work "provides a small but significant link between the modern UFO movement and occultism." Blavatsky, founder of Theosophy, "a nineteenth-century occult phenomenon that gave rise to much of the modern New Age movement," relates a strange incident involving the *Book of Dzyan*. In this purportedly ancient Indian chronicle is found the story of the arrival of extraterrestrials on planet Earth in a metal vehicle to set up a colony. The account relates that there was dissension in outer space leading to a battle involving weapons that are similar to modern guided missiles with nuclear warheads. The story bears some striking resemblances to tales of ancient astronauts. Though highly imaginary, the story is cited in numerous books on UFOs, and is related in Blavatsky's 1886 work *The Secret Doctrine*.[51]

Messengers of Deception

When investigating the backgrounds of those who have been abducted by UFOs it soon becomes apparent that many of the abductees have an

---

49. Vallee, *Confrontations,* p. 177
50. Ritchie, p. 30.
51. Ibid., p. 31.

established connection with occultic and New Age beliefs. The people who are carried off by UFOs are the people who have been dabbling in the paranormal, Eastern religions, and practices that are contrary to the biblical world and life view. Significantly, many of the messages channeled from aliens speak about man's oneness with the Christ and a cosmic consciousness. New Age writer and UFO devotee Brad Steiger denies that there will be a literal Second Coming of Christ. According to Steiger, the true doctrine of the Second Coming is that the human race will have a second opportunity to express its true Christ consciousness. It is in this way that mankind will take a giant leap forward. As Groothius observes, this is but an echo of the ancient Gnostic message loved by New Age theorists: "Humans are enmeshed in matter, but they can liberate the Christ energy within them."[52]

A common message channeled from alien visitors is that the established Christian religions have been engaged in a deliberate coverup which has masked Christ's true message. These messages claim that the Bible has been altered by Christian fundamentalists, or that the Bible is incomplete and needs some additional books which the "Church" has deliberately omitted from the canon of Scripture.

Well, then, where can we find the "true Bible"? Extraterrestrial entities, it is believed by some in the UFO cult, have been given the "true Bible." Known as *The Urantia Book,* this gigantic 2,097-page volume claims to have been assembled by extraterrestrial beings, known as "Revelators," bearing imposing names such as "Perfector of Wisdom," "Divine Counselor," "One Without Name," and channeled by an unidentified human. *The Urantia Book* has gone through eleven printings in the U.S. and has been translated into Spanish and Finnish, along with Russian and Dutch language editions. Over 770 are devoted to the life of Christ, much of it focusing on the eighteen "lost years of Jesus" between His twelfth and His thirtieth birthdays. Though the canonic New Testament is silent concerning this time period, *The Urantia Book* claims that Jesus traveled to differ-

---

52. Douglas Groothius, *Jesus in an Age of Controversy* (Eugene, OR: Harvest House, 1996), p. 203.

ent parts of the world learning much wisdom from the East. Supposedly, Jesus' teachings gleaned from these travels have been deliberately omitted by the New Testament writers.

Though it is impossible to give a detailed description of the contents of *The Urantia Book,* some of its teachings which conflict with the biblical revelation is the denial of the fall and depravity of the human race, the teaching that all humans have a "divine spark" within, and the erroneous notion that Jesus did not die to atone for the sin of mankind. "The Gospel of the Kingdom," declares *The Urantia Book,* is "the fact of the fatherhood of God, coupled with the resulting truth of the sonship-brotherhood of man."[53]

Production of a Hybrid Race by Naughty Aliens?

No discussion of UFOs would be complete apart from at least a cursory study of Genesis 6:1–4. Some claim that this passage has absolutely nothing to do with UFOs. Others, however, claim that it provides God's perspective on this marginal mystery that is becoming a major issue. We quote the passage:

> And it came to pass, when men began to multiply on the face of the earth, and daughters were born unto them, That the sons of God saw the daughters of men that they were fair; and they took them wives of all which they chose. And the LORD said, My spirit shall not always strive with man, for that he also is flesh: yet his days shall be an hundred and twenty years. There were giants [*nephilim*] in the earth in those days; and also after that, when the sons of God came in unto the daughters of men, and they bare children to them, the same became mighty men which were of old, men of renown.

Of vital importance is the identification of "the sons of God." Some maintain that they are the godly line of Seth who married unbelieving women. In this view the Sethites of chapter five ("the sons of God") married the

53. Ibid., pp. 206–207.

Cainites ("the daughters of men") of chapter four. In other words, they violated the principle that believers are to marry "only in the Lord" (1 Corinthians 7:39). This interpretation stands or falls on two questions: does the phrase "the sons of God" refer to godly men, and were the sons of Seth godly?

A second view is that "the sons of God" refers to the kings of the ancient world, closely associated with various deities, who wanted to build their harems and populate the Earth with their offspring. This view depends on being able to demonstrate that "the sons of God" is a reference to pagan kings. Does the Bible ever use that phrase in reference to pagan kings?

The third view maintains that "the sons of God" (*bne ha elohim*) is really a reference to angels. On at least three occasions that phrase is used in reference to angels (Job 1:6; 2:1; 38:7). A similar phrase (*bar elohim*) is used in Daniel 3:25 to refer to a superhuman figure. In Scripture the phrase "the sons of God" refers to beings directly brought into existence by Divine agency, such as Adam, angels, or born-again believers. Adam was created by God, as were angels. Likewise, of born-again believers Scripture says, "Which were born, not of blood, nor of the will of the flesh, nor of the will of man, but of God" (John 1:13). The only beings at the time of Genesis 6 brought into existence by direct Divine agency were angels. Significantly, of Adam it is said that he was made "in the likeness of God" (Genesis 5:1), but of his son Seth it is said that he was fathered in Adam's "own likeness, after his [Adam's] image" (Genesis 5:3).

The view that "the sons of God" is a reference to angels was the uniform view of ancient Jewish writers as well as the early church fathers. The ancient historian Josephus believed in this third view. In his *Antiquities of the Jews* (Book I, chapter 3, paragraph 1), Josephus writes: ". . . for many angels of God accompanied with women, and begat sons which proved unjust, and despisers of all that was good, on account of the confidence they had in their own strength; for the tradition is, That these men did what resembled the acts of those whom the Grecians call giants."

A footnote in the Whiston translation states: "This notion that the fallen angels were, in some sense the fathers of the old giants, was the constant opinion of antiquity." In Book V, chapter 2, paragraph 3, we find another reference to this incident: "There were till then left the race of giants, who had bodies so large, and countenances so entirely different from other men, that they were surprising to the sight, and terrible to the hearing. The bones of these men are still shown to this very day, unlike to any creditable relations of other men."

A common objection to the angel view is based on a statement that our Lord made, as recorded in Matthew 22:30 where our Lord was speaking to the Sadducees, a quasi religious group of the first century who denied some of the basic tenets of Judaism: "For in the resurrection they neither marry, nor are given in marriage, but are as the angels of God in heaven." This verse indicates, however, *that the angels of God in Heaven* do not marry. It speaks about marriage; but it does not rule out cohabitation on Earth outside of marriage.

Recent happenings make the angel view plausible. Remember, angels coming down from Heaven and cohabiting with women was something that happened in the days of Noah. And what did Jesus say about conditions on Earth at the time of His return? "But as the days of Noe were, so shall also the coming of the Son of man be" (Matthew 24:37).

Insight on the News for August 9, 1999, presented an article by Julia Duin entitled "Space Aliens Steal Kisses?" The article reports on some of the individuals who have given their testimony regarding what happened to them when UFOs abducted them. These individuals were speaking at the MUFON '99 International Symposium help just outside Washington, D.C. "MUFON" stands for Mutual UFO Network. "Essentially the scenario is the same," the article states. "Aliens snatch unsuspecting people and perform sexual experiments on them in the hopes of creating a hybrid human-alien race."

Perhaps the most unusual, and most important, testimony was that of Kelly Cahill of Australia. She told of a multi-witness abduction that occurred early in the morning of August 8, 1993. On that day, six individuals in three different cars reported to authorities that they were forced over on the side of the road. Cahill tells how these individuals got out of their cars to investigate what looked like a hovering craft with bright orange lights and how they were approached by a seven-foot-tall being cloaked completely in black who had luminous red eyes. Cahill claims that she was knocked to the ground and temporarily blinded. Reporter Duin writes: "Cahill remembers little after that, until she and her husband found themselves back in their car. Later, she found a triangular cut burned into her abdomen and began experiencing uterine bleeding. People in other cars claimed to have been taken into alien ships. Two of them, she says, emerged with strange-shaped slashes on their inner thighs and ankles."

Dr. Robert Jastrow, former head of NASA's Goddard Institute for Space Studies, has expressed that he is "open to the possibility of extraterrestrial life in the universe, but skeptical of proposed alien origin of UFOs due to lack of strong physical evidence that would support this hypothesis."[54]

We would think that the testimony of eyewitnesses such as Winston Churchill, Werner Von Braun, President Jimmy Carter, airline pilots, police officers, and thousands of others that we would consider reliable people, are credible accounts. Rev. Noah Hutchings believes such accounts, because as noted before, at the age of twelve he saw three unidentifiable objects—something that he will never forget. Still, governments refuse to acknowledge this evidence.

In this chapter, we have referenced a variety of reports from around the world by those of other countries, educational backgrounds, and cultures. Admittedly, some may be questionable, especially the UFO abductions. However, it is our conclusion that the majority are accounts of actual sightings and related events. The reports of UFOs of many sizes, shapes, and activities may be difficult to reconcile, but we really do not know if there is a standard UFO. The ones Rev. Hutchings saw were round, bright, steady, and traveled at a rapid course, stopping suddenly without slowing down. They lined up, indicating intelligence.

---

54. Wikipedia.org

Evidence That Cannot Be Refuted

On September 25, 2010, five retired Air Force officers and a Navy Intelligence officer testified at the National Press Club about their experience with UFOs appearing over nuclear missile sites, and then disarming the Minuteman intercontinental nuclear missiles (ICBMs).

The officers testifying were:

» Dwynne Arneson, USAF (ret.) Lt. Colonel, Control Officer, Malmstrom Air Force Base in Montana.
» Bruce Fenstermacher, USAF (ret.) Captain, Minuteman Launch Officer
» Robert Jameson, USAF (ret.), Missile Target Officer
» Jerry Nelson, USAF (ret.) 1st Lieutenant, Atlas Missile Launch Officer
» Robert Salas, USAF (ret.) Captain, Minuteman Launch Officer
» Patrick McDonough, USN (ret.) Master Chief, Naval Intelligence Command

All of these retired Air Force and Navy officers were directly involved with programming Minuteman or Atlas ICBMs. All of them testified that they had problems with UFOs in the form of round flashing objects, some thirty feet across, which disarmed missiles in their silos. One retired Air Force commander on a U.S. airfield in England testified that they had the same problems in England, and that Winston Churchill forbade the release of any information pertaining to UFOs, including UFOs flying alongside their fighter and bomber airplanes in World War II.

The description of the UFOs given by these retired USAF officers corresponds exactly with the three UFOs Rev. Hutchings saw in 1937.

The only answer as to what UFOs are, or what their mission is, is provided in the Bible under the subject of angelic activity. If so, then we can understand why UFOs would be concerned with disarming nuclear missiles. In the Book of Revelation we find that such angelic activity is to increase in the last days. The officers testified that the power and intelligence of the UFOs was beyond comprehension.

Evidently, on the basis of the testimony of the five retired U.S. Air Force officers, on February 5, 2011, the British government released its files on UFO activity, which included some 8,500 reports. The statement accompanying the release of the files included the following: ". . . The extra-terrestrial files released by the UK's National Archives illustrate how incidents were discussed at the highest level of government and by security services worldwide, including at the UN and CIA." These files confirm the evidences of UFOs, aliens, and discuss at length the ongoing alien invasion that is occurring around the world.

Well, the reader can see why this is such a complicated—and important—issue. Perhaps the aliens themselves will help solve the mystery. But that will probably happen in the Tribulation, and by then we will all be in glory with the Lord.

Though no one can be dogmatic about the UFOs, don't be surprised if you see something in the sky that defies explanation.

Mystery Monsters

Nessie, the Abominable Snowman, Bigfoot, and Dragons

In the Genesis account of creation, Moses recorded all the basic forms of life God created. Almost all of these forms are in evidence today. However, some species of birds and animals like the roc and the Tasmanian devil have been driven to extinction, or near extinction. There is even evidence in Scripture of giant animals—the dinosaurs?—that roamed the Earth. Job 40:15, for example, speaks of "behemoth." Some have argued that it is no more than a modern hippopotamus, but that seems rather doubtful since the scripture says, "He moveth his tail like a cedar . . ." (vs. 17). Hippos have small tails and it makes no sense to compare their tails to cedar trees.

Are They Around Today?

How long ago dinosaurs lived, and why they became extinct, is under discussion by scientists and Bible scholars alike. Some theologians believe that they were part of another creation on Earth that was destroyed in the so-called "gap" between Genesis 1:1 and Genesis 1:2. Others believe that they were destroyed in the Flood because the changes that God brought about in the environment following the Flood made it impossible for them to survive. The age in which they lived, according to evolutionary scientists, is given as millions or even hundreds of millions of years ago.

These greatly exaggerated periods of time are open to serious question. The archaic fish called the coelacanth (*SEE-la-kanth*), that supposedly became extinct 65 to 75 million years ago, has been captured by modern-day fishermen. Marco Polo, in his travels to the Far East, wrote about a giant flying bird called the "roc." Significantly, recent discoveries of the roc's egg shells, which are three times larger than the egg of an ostrich, indicate that this supposedly prehistoric fowl probably became extinct not more than five or six hundred years ago. Such discoveries lend a measure of credibility to the belief that many of the supposedly extinct life forms, such as the Loch Ness Monster and the Abominable Snowman, are still alive in our world today.

The Loch Ness Monster

In Lamentations 4:3 we read: "Even the sea monsters draw out the breast, they give suck to their young. . . ." There are several references to a sea monster called Leviathan in Scripture. Isaiah 27:1 seems to indicate that this beast is more than a hippopotamus, or an alligator: "In that day the Lord with his sore and great and strong sword shall punish leviathan the piercing serpent, even leviathan that crooked serpent; and he shall slay the dragon that is in the sea." There are thirty-nine references to "dragons" or "a dragon" in Scripture. In some of these references the dragon is described as the serpent that dwells in the midst of the sea.

In Australia, Wyoming, and in several other localities, the bones of huge lizards have been discovered. These giant reptiles grew to be thirty feet in length, and scientists expressed the opinion that they were the last of the dinosaurs, supposedly becoming extinct 30 million years ago. That's quite a number. Thirty million would be five thousand times the age of the recorded history of man. Is that a realistic figure? In the early 1920s a pilot was forced down on the remote and deserted island of Komodo, located in the South Pacific. He brought back stories of a monster lizard that could gulp down a hog or deer in a few bites. The Museum of Natural History assigned Douglas Burden to investigate. After a 12,000-mile journey, Mr. Burden, in June of 1926, saw this "thirty million–year-old, extinct neo-dinosaur." It has since been called "the Komodo dragon" and has survived on that remote island because it had no natural enemies.

This has happened so many times in the last 150 years. In 1860, British journalist H. M. Stanley related how Pygmies living in the tropical rainforests of the Congo captured a wild donkey which they called an *atti*. Zoologists were stumped as to what this creature could be because there were no donkeys living in the Congo. But was it perhaps a zebra? The answer was definitely "no." Zebras don't live in tropical rainforests.

In 1899, Sir Harry Johnston asked a group of Pygmies about the *atti*. To Johnston's surprise, they knew exactly what he was talking about because they had seen several! They called it the *okapi,* and said it was a mule with stripes like a zebra. Johnston did further research and sought more information about this strange creature. But the more information he found, the more bizarre the creature seemed. The *okapi* appeared to be some kind of a small horse with hooves like an antelope, ears like a donkey, and stripes like a zebra—that lived in the wrong place!

After hearing of Johnston's interest in the *okapi,* another British official sent him a skin and two skulls of the mysterious animal. Several zoologists studied the specimens and concluded that everyone thus far had been wrong about the *okapi*. It was not a horse, antelope, donkey, or zebra, but a short-necked relative of the modern giraffe! Of course, the *okapi* is not a hideous monster. It's just different. And it was not recognized by the scientific community at that time.

In the twentieth century, several other unusual and unknown creatures were discovered, such as the mountain gorilla and the pygmy chimpanzee. Perhaps the most amazing discovery of all has been the coelacanth, a six-foot-long fish resembling a prehistoric sea creature. And more unclassified creatures are being discovered. The International Society of Cryptozoology is a scientific organization devoted to the study of unusual creatures whose existence is not yet accepted by the scientific world. In 1982 the society chose the *okapi* as its symbol.[1]

---

1. Paul Robert Walker, *Bigfoot and Other Legendary Creatures* (San Diego: Harcourt Brace, 1992), pp. 1–3.

The recent catch of a coelacanth has significance for this present investigation. On December 22, 1938, a grouper-sized fish was caught off the mouth of the Chalumna River near East London, South Africa. No one on board had ever seen this kind of fish. A sketch of the fish was sent to J. L. B. Smith, a South African chemistry professor with a growing reputation for the study of the fishes of the Indian Ocean. Smith, hardly believing what he saw, concluded that the fish was a member of the coelacanth family, but wanted more convincing proof. He searched for some fourteen years, and then on December 21, 1952, Eric Hunt, an English ship captain trading among the islands of the eastern Indian Ocean, obtained a specimen from natives of the Comoran Archipelago, midway between East Africa and Madagascar.[2]

Evidently, there have been unusual creatures that have been around for a long time, and yet no one has admitted that they exist. Does the Loch Ness Monster fall into the same category? Is it another "extinct" monster that is still alive and well on planet Earth?

A History of Sightings

Loch Ness is a deep, dark lake in the highlands of Scotland. It runs in a southwesterly direction from Inverness. It is the largest freshwater lake by volume in Great Britain, and the third largest lake in Europe. Initially it was thought bottomless, through in this century research has shown that the average depth along the centerline of the lake is about 500 feet. There is one point which is 734 feet in depth. The bottom is covered generally with a thick mud or a stiff, yellow clay, except in two spots where there is nothing on the bottom but bare rock. The water of the lake is murky due to the suspended particles of peat, which lowers the visibility to only a few feet, or even less. The water at the bottom is anaerobic, which means that there is no oxygen of sufficient quantity to support either plant or animal life. Animals and people who have drowned in Loch Ness never return to the surface because of this feature.[3]

2. www.dinofish.com

3. Thomas G. Aylesworth, *Science Looks at Mysterious Monsters* (New York: Julian Messner,

Reports of Nessie, the affectionate term used by locals for the Loch Ness Monster, go back to at least A.D. 565 when the Irish missionary St. Columba was walking along the shore of the lake preaching to the Picts, Scots, and Northumbrians. When Columba drew close to a certain part of the shore he found some of the local people in the process of burying a man who had been mauled by a large monster.

Columba had a disciple, a man named Lugne, who swam across the narrowest part of the lake to bring back a small boat that had been left on the other side. As Lugne was swimming he was suddenly confronted by "a very odd beastie, something like a huge frog, only it was not a frog." The story goes on to relate that the monster was about to devour Lugne, but Columba shouted at the monster and said: "Go thou no further nor touch the man. Go back at once!" According to the biography of St. Columba, written in the eighth century A.D.: "On hearing this word . . . the monster was terrified and fled away again more quickly than if it had been dragged on by ropes, though it approached Lugne as he swam so closely that between man and monster there was no more than the length of one punt pole." The ancient report indicates that the local tribesmen were so impressed that they were immediately converted. Local legend teaches that St. Columba's work was so thorough that the Loch Ness Monster was not seen again until the late 1800s.[4] It would appear that local tribes of the northern regions have always known about these creatures. "The Vikings," writes Bauer, "had been very familiar with the saltwater sea serpents and had modeled the shapes of their vessels after the bulky bodies, long and tapering necks, and small heads."[5]

There have been several sightings of Nessie in the twentieth century. In 1933, over ninety people claimed to have seen the monster. In 1934, there were one hundred thirty reported sightings of Nessie. At the end of the twentieth century, some four thousand people had reported seeing

1982), pp. 84–85.

4. Ibid., pp. 85–86.

5. Henry H. Bauer, *The Enigma of Loch Ness* (Chicago: University of Illinois Press, 1986), p. 12.

the strange creature that appears from time to time in Loch Ness. Perhaps the strongest piece of evidence for the existence of Nessie is a photograph taken by Tim Dinsdale in 1960. It was analyzed in 1966 by British military intelligence experts who concluded that it was a photograph of a creature that was at least sixteen feet long. Initially, researchers thought that Nessie was a single, individual creature that had wandered into the Ness from the sea. Now it appears, however, that there is a large known population of "monsters" living and breeding in Loch Ness.[6]

In 1962, the Loch Ness Phenomena Investigation Bureau (later known as Loch Ness Investigation, or LNI) was founded by Norman Collins, Richard Fitter, David James, Peter Scott, and Constance Whyte. For about ten years LNI put together teams for surface photography, aerial surveillance by glider, night observation by searchlight and infrared equipment, sonar from shore- and water-based units, attraction of Nessies through baiting, and even underwater searches by submarine. In succeeding years the Academy of Applied Science came close to carrying out a search for the monster with sonar-triggered cameras and strobes mounted on dolphins, but one of the trained dolphins died before it could be brought to Loch Ness. In 1977, Doc Shiels, stage performer and psychic, attempted to bring Nessie to the surface through a variety of psychic means, and has obtained photos which have been attested to be genuine.[7]

Various attempts have been made to explain the identity of the Loch Ness Monster. Some thought that the creature had wandered into the lake from the sea during a heavy storm when the water in the River Ness was high. A view that is quite popular is that Nessie is a landlocked creature. Initially much of the northern hemisphere was covered by seawater. In other words, the oceans covered a great deal of what is now dry land. Following the Ice Age, the subsequent thaw which freed much of the land from the weight of the ice allowed the landmass to rise very slowly. Many of the fjords (long saltwater inlets situated between parallel mountain ranges) were inhabited by a variety of marine life that came to the

6. Walker, pp. 322–333.
7. Bauer, pp. 163–166.

fjords to find food. Some of these life forms were temporary visitors to the fjords and others took up residence there. With the rise of land, some of the fjords were cut off from the ocean waters and became more and more diluted with freshwater from rain, snow, and runoff from hills and streams. As the saltwater of the fjords became more diluted, these fjords became freshwater lakes (lochs). Some of the marine creatures that lived in these fjords adjusted to the freshwater, but others could not adapt and simply died off. Bauer explains:

> In a number of the newly-formed lakes of the Northern Hemisphere there had been trapped members of that rare, still-not-well-known sort of marine animal, the long-necked sea serpent. These large fish-predators adapted well to the progressive lowering of the salinity of the water, but their continued existence depended on the presence of a large stock of fish to support a viable breeding population—not less than twenty or thirty individuals. . . . Hence, in many of the smaller lakes the sea serpents died out; they could survive nowadays only in such very large lakes as Morar, Ness, and Shiel in Scotland, Okanagan and Champlain in North America, Lagerflot in Iceland, and possibly a few others.[8]

Some have argued against the idea that Nessie is a giant sea creature trapped in the fjords. They have contended that Nessie is a plesiosaur—a group of water-dwelling dinosaurs with small heads, long necks, and large bodies—fitting the descriptions given of Nessie. Those opposed to the plesiosaur theory point out, however, that plesiosaurs have been extinct for 60 million years. Moreover, plesiosaurs were cold-blooded and received their heat from the surrounding environment which, at that time, was allegedly tropical. A true plesiosaur, therefore, could not receive sufficient heat from the cold waters of Loch Ness. Furthermore, plesiosaurs were air-breathing creatures. If Nessie was a plesiosaur, Nessie would have to surface very frequently to breathe. The infrequency of the Nessie

---

8. Ibid., p. 12.

sightings throws this whole theory into question.[9] Interestingly enough, though there has not been enough data gleaned to scientifically classify the Nessies, nevertheless a formal scientific name has been given to them so that official governmental protection could be extended to them as a species. The name given is *Nessiteras rhombopteryx,* meaning "Ness marvel with a diamond-shaped fin."[10]

But have any photographs of Nessie been taken? As a matter of fact, photos have been taken. The LNI has footage of film shot that seems to confirm that Nessies like to eat fish, since salmon are seen in some of the footage jumping out of the water with a Nessie in pursuit. According to Bauer:

> The AAS [Academy of Applied Science] has obtained the best details yet: in 1972 a diamond-shaped flipper about six feet long and two feet wide was captured at two different angles in underwater photographs taken forty-five seconds apart. . . . And in 1975 the Academy had real luck. One shot . . . captured the front of a Nessie, showing parts of two flippers and the long neck, a total length of about seventeen feet. Another shot . . . was claimed to be of the head, indicating the presence of the horns or stalks occasionally mentioned by eyewitnesses, but showing little other detail.[11]

Did the work of the AAS remove all doubts and prove that Nessie is real? Nessie believers thought so, but others were reluctant to reach that conclusion. Scientists at the British Museum in London harshly criticized the photos taken by the AAS. They claimed that their studies showed that the images had been "doctored" through the use of computers. Others voiced the opinion that the photos were just not sufficiently clear to remove all doubts that this was a real creature. By now, the public began to grow

---

9. Elaine Landau, *The Loch Ness Monster* (Brookfield, CT: The Millbrook Press, 1993), pp. 11–12.

10. Bauer, p. 25.

11. Ibid., p. 17.

impatient over all of the uncertainty. There was a cry for closure to the mystery. At one point there was even the demand that the lake be drained to solve the mystery once and for all. But since Loch Ness contains some 263 billion cubic feet of water, it would take years to finish the project. Besides, where would all that water be stored?[12]

Sightings in Other Places

There are several reports of Nessie-type water monsters in other places. In the eighteenth and nineteenth centuries there were reports of a lake monster in Sweden, and the reports have continued into the twentieth-first century. "Champie," the sea monster of Lake Champlain in northeastern New York State, has been sighted several times, as well as creatures in other Scottish lakes and at various locations in Ireland and Russia.[13]

In the mid-1800s there were reports of monsters in some of the lakes in Canada. One of the most famous of the Canadian monsters is Ogopogo. In 1854, an Indian was taking a team of horses on a raft across Lake Okanagan in British Columbia. The Indian told of being grabbed by a gigantic hand that tried to pull him off of the raft. The terrified man managed to escape, but the horses were not so fortunate.

Indeed, Ogopogo seems to have a fondness for horse meat. In another account, a pioneer by the name of John McDougal related an experience that was similar to that of the Indian. McDougal escaped, but the horses were taken and were never seen again. More recent sightings indicate that Ogopogo has a long sinuous body, thirty or more feet in length, consisting of several undulations, perhaps as many as five.

In 1959, R. H. Millar, the owner-publisher of the small-town Vernon *Advertiser,* claimed that he also saw Ogopogo. In the July 20 edition of his newspaper he wrote the following account.

> Returning from a cruise down Okanagan Lake, traveling at ten miles per hour, I noticed, about two hundred fifty feet in our wake, what ap-

---

12. Landau, p. 35
13. Walker, p. 34.

peared to be the serpent. On picking up the field glasses, my thought was verified. It was Ogopogo, and it was traveling a great deal faster than we were. I would judge about fifteen to seventeen miles per hour.

The head was about nine inches above the water. The head was definitely snakelike with a blunt nose. . . . Our excitement was short-lived. We watched for about three minutes, as Ogie did not appear to like the boat coming on him broadside; he very gracefully reduced the five humps which were so plainly visible, lowered his head, and gradually submerged. At no time was the tale visible. . . . The color is very dark greenish. . . . This sea serpent glides gracefully in a smooth motion. . . . This would lead one to believe that in between the humps it possibly has some type of fin which is works . . . to control direction.[14]

Ogopogo has many Canadian "relatives." There is Manipogo, a serpent-like monster sighted in Lake Winnipeg in Manitoba. The monster is said to have a loud bellow like a train. Other Canadian lake monsters are Igopogo, the dog-faced monster of Lake Simcoe, located forty miles north of Toronto, and T-Zum-A in Lake Shuswap, British Columbia. In addition, lake monsters have been reported in upstate New York and in Utah.[15]

Yeti, or the Abominable Snowman

Another marginal mystery that continues to mystify is the "Abominable Snowman," known as "Yeti" by the peoples of the Himalaya mountain range. "Yeti" is the anglicized version of *yeh-teh*, a Nepalese word that means "snowman." "Abominable Snowman" comes from, the Tibetan name given to the creature, *metoh-kangmi*, meaning "disgusting snowman."[16] The local people who have seen yetis claim that they are so strong that they can toss huge boulders as though they were small stones, and have been seen uprooting deep-rooted shrubs. They are said to give off a disgusting odor, hence their name. According

---

14. Aylesworth, pp. 108–109.
15. Ibid., pp. 109–110.
16. Walker, p. 19.

to the descriptions of this creature, it is hairy and strong, and lives at extremely high altitudes. Hairiness is believed to be an indication of wildness. Esau had hair over his body, and he "was a cunning hunter" (Genesis 25:25; 27:11–32).

Mysterious wild men have been seen in the Himalayan region for hundreds of years. The Sherpas, a tribe of hardy people living beneath Mount Everest in Nepal, tell many stories of yeti. Its fondness for *chang,* a beer-like beverage, is part of the local folklore and, supposedly, it has been used by the Sherpas to drug the yeti, who has an insatiable urge to drink all the *chang* it can get.

Incident at 20,000 Feet

It was not until 1951 that the yeti received international attention. In that year, a British mountain climber, Eric Shipton, came across a strange set of footprints on the Menlung Glacier situated at an elevation of almost twenty thousand feet—almost four miles above sea level. On the same day, Shipton discovered another footprint. This one was clearly defined. The creature that made the footprint only had four toes. Measuring thirteen inches in length and eight inches in width, it showed clearly defined toes. Shipton took several photographs of the footprints. While footprints that have melted usually increase in size, these prints had not yet melted and the measurements accurately reflected the size of the foot that made the print. Shipton and his companion, Michael Ward, followed the tracks for about one mile before the prints disappeared in thinning snow and windswept rock. The London Zoological Society and the natural history department of the British Museum concluded that the footprints had been made by a langur monkey, or perhaps a red bear. That view has been challenged. While bears do walk on two feet, they do so only for a few steps at a time, and then go back to walking on all fours. Against the langur monkey view is the observation that langur monkeys are relatively small in comparison to the size of the footprints that Shipton and Ward had followed, and langur monkeys generally walk on all fours. *The Lancet,* a highly respected British medical journal, defended Shipton and Ward's conclusions, and in 1960 published an article that tentatively admitted the possibility of such a large creature.[17]

There have been more recent reported sightings of the yeti. In 1986, German mountaineer Reinhold Messner claimed that he got to within thirty feet of a yeti. In that same year, British physicist Anthony Wooldridge photographed footprints of a large, high-altitude creature that he believed had been made by a yeti. Wooldridge "proved" that the yeti Messner saw was a strange rock formation, but he was unable to explain the footprints.[18]

Initially, scientists and explorers believed that the yeti lived in a small, isolated region of the Himalayas. However, yeti-like creatures have been sighted in Russia, China, and Mongolia. The alma (*alma* being a Mongolian term meaning "wild man") has been investigated by Dr. Marie-Jeanne Koffman who, by 1966, had gathered over three hundred eyewitness reports from which she was able to describe a "typical" alma. Early conclusions about the alma was that the alma and the yeti were regional names for the same creature. Later research, however, has led to the conclusion that there are at least two different species of "snowmen" in Asia.[19]

Strange Tales?

There are a variety of stories concerning yeti encounters, but perhaps the most dramatic occurred in 1938 and involved Captain d'Auvergne, the curator of the Victoria Memorial near Chowringhee in Calcutta, India. D'Auvergne relates he was travelling by himself in the Himalayas, suffering terribly from the effects of extreme cold and high altitude, when a nine-foot yeti appeared. The creature carried the man several miles to a cave where it fed and nursed him back to health. The curator developed the theory that the yetis were really members of an ancient tribe, the *a-o-re,* who had fled into the mountains centuries earlier to escape persecution. After living for centuries in the harsh mountain environment, the tribe

---

17. Aylesworth, pp. 11–12.
18. Walker, p. 19.
19. Ibid., pp. 26–27.

"evolved" into huge hairy beasts suited to living in that environment.[20]

Many of the yeti encounters, such as the previous one, are anecdotal and open to alternate interpretations. D'Auvergne, for example, could have been suffering from snow blindness and high-altitude sickness. The "nine-foot yeti" could have been an hallucination.

While there seem to be some credible reports of yeti encounters, its existence seems to be wrapped in legend and folklore—though of course there are usually kernels of truth behind legends and folklore. The mountain people who affirm yeti's existence believe that if one is chased by a yeti, the best thing to do is to run downhill. When the creature chases you going downhill, its long hair will fall over its eyes and it will be unable to see. On the other hand, if you are being chased on level ground, you are told to pick up as many stones and sticks as you can carry. Throw them, one by one, at the yeti, who will catch them all, but it won't want to put them down. Soon both of its arms will be weighted down with stones so that it won't be able to chase you. We should point out that the yeti is a good tourist attraction that brings in large sums of money from visitors. In 1960 King Mehendra of Nepal was questioned about his belief in the existence of the yeti. His answer was that "his majesty is no expert, no anthropologist, or zoologist, so he cannot say anything definite about this creature. But all the same," the king said, "it pays us to keep the mystery alive." In certain regions those who want to look for the yeti need a government permit that costs $10,000 per individual.[21]

Not only does the existence of the yeti satisfy a financial need, it may also satisfy a psychological one. Angus Hall, for example, states:

> Perhaps this is the function that the yeti serves for most of us. We need creatures to inhabit the strange borderland between fact and fantasy, and our interest lies not so much in whether they really exist, but in the possibility that they may exist. It is as if the very uncertainty, the remoteness, and the scanty evidence on which our ideas are based, increases the hold

---

20. Aylesworth, p. 16.
21. Ibid., p. 24.

on us, and gives life an extra dimension it would lose if final proof came. These large creatures hovering between man and ape, grappling with nature to survive, satisfy a psychological need for many of us—just as dragons and mermaids did for our ancestors.[22]

Bigfoot or Sasquatch

The mysterious creature known as "Bigfoot," called "Sasquatch" by the Indians of Canada, is a large, hairy, apelike being that walks upright on two feet, and is the North American counterpart to yeti.[23]

The description given by those who claim to have seen this elusive creature corresponds to that of the Himalayan phantom: six or seven feet tall, weighing three hundred pounds or so, humanlike in appearance, reddish-brown hair covering its body, and leaving usually large footprints. Bigfoot has been reported to give off a strong odor which is caused, according to some, by improperly cured animal skins that it wears for protection.[24]

The first sighting of a Bigfoot track by a European most likely occurred in 1811 near what is now known as Jasper, Alberta, Canada. David Thompson, an explorer and fur trader, found a set of strange footprints in the snow. The prints measured fourteen inches long and eight inches wide. They showed four toes, which led Thompson to conclude that whatever made the tracks was not a large bear because bears have five toes.

The earliest written account of a Bigfoot sighting in the U.S. is recorded in an historical pamphlet dated January 2, 1886. It records an event that happened in the Siskiyou country of northern California. The pamphlet called the creature a "wild man" and described it in this way: "The thing was of gigantic size—about seven feet tall—with a bulldog head, short ears, and long hair; it was also furnished with a beard, and was free from hair on such parts of its body as is common among men."[25]

22. Ibid., p. 26.
23. Ibid., p. 27.
24. Walker, p. 58. See also Robert Michael Pyle, *Where Bigfoot Walks: Crossing the Dark Divide* (Boston: Houghton Mifflin Co., 1995), p. 280.
25. Aylesworth, p. 30.

One of the most notable reports concerning Bigfoot was made by President Theodore Roosevelt, who was himself an avid outdoorsman. The story appeared in *The Wilderness Hunter* published in 1893. The account given by Roosevelt related that some kind of a wild beast had killed a man and had eaten half his body in a mountain range between the Salmon and Windom rivers. The following year, two hunters were camping in the same area when they became aware that they were being watched by a strange creature walking on two legs. The next day, the hunters separated. One of the hunters arrived at camp to find the other hunter dead with his neck broken and severe wounds to the throat area. In the article, Mr. Roosevelt reported his belief that the hunter was killed by "something either half-human or half-devil, some great goblin-beast."[26]

The United States has provided some dramatic sightings. In 1924, near Mount St. Helens, in an area that was later called "Ape Canyon"—a fit name in view of what is reported as having taken place there—a group of coal miners were viciously attacked by several Bigfoot. Precisely what triggered the attack is uncertain, since there are two stories of the event that are very similar except in this particular.

One version reports that the miners saw a large apelike creature staring at the group. One of the miners grabbed his rifle and shot the creature in the head, and another miner shot it in the back. It fell off the cliff where it was perched and was never found. The other version states that one of the miners was alone when he met the creature and killed it with three shots in the back. At any rate, the shooting of this individual Bigfoot irritated its companions. Several came out of the woods and assaulted the miner's cabin. One of the accounts reveals the following:

> At night the apes counterattacked, opening the assault by knocking a heavy strip of wood out from between two logs of the miners' cabin. After that there were assorted poundings on the walls, door, and roof, but the building was built to withstand heavy mountain snows and the apes failed to break in. . . . There was . . . the sound of rocks hitting the

---

26. Noah Hutchings, *Marginal Mysteries,* first ed., p. 31.

roof and rolling off, and [the miners] did brace the heavy door from the inside.

They heard creatures thumping around on top of the cabin as well as battering the walls, and they fired shots through the walls and roof without driving them away. The noise went on from shortly after dark till near dawn. . . . The cabin had no windows and of course no one opened the door, so in fact the men inside did not see what was causing the commotion outside.

Nor could Mr. Beck say for sure . . . that there were more than two creatures outside. There were [at least] that many because there had been one on the roof and one pounding the wall simultaneously. However many there were, it was enough for the miners, who packed up and abandoned their mine the next day.[27]

Perhaps one of the most important Bigfoot sightings occurred in 1967. On October 20 of that year, Roger Patterson and his friend Bob Gimlin were in the mountains of northern California. Patterson states that while he was riding on horseback, something spooked his horse, causing the animal to fall. Patterson was able to get his movie camera out of his saddlebag and was able to take twenty-nine feet of sixteen millimeter colored film. Experts have studied the film. Some claim that it is genuine, including a Hollywood special effects expert who checked the film to see if it was "doctored."[28]

Does Bigfoot really exist? To date, more than two thousand people have reported seeing Bigfoot. Even more significant is the fact that Bigfoot tracks have been found in remote regions of northern California, Oregon, Washington State, and British Columbia. The tracks resemble human tracks, but are much larger, farther apart, and, because of the greater weight of the creature making the tracks, pressed further into the soil. Some of the prints are as much as eighteen inches in length and seven inches in width. On the basis of some of the sightings and the size of the

27. Aylesworth, pp. 32–33.
28. Ibid., p. 35.

larger prints, Bigfoot has been estimated to grow as tall as eight feet and to weight up to eight hundred pounds. Since many of the footprints have been found in remote, highly inaccessible areas, it would seem hard to "fake" them with some kind of a footprint machine (see Walker, p. 10). The California Bigfoot Sightings List[29]

> Hundreds of people have reported seeing a large, hairy, human-like creature lurking in the remote regions of California, mostly Northern and central California. . . . The highest rate of sightings and recovered footprints are in the Northwesternmost part of Northern California near the Oregon border around the Humboldt Forest, Bluff Creek, Hoopa, Weitchpec, Orleans, Somes Bar and Willow Creek, located between Crescent City to the North and Eureka to the South; between Interstate 5 and Highway 101 on Highways 299 and 96. Why this general location has more sightings reported is not known. Perhaps because an increase in summer back-packers, bikers, campers, fisherman, would-be trackers and the fact that much has been written about this general area and Bigfoot. . . . Unlike the Eastern reports, the California Bigfoot is extremely shy, illusive and while he seems curious, he is rarely aggressive when confronted by humans. . . . Bigfoot is a good swimmer and are often seen near and around bodies of fresh water—streams, lakes and rivers. They are notable for a putrid, rank odor. Bigfoot enjoys a broad diet ranging from fish, rodents, and deer to fruits, berries and various vegetation. . . . Most of all, the Sasquatch is huge in stature: specimens up to 14 feet tall have been reported (tallest in Canada) with human-like tracks ranging from 11 to 21 inches long but averaging about 16 inches here in California. . . .

Recent reports of sightings in China are becoming more publicized, and Chinese scientists are trying to get hard "proof" that Bigfoot is real. In August of 1999, a hunter reported sighting a seven-foot-tall animal covered with long, red hair, which was moving very quickly.

---

29. www.bigfootencounters.com/sightings.htm

"After examining the evidence, Yuan Zhenxing, an established paleo-anthropologist from the [Chinese Academy of Sciences], ruled that the mystery animal was in fact a bear," an Internet report stated. Scientists have unearthed many fossilized teeth of an extinct giant ape in the Shennongjia National Nature Reserve, and some Chinese scientists have speculated that the reported Bigfoot might be a descendant of one of the giant apes. The Chinese government has launched several searches for Bigfoot, but have come up with no conclusive evidence. There are a few scientists, however, who believe that "the possibility exists that such an animal is still there."[30]

There are many questions about Bigfoot that need to be raised. How is it, for example, that in an area such as California and Oregon, where there are so many hikers and backpackers, and there is a relatively high use of trails in the backcountry, that there have been no bona fide skeletal remains found, that dogs have not killed some of its young, or that hunters have not treed one? But added to that question must be the question: How can you deny the large numbers of sightings and the actual film footage?

It would appear to us that the question of the existence of these "ape men" hinges upon whether or not they are demons inhabiting the bodies of animals in the same manner as the devils from the demoniac went into a herd of swine. The fact that (as in the case of UFOs) all, or almost all, of the encounters involved non-Christians may suggest either that there aren't that many Christians roaming the wildest reaches of the Earth, or, in the event that is not a sound conclusion, that these are demon forces manifesting themselves on planet Earth.

Dragons

The Bible has some horrific monsters in it that no one would want to meet on a dark street, or any other place, for that matter. There are beasts and monsters, some quite intimidating. The following is just a small sample of the passages mentioning dragons.

---

30. Ibid.

» Jeremiah 51:34:"...the king of Babylon hath devoured me ... he hath swallowed me up like a dragon. . . ."

» Jeremiah 51:37:"And Babylon shall become heaps, a dwelling place for dragons, an astonishment, and a hissing, without an inhabitants.

» Revelation 12:3:"And there appeared another wonder in heaven; and behold a great red dragon, having seven heads and ten horns, and seven crowns upon his heads."

On the basis of statements like this some have concluded that the term "dragon" is merely a metaphor for Satan. However, it would be better to say that real-life dragons provide a visible representation of Satan's character, just as the skull and crossbones is a proper emblem to put on a container marked "poison."

There is much in ancient lore about "dragons." Dragon legends are multitudinous and are similar in many respects. This similarity suggests that there is a common core truth that is at the root of these legends. Some of the legends have dragons controlling the weather and the seas. Only God does that.

However, just as Noah's Flood has produced flood legends in different cultures, many researchers have concluded that real dragons are at the core of many dragon legends. But what are dragons?

Dragons were an accepted part of the culture and literal events in the minds of the populace. They were as real as the world around us today because they actually existed at some point in history. Just as we categorize many kinds of distinctly different animals as "dinosaurs"—a word coined relatively recently in 1841—these same creatures could have once been collectively categorized as "dragons." Long extinct, their powerful and terrifying presence has lingered to this day.[31]

Could the dragons of the Bible have been dinosaurs? Those who hold to the evolutionary hypothesis would argue that men and dinosaurs were not on the Earth at the same time. Those who hold to this view would

---

31. *Dragons: Legends & Lore Of Dinosaurs.* (Green Forest, AR: New Leaf Publishing, 2011), p. 13.

have to argue that dragons are simply mythical creatures with no basis in reality. However, the biblical accounts do not portray dragons as being mythical, but real. Given a young Earth cosmology, we can hold to the view that dragons were simply dinosaurs living on Earth with men and women who preserved their encounters in numerous legends that have their root in real-life encounters as recorded in the Bible.

As to the solution of this marginal mystery, we again must state that we will have to wait until Jesus Christ sits as the Universal Judge to judge not only all men who have died in sin, but also the fallen angels and the demon hordes of Satan.

Nostradamus

The Mystery of the Prophetic Poet

Early in the nineteenth century the citizens of Salon, France, after having saved most of the homesite of Nostradamus, erected a marble plaque in front of his house. The plaque has these words written on it.

In This House
Lived And Died
Michel Nostradamus
Astrologer
Physician-in-ordinary to the King
Author of the "Almanacs" and
of the Immortal "Centuries" 1503–1566

We've all lost car keys and misplaced our glasses, but wouldn't it be handy to have someone around who can tell us where they can be found? And it would really be great if that person could tell us exactly what's in our food, too. Did Nostradamus have the powers to do such things, and if so, where did those powers originate?

He Couldn't Be Fooled

One day a wealthy man by the name of Monsieur de Florinville was chat-

ting with Nostradamus. As they were walking on the grounds of de Florinville's chateau, or castle, they saw two suckling pigs, one white and one
black. Monsieur de Florinville, who had heard of Nostradamus' powers
and who wanted to discredit the seer, asked: "What will happen to these
two animals?" Nostradamus replied: "We will eat the black one and the
wolf will eat the white one."

De Florinville took his cook aside and commanded the cook to kill
the white pig and present it for supper. The cook dutifully obeyed. He
killed the white pig, prepared it, and placed it on the spit for roasting at the
designated hour. However, while the cook was gone to run a few errands,
a wolf cub that was being raised on the chateau saw the little pig and ate
part of the carcass. When the cook returned and saw that the pig had been
partly mangled, he was thrown into a fright. He would not dare to present
a partially eaten pig for supper. So, fearing the anger of his master, he took
the black pig, killed it, prepared it, and roasted it for supper.

As they were eating, Monsieur de Florinville, wishing to prove Nostradamus in error, boldly turned to Nostradamus and said, "Well, sir, we
are now eating the white pig and the wolf will not touch it here." Nostradamus smiled and simply said, "I do not believe it. It is the black one
which is on the table." Monsieur de Florinville smiled and explained his
command to the cook and how he had prepared the white pig. The cook,
who was totally amazed by the accuracy of what Nostradamus had predicted, hastily explained that Nostradamus was right. Indeed, they were
eating the black pig, as Nostradamus had predicted.[1]

Nostradamus' reputation grew because of incidents such as this.
Though he often suffered poor health, it was during one of his bouts with
gout, at which time he had been confined to his home, that another incident raised his reputation even more. Late one night while he was engaged
in his "secret studies," he was interrupted by insistent knocking at his front
door. Angered by this late-night interruption, Nostradamus hobbled over
to the door and angrily opened it to see who had come at such a late hour.
There standing before him was a page from the illustrious family of Beau-

---

1. Edgar Leoni, *Nostradamus and His Prophecies* (New York: Random House, 1982), pp. 20–21.

veau. The page was deeply apologetic and asked Nostradamus to forgive him for the interruption. But before the page could explain the nature of his visit Nostradamus angrily said, "What's the matter, king's page? You are making a lot of noise over a lost dog. Go and look on the road to Orleans. You will find it there, lead on a leash." The page, who was astounded that Nostradamus knew the nature of his problem before he could even explain it and that the seer had already provided the answer, humbly bowed and went to the location indicated by Nostradamus. He wandered around a bit and, to his surprise, found a servant leading the dog back.[2]

We are reminded of two events recorded in the New Testament. In Luke 22:8–13 we read:

> And he sent Peter and John, saying, Go and prepare us the passover, that we may eat. And they said unto him, Where wilt thou that we prepare? And he said unto them, Behold, when ye are entered into the city, there shall a man meet you, bearing a pitcher of water; follow him into the house where he entereth in. And ye shall say unto the goodman of the house, The Master saith unto thee, Where is the guestchamber, where I shall eat the passover with my disciples? And he shall shew you a large upper room furnished: there make ready. And they went, and found as he had said unto them: and they made ready the passover.

In Matthew 21:1–3 we have another, similar incident:

> And when they drew nigh unto Jerusalem, and were come to Beth-phage, unto the mount of Olives, then sent Jesus two disciples, Saying unto them, Go into the village over against you, and straightway ye shall find an ass tied, and a colt with her: loose them, and bring them unto me. And if any man say ought unto you, ye shall say, The Lord hath need of them; and straightway he will send them.

Christians do not find anything unusual about these accounts. As the eternal Son of God, Jesus Christ knew about the upper room, and also knew

2. Ibid., p. 28.

how the man with the animals would react to His disciples coming to get his animals. But what about Nostradamus? Was he manifesting Divine power and knowledge?

The Man Nostradamus

"Nostradamus" is the Latinized last name of Michel de Nostredame, a French doctor, astrologer, and prognosticator who lived from 1503 to 1566. There has been a revival of interest in Nostradamus since the 1930s when many began to understand his prophecies were predicting the rise of Adolph Hitler and the events of World War II.

Nostradamus' biographer, Chavigny, writing around the middle of the seventeenth century, described Nostradamus in the following way:

> He was a little under medium height, of robust body, nimble and vigorous. He had a large and open forehead, a straight and even nose, gray eyes, which were generally pleasant but which blazed when he was angry. . . . He approved of the ceremonies of the Roman Church and held to the Catholic faith and religion, outside of which he was convinced there was no salvation; he reproved vigorously those who, withdrawn from its bosom, abandoned themselves to eating and drinking of the sweetness and liberties of the foreign and damned doctrines, affirming that they would come to a bad and pernicious end. I do not want to forget to say that he engaged willingly in fasts, prayers, alms, and patience; he abhorred vice and chastised it severely; I can remember his giving to the poor, toward whom he was very liberal and charitable, often making use of these words drawn from the Holy Scriptures: "Make friends of the riches of iniquity."[3]

Nostradamus' major work, *Centuries*, was written as a collection of prophetic quatrains with no discernible chronological order. These *Centuries* are not true almanacs because the latter usually contain predictions and

---

3. Ibid., p. 38.

information for one year in advance. Nostradamus' *Centuries,* however, reach out for centuries, culminating in predictions for the year 3797. Each century contains one hundred quatrains, or four-line verses.

Nostradamus states that he wrote his *Centuries* because he believed that the signs of his day signaled the coming of unprecedented suffering and woe, and he wanted his writings to be of help. One of his biographers states that at first Nostradamus did not want to publish his *Centuries.* However, he was "finally overcome by the desire that he had to be of service to the public." Since many of his quatrains are quite obscure and seemingly incomprehensible, it is hard to understand how he could "be of service to the public."[4] He also wrote numerous other works, such as letters and *presages* (predictions).

Nostradamus' writings have fascinated men and women for centuries. After more than four centuries, the works of this "Seer of Provence" have been in continuous print and are being studiously investigated. More than four hundred books and learned essays about his work, especially his predictions, have been published since his death in 1566.

The Times In Which He Lived

Nostradamus received his license to practice medicine in 1525. It was in that year that there was an outbreak of the ever-recurring plague that was particularly aggressive in southern France. In the town of Montpelier, Nostradamus earned an impressive reputation as a healer. He was extremely bold when it came to exposing himself to the plague for the sake of a patient. Moreover, though some of his "treatments" were considered unorthodox, the fact that he healed many—whether through concoctions, psychological influence, or in some other way—won him a large following of devoted admirers.[5]

In addition to the deadly outbreak of plague, other things were happening that made mid-sixteenth century France a place of turmoil. In the year 1554, a "monstrous child" was born in Senas. Having two heads, this

---

4. Ibid., p. 26.
5. Ibid., pp. 17–18.

child was regarded as some kind of an omen. Within a month and a half, a two-headed horse was born near Salon.[6]

The religious situation in France at that time was marked by strife and war. Staring in 1562 there were more than thirty years of religious wars. R. R. Palmer writes:

> They were not civil wars of the kind where one region of a country takes up arms against another, each retaining some apparatus of the government, as in the American Civil War or the civil wars of the seventeenth century in England. They were the civil wars of the kind fought in the absence of government. Roving bands of armed men, without territorial base or regular means of subsistence, wandered about the country, fighting and plundering, joining and separating from other similar bands, in shifting hosts that were quickly formed or quickly dissolved.[7]

The Inquisition—the Roman Catholic Church's attempt to suppress all religious dissent—also added to the confusion. Barbaric in the extreme, the Inquisition was a reign of terror launched by the church. In order to escape the most horrible of tortures, individuals who had been accused and convicted could confess to unspeakable acts that they had not committed in order to "enjoy" immediate execution, sometimes by strangulation. Church officials would go easy on the accused if the accused would confess their own sins and implicate others. Countless numbers of innocent individuals were punished on the basis of these false accusations.[8]

Nostradamus had invoked the wrath of the Inquisitors in 1534. Nostradamus had seen a workman cast a bronze model of the Virgin Mary and made the comment that the man "was only making devils." Some have been of the opinion that Nostradamus was not making a comment about the Virgin, but rather about the man's workmanship. The Inquisi-

---

6. Ibid., p. 25.
7. R. R. Palmer, *A History of the Modern World,* rev. ed. (New York: Alfred A. Knopf, 1963), p. 116.
8. James Randi, *The Mask of Nostradamus: The Prophecies of the World's Most Famous Seer* (Buffalo, NY: Prometheus Books, 1993), p. 41

tion, however, did not regard it as an innocuous statement. By 1538 an official order was sent to Nostradamus requiring him to appear before the Inquisitor in Toulouse. Fearing the worst, Nostradamus went into a period of wandering from town to town during the years 1538 to 1544. It was during this period that Nostradamus sought to add to his medical and pharmaceutical knowledge by visiting astrologers, alchemists, cabalists, and magicians.[9]

It should not be thought strange that Nostradamus would have been alarmed by the invitation to appear before the Inquisitor, since others had suffered horribly at his hands. Joan of Arc (1411–1431) knew the prophecy that France would be restored by a virgin-warrior from Lorraine. She, of course, was that person. From 1424 and following, Joan felt a calling to free France from England, claiming that she was urged on in her calling and mission by the voices of St. Michael, St. Catherine, and St. Margaret. She and those under her enjoyed several military victories, but Joan was captured in May of 1430 and burned at the stake in May of 1431 because her visions incurred the wrath of the Inquisition and the University of Paris. Knowledge of her fiery demise no doubt cautioned Nostradamus.[10]

There were other things about Nostradamus that put him in jeopardy with the church as well. To prophesy about the future led many authorities in the church to believe that he may have been in league with the devil. All prognosticators came either from God or from Satan, and since Nostradamus had Jewish ancestry some clerics were convinced that his abilities had a diabolical origin. Randi believes that the church took a dim view of astrology and prognostications "because they brought into question the doctrine of free will and implied a predetermined future for everyone that might not be changed, even by prayer. Without free will, sin is impossible. Without sin and the prescribed penalties, the need for the church becomes less clear and less persuasive."[11]

---

9. Leoni, p. 20.
10. Erica Cheetham, *The Further Prophecies of Nostradamus: 1985 and Beyond* (New York: Perigee Books, 1985), p. 17.
11. Randi, p. 90.

Nostradamus and the Royal Family

Nostradamus had many admirers, but the most influential of all—a great blessing when facing the terrors of the Inquisitor—was the superstitious and astrology-conscious queen, Catherine de Medici. Catherine was given to believing every charlatan and would-be miracle worker or teacher who claimed to have a message from on high. Many of the books written on occult topics were dedicated to her. *Mirror of Astrology,* written by Catherine's contemporary Friar Francesco Giuntini, devotes some six pages of dedication to Catherine.

Catherine was married to Henry II, but she struggled through life in the shadow of the beautiful Diane de Poitiers, Henry's gorgeous mistress. Henry met a tragic end. Some claimed it was divine judgment for his immoral lifestyle. In 1559, while engaging in a jousting tournament, Henry was accidentally struck in the eye. The wound went deep into his head and caused excruciating pain. The court physicians were not quite sure how to treat the king. In their desperation, they had four prisoners executed immediately so that they could open their heads to see what kind of remedial surgery would be of benefit to Henry. The prisoners all died, of course. But so did the king.[12]

With the death of Henry, the perpetuation of the Valois line depended on Catherine's three sons. The eldest, Francis II, was mentally and physically feeble. Ascending the throne at the age of sixteen, Catherine had him married to the daughter of King James V of Scotland, Mary Stuart, who became famous under the name Mary, Queen of Scots. Francis lived to reign—and that by title only—for one year. He died of tubercular meningitis.

Catherine's next son, Charles IX, ascended the throne at the tender age of nine. He did not make much of a contribution to the well-being of France other than engage in his boyhood zeal for decapitating horses with a single blow of his sword, something in which he excelled, according to contemporary reports. The only other contribution to humanity

---

12. Palmer, p. 351.

under Charles' reign that can be noted was the introduction of the use of tobacco in France as a popular pastime for those who had both the time and money to use it. Tobacco was also promoted as a cure for ulcers and other ailments. Catherine had high hopes for Charles and asked that Nostradamus would give a prophecy in his behalf. Her letter, which was dated 1564, describes her wishes in this. The letter reads, in part: "To my godfather, the Milord Conetable . . . and as we were passing through the Salons, we have seen Nostradamus, who has promised to my son, the King [meaning Charles IX], everything good, and also that he shall live as long as you yourself, who he says shall see your ninetieth year ere passing his life."

Randi, who is skeptical of Nostradamus' powers, points out that if we can believe what Catherine says about Nostradamus and his promise, then Nostradamus can be proven wrong. Milord Conetable died at the age of seventy-seven years, and Charles died at the age of twenty-four. Nostradamus was, therefore, off in his prediction. Conetable missed his ninetieth birthday by thirteen years, and Charles missed it by sixty-six years.[13]

Charles reigned for fourteen years and died childless of intestinal tuberculosis. His brother, Henry III, replaced him. Randi's description of Catherine's third son is as follows: ". . . an infamous transvestite who scandalized the court by appearing in public dressed in outlandish costumes with his parading *mignons* [effeminate young men] at his side. Chroniclers of the day, particularly those of other national origins and ambassadors reporting to the home office, delighted in describing Henry's latest apparel, often in great detail. His jeweled brocades, platform shoes, and comical corsets were caricatured at home and abroad."[14]

When Catherine, and shortly thereafter Henry III, died, there was no one to carry on the Valois line. The family vanished from the scene, to be replaced by the Bourbons. Nostradamus had predicted great success for the Valois family. With "success" like that, who can survive failure?

---

13. Randi, p. 43.
14. Ibid., p. 44.

Nostradamus' Method

Many who claim success in any venture often have their own particular method that works best for them. Nostradamus explains his personal method of divination in *Century* I, Quatrain 1:

> Sitting alone at night in a secret study;
> it is placed on the brass tripod.
> A slight flame comes out of the emptiness
> and prophecies that should not be believed in vain.

Nostradamian Erika Cheetham believes that this shows that Nostradamus used the methods of the fourth-century neo-Platonist Iamblichus, whose book *The Mystery of Egypt* (1547) was known to Nostradamus, since he frequently quoted from it.

Nostradamus proceeds by sitting in his quiet study reading secret and esoteric books which inspire him. The reference in the above quatrain to the brass tripod comes from Iamblichus. He would place a bowl of water on the tripod and stare at the water until it became clouded and precognitions of the future were revealed. The "slight flame," according to Cheetham, "is almost certainly meant to indicate the inspiration which possessed Nostradamus as, despite himself, he begins to prophesy."[15]

Quatrain 2 continues to explain the method of Nostradamus:

> The wand in the hand is placed in the middle of the legs of the tripod.
> He sprinkles both the hem of his garment and his foot with water.
> A voice: Fear: he trembles in his robes.
> Divine Splendor. The God sits beside him.

Nostradamus indicates that he touches the center of the tripod with his wand, and then moistens his feet and the edge of his robe with the water that drops from his wand. This is a symbolic presentation of being freed from earthly ties. Cheetham explains:

---

15. Cheetham, pp. 24–25.

It seems that Nostradamus fears the power he evokes. It is important to note that he hears as well as sees it, and it speaks to him as he writes down the Prophecies. Once the gift has possessed him, he is not afraid. I feel that this duel aspect of his prophetic vision is very important to our interpretation of Nostradamus' gifts, and he has something in common with the modern American predictor Jeane Dixon, in that his visions appear to more than one sense.[16]

Though Nostradamus saw himself as an imperfect individual, he did attribute a certain infallibility to his words, as can be seen in the preface to the first edition of his *Centuries,* which consists of a letter of dedication to his son, Cesar Nostradamus. We quote one paragraph that reveals what Nostradamus thought of himself and his prognostications:

Therefore, my son, thou mayest, notwithstanding thy tender brain, comprehend things that shall happen hereafter, and may be foretold by celestial natural lights, and by the spirit of prophecy, not that I will attribute to myself the name of a prophet, but as a mortal man, being no farther from Heaven by my sense that I am from Earth by my feet. *'Possum non errare, falli, decipi,'* [meaning: "I am able not to err, be deceived nor fail"). I am the greatest sinner of the world subject to all human afflictions. But being surprised sometimes by a prophetical mood, and by a long calculation, pleasing myself in my study, I have made Books of Prophecies, each one containing a hundred Astronomical Stanzas, which I have joined obscurely, and are perpetual prophecies from this year [1555] to the year 3797, at which some perhaps will frown, seeing so large an extension of time, and that I treat of everything under the Moon. If thou livest the natural age of a man thou shalt see in thy climate, and under the Heaven of thy nativity, the future things that have been foretold.[17]

---

16. Ibid., p. 25.
17. Henry C. Roberts, *The Complete Prophecies of Nostradamus* (Oyster Bay, NY: Nostradamus Co., 1981), pp. 5–6.

It will be remembered by the reader that the plaque erected in front of Nostradamus' house, as presented in the opening of this chapter, indicates that Nostradamus was regarded as an "astrologer" as well as a "physician." We may wonder what is the connection between astrology and the healing arts, at least as viewed by Nostradamus and his contemporaries.

In the middle of the sixteenth century there were old practices that were continuing in use, as well as new ones that were being developed. Astrology and magic were commonplace in the Middle Ages and were continued in Nostradamus' time, and evidently by Nostradamus himself. They utilized a variety of potions, ranging from herbal mixes of the mustard plaster and perennial mud baths to a variety of other concoctions of various substances including a mixture of ground animal glands. All of this was used with the ever-popular practice of "bleeding" patients, something that contributed to the enfeeblement rather than to the healing of the patient. Astrology fits into all of this because it was believed that certain concoctions were especially effective during certain astrological configurations and that some of the concoctions might actually prove fatal if not used in strict accordance with the astrological disciplines. The ancient notion predominated that various parts of the body, and various organs, are in some way governed by the particular zodiacal signs assigned to them. In ancient Egyptian astrology the human body was divided into thirty-six parts, with a particular planet assigned to each part. One aspect of "treatment" that was rather new in Nostradamus' day, however, was the growing use of a variety of nonorganic chemicals containing metals such as lead, mercury, copper, and selenium. The effects were often quite dramatic. The patient's suffering was terminated through the onset of coma and death![18]

Nostradamus and the Twentieth Century

What did Nostradamus have to say about the twentieth century? Do his prophecies tell us anything about modern weapons, and even about contemporary disasters? Are missiles and nuclear weapons envisioned in his

18. Randi, p. 56.

quatrains? Though a lot of what Nostradamus writes is enigmatic and puzzling, some of it has a contemporary flavor, as in the following quatrain:

> The city is almost burned down by fire from the sky, water again threatens Ceucalion . . . (II.81).

Cheetham writes: "Whatever object Nostradamus visualizes here, it is certainly no cannon ball but some object of modern warfare, probably atomic."[19]

Another quatrain (II.6) has been applied to the devastation of Hiroshima and Nagasaki. It reads:

> Near the harbor and in two cities will descend two scourges the like of which have never been seen before.

Both of these Japanese cities were the first to experience the effects of a nuclear bomb. The words "two scourges the like of which have never been seen before" would seem to fit the use of these new weapons of mass destruction.

The next line of this quatrain reads:

> Hunger, plague within, people thrown out by the iron thing will cry out for help from the great immortal God.

Cheetham finds the words "plague within" [*dedans peste*] important for an understanding of the passage. The plague that was common to southern France in Nostradamus' day was defined as *charbon,* "because its victims were covered with large black pustules. Radiation burns turn black too," she writes, but observes that it is not the same kind of plague. Something future is being described.[20]

---

19. Cheetham, p. 69.
20. Ibid.

Cheetham also understands Nostradamus to predict World War III and that it will begin with an attack on New York—both city and state. New York is located in between the fortieth and forty-fifth parallel and this could be a locator:

> The sky will burn at forty-five degrees.
> Fire approaches the great new city.
> Immediately huge, scattered flame leaps up . . . (VI.97).[21]

Some writers fault some of the translations of Nostradamus' *Centuries*. For example, John Boanerges looks at quatrain 63 of *Century 1*, which reads in the French: *Seur marchera par la ciel, terre, mer and Onde*. The last two words, *mer* and *onde*, literally mean "sea and wave." Boanerges observes, however:

> Although implicitly almost correct, this translation already incorporates interpretative features. That is a no! because the actual interpretation will be an outcome of the translation. Furthermore, I have found that all translations ignore the meaning of the word "Onde," as if it weren't even there, or incorporate it as part of "mer." This is a gross oversight, for the word "Onde" must also be translated. Nostradamus did not place it there only for metrical reasons. This word is emphatic, which means that "Onde" is very important and signifies more than "sea," which he has already covered with "mer." My translations will strive to avoid such oversights. In this particular line, my interpretation of "Wave" is that of electromagnetic waves of communication—radio, television, telemetry, facsimile—a very important revelation.[22]

Does the Spirit of Nostradamus Live On Today?

The accuracy of Nostradamus' prognostications are questioned by some, though accepted by others. Prognosticators often use a great deal of figurative and symbolic language and speak metaphorically, using images of ani-

---

21. Ibid., p. 108.
22. John Boanerges, *NostrApocalypse* (San Francisco: John Peniel Publications, 1992), pp. ix–x.

mals, obscure names and references, and other devices that can be molded to fit a variety of situations. In his *Centuries,* Nostradamus makes mention of "Neptune," which was a reference to England. However, "lion" can also mean "England," or "royalty" in general. There is another possible meaning to "lion," however. It can be a reference to Lyon, France. The same is true of "wolf," which can have a variety of applications that will give the prognosticator more latitude to allow for possible "mistakes." Randi states that "wolf can stand for either Italy or Rome, since Romulus and Remus, the mythological founders of Rome, were suckled from a wolf."[23] At any rate, many prognosticators often credit God with their success and blame themselves for their errors. In this way the prognosticator can force his detractors into a corner in which they end up "fighting God."

The normal way for gaining a perception of things is through the senses. We see, hear, taste, touch, or smell something. Our perception of these things through the senses can be explained scientifically. We explain hearing in terms of sound waves and auditory nerves. In the same way, we explain sight scientifically by referring to the structures of eye and brain. But in recent years individuals are once again exploring the possibility of receiving information through "other channels." There are several processes that can be mentioned:

Telepathy—an individual's awareness of another person's thoughts in the absence of communication through the normal modes of communication, i.e., speaking, writing. Telepathy is said to occur when the person receiving the message (the percipient) comes to know what the sender (the agent) is thinking about. Telepathic communication takes place without the sender using any special apparatus—telephone, voice, written messages, and so on. Of course, to read someone's thoughts is not necessarily telepathy. Oftentimes individuals can read someone else's thoughts by looking for nonverbal signals, such as facial expressions, skin color, and posture.

Clairvoyance—knowledge of an object or event without the use of the senses. In clairvoyance, only one person is involved. The person who

---

23. Randi, p. 34.

is being tested for clairvoyant abilities is told to look at a shuffled deck of cards and to guess the identity of the cards, and their order in the pack.

Precognition—knowledge of another person's future thoughts (precognitive telepathy) or of future events (precognitive clairvoyance). Precognitive clairvoyance takes place when a person knows the identity of the cards and their order after they have been shuffled. If scores above the chance level exist, the subject is said to possess precognitive clairvoyance.[24]

Psychokinesis—the ability to influence a physical object simply by thinking certain thoughts about that object.[25] Psychokinesis takes the above a step farther. If the person seeks to influence the order of the cards simply by thinking about that order, or if the person can influence the fall of dice so that a particular face or faces will land uppermost, the person is exhibiting psychokinetic influence.

Do these powers and abilities exist, or are people who make claims of ESP and other abilities frauds? Some have flatly denied the reality of these phenomena on the grounds that belief in them is not scientific or that it simply does not make sense. Of course, creationism has been denied on similar grounds. Aldous Huxley (1894–1963) gives the classical response to all who deny ESP when he writes:"That a man of science should allow a prejudice to outweigh evidence seems strange enough. It is even stranger to find a psychologist rejecting a psychological discovery simply because it cannot be explained. Psi (the process of ESP) is intrinsically no more inexplicable than, say, perception or memory; it is merely less common."[26]

One thing is certain, however. Those who seek to develop these powers of clairvoyance, ESP, and psychokinesis appear to be spiritualists. On August 26, 1882, a letter by Douglas Blackburn, at that time editor of *The Brightonian,* was published in the spiritualist magazine *Light.* Blackburn's letter describes an experiment in mental telepathy.

---

24. C. E. M. Hansel, *ESP and Parapsychology: A Critical Reevaluation* (Buffalo, NY: Prometheus Books, 1980), pp. 14–17.

25. Ibid., pp. 3–4.

26. Ibid., p. 7.

The way Mr. Smith conducts his experiment is this: He places himself *en rapport* with myself by taking my hands: and a strong concentration of will and mental vision on my part has enabled him to read my thoughts with an accuracy that approaches the miraculous. Not only can he, with slight hesitation, read numbers, words, and even whole sentences which I alone have seen, but the sympathy between us has developed to such a degree that he rarely fails to experience the taste of any liquid or solid I choose to imagine. He has named, described, or discovered small articles he has never seen when they have been concealed by me in the most unusual places, and on two occasions, he has successfully described portions of a scene which I either imagined or actually saw.[27]

Various police departments around the world are employing psychics to help them solve crimes. When movie actress Sharon Tate—pregnant with her first child—and four friends were brutally murdered in Tate's home, the world was appalled at the savagery of the killers. The police department called in psychic Peter Hurkos, a man who discovered his psychic abilities after he had an accident in which he had fallen from a ladder and was rendered unconscious. As Hurkos was coming out of his coma in a hospital room, he found that he could read people's thoughts and had a knowledge of future events. On one occasion when a nurse came to take his pulse, he told her to be careful since she was in danger of losing a suitcase that belonged to a friend. When Hurkos made that statement, the nurse looked at him with incredulity. She explained that she had just arrived at the hospital by train and had left her friend's suitcase behind in the dining car.

In 1958 the Miami, Florida, police department asked Hurkos to solve the murder of a cab driver. As Hurkos sat in the seat of the cab, he closed his eyes, went into deep contemplation, and began to describe the murder of the cab driver down to the minutest of details. Hurkos then began to describe the killer: a tall, thin man with a tattoo on his right arm and a rolling walk like a sailor. Hurkos said the man's name was "Smitty," and,

---

27. Ibid., p. 30.

said Hurkos, "Smitty" was responsible for another murder in Miami—the murder of a man shot to death in his apartment. The police were stunned. They knew of the murder of a man who was shot to death in his apartment, but they did not see any connection with the murder of the cab driver. They searched their files and came up with a photograph of an ex-sailor named Charles Smith. In the process of investigating the murder, the police interviewed a waitress who recognized the man in the photograph. She remembered that the man had boasted of killing two men. Smith was arrested in New Orleans and sent back to Miami where he confessed.

Gerard Croiset has been employed on numerous occasions by the Dutch police, and has often enjoyed remarkable success. Croiset is known as a "psychometrist." He has the ability to read the past associations of an object by simply holding them in his hand. In 1949 he was asked to help solve a rape case. The police spoke to Croiset and placed two packages in his hands. One of the packages contained an object that was a tobacco box. Croiset identified the house from which it came and also the two middle-aged brothers who lived there. He gave detailed descriptions of the brothers and identified them as the rapists. The second package contained a sack. As Croiset handled this package he saw a cow in his mind. He then described to the police how the two brothers had taken the girl to the cowshed and raped her. Interestingly, his son, Gerard Croiset, Jr., has also helped police solve many crimes. Gerard Junior demonstrated that he was endowed with his father's powers when he assisted in the case of two missing girls in South Carolina, and he did it while he was thousands of miles away.[28]

Erika Cheetham, Nostradamus researcher and psychic, was first introduced to the works of Nostradamus while a student at Oxford University. She began to dabble in what many would call "strange practices" such as "reading hands" and "Tarot cards." Cheetham evidently had already been telling fortunes and had built a reputation as a fortune-teller. She was having supper with a friend and one of the guests was a wealthy Egyptian student who was about twenty years of age. Cheetham explains:

28. Colin Wilson, *Mysterious Powers* (London: Aldus Books, 1975), pp. 122–130.

I hardly knew him except by sight and was amazed when on taking his hand to be surrounded by a feeling of deepest gloom and despair, and was momentarily unable to say anything. I laughed the situation off, made light of it, saying I was feeling tired. Nevertheless the feeling of unease remained. Two days later I learned that he had flown to Rome for the weekend, the day after the party, and had been shot dead at the airport by the irate husband of one of his mistresses.[29]

Cheetham relates that she also began to have precognitive [predictive] dreams "which seemed to come true," to use her own words. One dream was about a friend who had a serious automobile wreck. She notes that the friend did not own a car and it was therefore highly unlikely that she would have an automobile wreck. But several days after her dream, her friend borrowed a car and had a serious crash on the way to London. Another episode that Cheetham relates was in the form of a vivid and troubling dream about a man being murdered.

One final dream which happened very recently, long after I had become involved with Nostradamus and was becoming more and more involved with the problems of time and space, occurred on June 4, 1981. I was living in Chelsea at the time and had a vivid dream of a man being shot three times in the head. I recognized the area as being somewhere in Park Lane or Mayfair. I awoke seriously shaken. The experience was so real and terrifying that I telephoned a friend and told him of it. He, being highly practical, without my knowledge wrote down the time of my telephone call. According to his notes, I rang at 12:45 a.m., i.e., 11:45 Greenwich Mean Time. Checking next day with Reuters, the attempted assassination of the Israeli ambassador in Mayfair was first announced at 12:22, then at 12:29, and 12:48 GMT. The fact that he had been shot in the head was not reported until 3:51 a.m., and only then was it specified that he had been shot three times.[30]

29. Cheetham, p. 3.
30. Ibid.

History is replete with accounts of this sort. As the story goes, Julius Caesar did not act upon the warning of a soothsayer to be extra careful at the Ides of March. As it turned out, that was the day he was murdered. Other warnings are said to have been given to Caesar, but he ignored these, too. No one will ever know for sure, but the question is intriguing: Did Caesar choose to die, or was he so sure of his personal security that he felt that he could ignore the words of the soothsayer?

In 1 Samuel 28 we read that King Saul, in deep desperation, went to a medium. Saul was filled with fear because the Philistines were poised at Shunem, ready to enter into battle against the Israelites. We pick up the account in verse 6:

> And when Saul enquired of the LORD, the LORD answered him not, neither by dreams, nor by Urim, nor by prophets. Then said Saul unto his servants, Seek me a woman that hath a familiar spirit, that I may go to her, and enquire of her. And his servants said to him, Behold, there is a woman that hath a familiar spirit at Endor. And Saul disguised himself, and put on other raiment, and he went, and two men with him, and they came to the woman by night: and he said, I pray thee, divine unto me by the familiar spirit, and bring me him up, whom I shall name unto thee. And the woman said unto him, Behold, thou knowest what Saul hath done, how he hath cut off those that have familiar spirits, and the wizards, out of the land: wherefore then layest thou a snare for my life, to cause me to die? And Saul sware to her by the LORD, saying, As the LORD liveth, there shall no punishment happen to thee for this thing. Then said the woman, Whom shall I bring up unto thee? And he said, Bring me up Samuel. And when the woman saw Samuel, she cried with a loud voice. . . . And Samuel said to Saul, Why hast thou disquieted me, to bring me up? And Saul answered, I am sore distressed; for the Philistines make war against me, and God is departed from me, and answereth me no more, neither by prophets, nor by dreams: therefore I have called thee, that thou mayest make known unto me what I shall do.
>
> —1 Samuel 28:6–15

Saul wanted to know what to do and, contrary to his own policies as king of Israel, he went, under disguise, to a woman who had "a familiar spirit," someone who practiced necromancy, that is, consulting the dead to determine the future. To Saul's consternation, the woman predicted Israel's defeat and Saul's death. This is exactly what happened (1 Samuel 31).

Poetic prophets, prognosticators, dreamers, and clairvoyants—what are we to think of them? Though Satan is not omnipresent, the Bible does call him "the god of this world" (2 Corinthians 4:4). In a world of dark and unseen forces, it is no wonder that there are things that we find hard to explain.

Grigori Efimovich Rasputin

The Unholy Villain Who Tumbled an Empire

For those of our readers who may be unfamiliar with this strange man, a statement of Jane Oakley's study of Rasputin gives us a summary insight into the man and his life:

> Rasputin's life was a powerful mixture of bizarre fictions and even more remarkable fact. The legend reached mythological proportions in his own lifetime and in the seventy years since his death, Rasputin has joined Cesare Borgia, Genghis Khan, and Caligula, amongst others, in the pantheon of satanic supermen. The name Rasputin is recognized universally with a frisson of excitement and recoil; "The Mad Monk" and "Russia's Greatest Love Machine" are just two of the sobriquets of the man who, single-handed, it was claimed, brought down the Romanov dynasty in an orgy of sex and intrigue and dark satanic practices.[1]

His Childhood Years

It gets cold in Siberia, especially in January. When there are no clouds, all heat seems to escape from the frozen earth and dissipates into the twinkling sky. On one particular January night, a shooting star was seen

---

1. Jane Oakley, *Rasputin: Rascal Master* (New York: St. Martin's Press, 1989), p. 7.

by several peasants. Believing that the shooting stars were omens of some momentous event, some of them started speculating as to the meaning of the shooting star. Rasputin was born on that night—January 23, 1871—in the Siberian village of Pokrovskoye, located some two hundred miles east of the Ural Mountains and sixteen hundred miles east of St. Petersburg, Russia.

Though Rasputin had hardly any formal education, he had an unbelievably retentive memory and could retain whole passages from the Bible after just one reading. Though his childhood was normal in many ways, it was evident that he had an uncanny ability to calm fearful farm animals, and to even heal them. On one occasion, as the family sat down at the table for a meal, Rasputin's father mentioned that the family horse had gone lame. Without saying a word, Rasputin left the table, went to the stable, and placed his hand on the horse's tendon. Rasputin stood up, closed his eyes, and tilted his head back, apparently deep in concentration. After a few minutes he came out of his reverie, patted the horse, and was heard to say, "You're all better."[2]

"He Stole the Horse!"

It did not take very long for rumors to develop and grow regarding Rasputin's abilities. The story is told of how the young Rasputin was sick with a fever. Because his father served sort of like a local constable, a number of the townspeople came to see his father to report the theft of a horse— something that frequently happened in Siberia. Several of the men began to voice their personal opinions regarding the identity of the culprit. Most of the men came to the conclusion that it must have been one of the *brodyagi*. They were vagabonds, gypsies who traveled from one village to another. They were known for being dishonest and uncouth. Yes, the thief must be one of the *brodyagi*. Surely, none of the local townspeople would do such a terrible thing.

It was at that moment that Rasputin surprised everyone. He rose from his sickbed and pointed his finger at one of the most respected men

2. Ibid., pp. 18–19.

in the whole town of Pokrovskoye. "He stole the horse," Rasputin said, as everyone cringed with fear. How could Grigori say that? He had not seen the thief. Surely, they thought, the boy has gone mad because of his fever. The accused vehemently denied that he stole the horse. Deeply embarrassed, Rasputin's father harshly reprimanded his son. How dare Grigori make such an outlandish accusation! Yet Rasputin's reputation was growing. Some of the men in the room were surprised at the authority and conviction with which Rasputin spoke as he said, "He stole the horse."

That night these men decided to follow the man whom Rasputin had accused. They watched the accused go into his barn, and they were amazed as they saw him exit the barn leading the very horse he had denied stealing![3]

The Death of Dmitri

When Rasputin was about twelve years of age, a tragedy occurred that affected him deeply. On a warm day in the summer of 1883, Rasputin and his brother, Dmitri, went swimming. It was not their usual spot and they were unfamiliar with the River Tura at that particular spot.

Dmitri was the first to jump in with a headlong rush characteristic of adventurous youth. The water was deep. Instead of finding sure footing, Dmitri disappeared beneath the surface. Rasputin tried to help him out, but tumbled in himself. The two youngsters were swept downstream in the swirling waters. They were quickly chilled and unable to regain their footing. It was a terrifying experience. A farmer heard their cries, ran down to the river, and was able to fish them out. Both boys contracted pneumonia. Rasputin's health got progressively better, but Dmitri was quickly overcome and succumbed. According to their mother, the death of Dmitri cast Rasputin into a profound depression. His behavior changed drastically and he began to manifest sudden mood swings. At one moment he would be happy and joyous, but suddenly his elation would disappear and he would sink into the pits of despondency.[4]

3. Ibid., p. 20.
4. Ibid., pp. 21–22.

His Marriage

When he was nineteen years of age, Rasputin married Praskovia Dubrovina, a woman with black eyes and blond hair. Unlike the other girls whom Rasputin met, Praskovia would not give in to his advances, reminding him that they were not yet husband and wife. They were married six months after they first met.[5]

With Rasputin's growing fame, there was also a growing opposition and vilification. Rumors of his debauchery circulated and people began to suspect that he was using religion as a cloak to satisfy his own personal desires. The nastier the stories, the quicker they traveled and, perhaps, became embellished along the way. After marriage, Rasputin's reputation as a lady's man continued to grow, but his wife continued with him and did not seem to mind his extramarital affairs.[6]

Rasputin and the Blessed Virgin

Shortly after his marriage Rasputin became involved in two other vices: drunkenness and thievery. Rasputin would be drunk for days on end, having imbibed enough vodka to cause ten men to stagger. He was also caught stealing pieces of a neighbor's fence and other yard items. Rasputin was tried and convicted. His sentence was banishment from Pokrovskoye. Rasputin offered a different penalty: he would personally do penance at the monastery of Verkhoturie, 260 miles northwest of Pokrovskoye. The authorities agreed. Rasputin journeyed to the monastery around 1885. His biographers agreed that the trip to Verkhoturie was a turning point in his life.

At the monastery of Verkhoturie, Rasputin met the celebrated hermit Makariy. The man was a true hermit. He lived in a simple hut seventy miles from the monastery and wore chains to punish his flesh. Makariy told Rasputin that the recent death of his son was a sign from God and that God had a mission for him. This had such an impact on Rasputin that he gave up alcohol and tobacco and refrained from eating meat.

5. Joseph T. Fuhrmann, *Rasputin: A Life* (New York: Praeger, 1990), p. 5.
6. Oakley, p. 28.

Fuhrmann describes Rasputin when he returned to Pokrovskoye from his pilgrimage and what his neighbors concluded:

> Rasputin's neighbors concluded that he had joined the *khlysty,* or "Flagellants," a radical religious sect. Russians believed the members of this secret group blended religious ecstasy and sex. The one hundred twenty thousand *khlysty* scattered from Tobolsk to Kazan and Saratov were said to gather at night in houses or remote places. Forming a circle, they supposedly moved in a ring, holding hands as they chanted, sang, and prayed. The leader . . . whipped any member who flagged or broke formation. When the ritual reached a certain point, the *khlysty* cast off their white linen gowns and joined in sexual intercourse.[7]

Rasputin gave much thought to Makariy's words, especially his comment that God had a special work for him to perform. But what kind of work was it, and how would Rasputin know that it was God's will for him?

These thoughts much occupied Rasputin and he decided that he needed a special visitation from Heaven. He didn't have long to wait. As he was plowing, there was a sudden glowing apparition of Mary. The Virgin was looking at him and making gestures with her hand. Mary did not say a word to Rasputin, but by her gestures Rasputin concluded that she wanted him to become a *strannik,* one of the pilgrims who wandered throughout the countryside, exchanging teaching and counsel for food and lodging along the way.

A Growing Reputation

Rasputin often disappeared from home for weeks on end—sometimes even for months—and stayed at monasteries where he would discuss the Bible with the monks. It was during these times of wandering through the forests and over the steppes of Russia, that he desired female companionship.

Rasputin was grieved at this and struggled with his thoughts. He was

---

7. Fuhrmann, pp. 5–6.

plagued with terrible feelings of guilt, being almost certain that he had failed God and that he must separate himself from these feelings and seek the more perfect way of holiness. He never attained that desired end. In fact, his thoughts and desires troubled him even more.

One day Rasputin was deep in the forest. He was mysteriously drawn by the singing of a lone bird. Making his way through the thick forest and following the sound of the bird's singing, Rasputin finally saw the bird. It was high in a tree and it was singing a song of courtship to another bird. Rasputin thought, "Surely, there is a message from God here." The conclusion he reached put his heart at ease. His struggles were over. "If this bird with his celestial song was moved by desire, how could it be so evil?"[8]

By the late 1890s Rasputin's reputation had spread throughout Russia. Known as a *starets*—a peasant holy man—his listeners claimed that he had the ability to convincingly explain the meaning of Scripture. His explanations were heightened by his reputation for healing and foretelling the future. He also had a growing reputation as a man who had a strange and hypnotic power over women, often taking advantage of them to suit his own desires. Rasputin may have been influenced in this kind of licentious-religious lifestyle by a group of Russian mystics known as the *skoptsi*. They judged an individual's piety by the ability to bear pain and often indulged in inflicting pain on their own bodies. The *skoptsi* were an offshoot of the *khlysty,* a religious group whose members alternated their style of living between the extremes of a harsh asceticism—practicing the most rigorous forms of self-denial—and ecstatic and religious immorality.[9] It must also be remembered that the Tungus of the Ural Mountains of Russia were known to have strange powers over people and Rasputin may have been influenced by them.[10]

At any rate, Rasputin made an imposing impression on some people. His hair and beard were long and matted. He refused to use a napkin and those eating with him noticed bits of food caught in his beard. Perhaps

---

8. Oakley, p. 33.

9. Ibid, pp. 57–58.

10. Colin Wilson, *Mysterious Powers* (London: Aldus Books, 1975), p. 26.

the most riveting aspect of his appearance was his piercing, blue eyes. His stare was absolutely penetrating. His daughter, Maria, stated that he could contract and dilate the pupils of his eyes at will.[11]

With such an appearance, it is hard to understand what magnetism he possessed that drew all of the ladies to him. Yet his "female followers had taken this greasy, smelly, unkempt peasant in hand and civilized a few of his superficial characteristics." He began to keep his nails trimmed, nails which, up to this time, were unsightly with dirt—and, though he never really gave up his traditional peasant outfit of baggy trousers and shirt, he began to wear the silk shirts his adoring ladies embroidered for him.[12]

Rasputin's power manifested itself in two forms: clairvoyance and healing—sometimes even healing at a distance. On one occasion a monk charged Rasputin with being a fake and a womanizer. Rasputin was not present, but later he confronted the monk and said, "So, you think I am a fake and a womanizer." Of course, Rasputin could have been tipped off, but it was believed that Rasputin had special powers that gave him knowledge of what happened behind closed doors.

Healing at a distance also caught the attention of many. A lady whose niece was seriously ill writes of the niece's healing and the role Rasputin played in that healing:

> Then something so strange happened that I cannot explain it. . . . However hard I tried to understand, there is nothing I could do. I don't know what happened, but I will describe it all in detail. He [Rasputin] took my hand. His face changed and he looked like a corpse, yellow, waxy, and dreadfully still. He rolled his eyes till the whites alone were visible. He took my hand roughly and said in a dull voice, "She won't die. She won't die." Then he let my hand go and the blood flowed back into his cheeks again. He continued talking as if nothing had happened.[13]

11. Oakley, p. 26.
12. Ibid., pp. 125–126.
13. Alex de Jonge, *The Life and Times of Grigori Rasputin* (New York: Coward, McCann and Geohegan, 1982), p. 147.

Rasputin's "Justification" of His Sensual Behavior

Rasputin was engrossed in a search for salvation. Most writers will agree that this was his all-consuming passion: how to be right with God. Driven by his carnal desires, Rasputin often languished in guilt and pain over his drinking and his womanizing. We would fail to understand what drove Rasputin if we fail to see that his life was a struggle for morality. How did Rasputin solve the problem of his immoral tendencies since he was unable to control his conduct? "Rasputin resolved the conflict by making his behavior a virtue and the basis of his religious outlook."[14] He developed a religious explanation for his immorality and made his womanizing the basis of personal redemption.

Rasputin concluded that repentance is absolutely essential to salvation. In fact, he believed that repentance was important because Jesus' first command was, "Repent." But how can a man repent if he has no sin? reasoned Rasputin. Sin is necessary to put us in the way of salvation and rid us of all pride. Rasputin developed this theory by asking why people resist temptation. Certainly not because they don't like sin. If sin were not attractive, it would have no appeal. People resist temptation because they are afraid they will have to repent of their sin, and such repentance is damaging to human pride. To fall into sin, and then to repent, is the height of Rasputin's piety. He felt sin was the best way to brokenness before God. Those who do not sin are not fit for communion with God because their "moral" behavior causes them to forget their need of God. According to Fuhrmann, Rasputin felt that "only humility makes us realize what abject sinners we are and might become. The Christian must 'commit a great sin in order to remind himself of the greater sin that awaited him in his pride, in his righteousness.' One might reach the depths of sin through sex. But from those depths regeneration may come, and then sinlessness."[15]

Rasputin had a strange charm over women. Most women did not need a lesson in theology to surrender themselves to his advances. But if some of his women rejected his advances he would quickly counter

14. Fuhrmann, p. 42.
15. Ibid.

by saying, "You have too much vanity. You must humiliate yourself." This did not always work, but on many occasions it was "convincing" to those women who had been "discipled" by him.

It seems strange that he would be able to pass his carnality off as religion. Most of the women he seduced led sheltered lives and had never sinned in ways that he was suggesting to them. They were virtuous, and they admired their virtue; but here came this wild-looking man telling them that the life that they had been following was just the opposite of virtuous. Rasputin pressed his point home, however, and argued that to have him as their lover must be seen as real virtue. "What appeared to be sin was really—in this case, at any rate—a path to salvation."[16]

Strange as these beliefs seem, Rasputin was regarded by many as a man of God. His daughter, Maria, saw her father spend hours in meditation and wrote that he would meditate, pray, and strike his head on the ground "until the skin became red."[17]

There was enough "good" in Rasputin's activities that those who were supporters could find something good to say about him. Some of the women even claimed that he never seduced them and that his relationship to them was always right and proper. Rasputin's various "faces" seemed contradictory, as though the man had some kind of a split personality. When Rasputin was confronted by his own scandalous behavior he would cite some of his supporters and friends who had spoken out in his behalf. If he was pressed even more, however, he would admit that perhaps some of the charges were true and that "all men sin, and I, being a man, am also a sinner." There was enough conflicting information to make Rasputin into whatever one wanted. If a person was convinced that he was a man of God, there was something that could be cited to support that view—some miracles or healing. Opposite claims were also reported by reports and testimonies, but they were sometimes discounted as misinformation or outright lies against a man of God. One thing that greatly aided Rasputin was that Christianity was being held in disrepute in Russia at the turn of

16. Ibid., p. 43.
17. Ibid., p. 45.

the twentieth century. Many of his opponents were rationalists who were hostile to religion of any sort. Hence, those who leveled charges against Rasputin were often labeled as enemies of Christianity and unbelievers who were seeking to attack the Christian faith.[18]

Rasputin and the Royal Family

The years 1904 and 1905 were tumultuous years for the Russian people. There was fear and near hysteria in the population. In 1904 the Russian navy suffered some serious defeats in its conflict with Japan. There was an intense hatred of government officials in St. Petersburg. Plehve (the hated police chief who argued in favor of war for the purpose of increasing the tsar's popularity) was assassinated by a bomb blast in the summer of 1904.[19]

On January 22, 1905, a deputation of workers approached the tsar's winter palace in St. Petersburg. A crowd of workers, along with their wives and children, stood outside of the palace and called to their "Little Father," as the Russian people affectionately called the tsar. Suddenly, the palace guards opened fire on the crowd. Mounted Cossacks charged the crowd, cutting down people with their swords and clubbing them on their heads with the butts of their rifles.

This was a terrible time for Russia—a period of turmoil and unrest. The crew of the Russian battleship *Potemkin* mutinied, murdering the ship's officers. In addition, peasants revolted and murdered their landowning masters. Government troops turned against their superiors. As a result, Tsar Nicholas offered the Russian people a constitution that allowed freedom of speech, conscience, and freedom of association. It was proposed that the Russian people be allowed to elect their own representatives for the Duma, the Russian parliamentary assembly. This seemed to quell the spirit of revolution, but only for a short time.

Sometime in November 1905 a priest with whom Rasputin was lodging wrote a letter to Tsar Nicholas asking the tsar to receive a holy man, one Grigori Rasputin, who had come from Siberia to present the

18. Ibid., p. 16.
19. Oakley, p. 102.

tsar with an icon of St. Simon, the patron saint of the monastery of Verkhoturie. The tsar agreed, and it was in this way that Rasputin was invited
to the royal family's home at Tsarkoe Selo. The entire royal family, including the children, came to meet Rasputin. He endeared himself to the
royal family by presenting each child with a miniature icon and a piece of
consecrated bread.[20]

Rasputin and Tsarevich Alexei's Hemophilia

Hemophilia, or "bleeder's disease," has been given as "the sole reason for
Rasputin's influence on the tsarita [Alexandra] and therefore on the tsar
and the government of the whole Russian empire."[21]

Though women carry the defective genes, they rarely suffer from
the disease. It is their sons, though not all of their sons, who are afflicted.
Sufferers from the disease bleed profusely and uncontrollably even from
minor cuts and abrasions, such as those often associated with childhood
and the fun games children play. When bumped or bruised, sufferers bleed
internally which causes excruciatingly painful swelling, fever, and even
death. Tsarevich Alexei was afflicted with hemophilia, having "inherited
this faulty gene from his mother who was one of the network of children
and grandchildren of Queen Victoria."[22]

The tsarita loved her husband, Tsar Nicholas, but did not have a male
son for quite some time. She fervently prayed to God that He would
provide a son for the royal line through her. With the birth of Alexei, Alexandra rejoiced that she had provided her husband with the longed-for
heir for his ancient Romanov line. Life, however, seemed to have thrown
her a painful dart when she found that the tsarevich was blighted with this
strange and incurable disease. Alexandra often went through agony as she
saw her little boy in pain, often bleeding copiously from the minor scrapes
and bruises that all healthy children survive in their childhood experience.

One of the most dramatic healings that Rasputin ever performed

20. Ibid., p. 105.
21. Ibid., p. 123.
22. Ibid., p. 130.

were those done in connection with Alexei's hemophilia. On one occasion, the tsarevich had been suffering terribly from a bump he had received and was bleeding internally in the groin area. The Grand Duchess Anastasia had heard that the tsarevich was in desperate straits and went to summon Rasputin to help the royal family. The story is somewhat amusing, but seems to be typical of much of Rasputin's life.

The story relates how Rasputin used to love to dance and drink with the gypsies at the encampment of Novaya Derevnya. When the messenger finally located Rasputin, he was dancing wildly and covered with perspiration. His eyes were inflamed with strong drink and his temples were pounding. But when Rasputin realized why the messenger had come, a sudden change came over him. His eyes suddenly became focused on something in the distance and, falling on his knees, he began to pray. The story relates how the gypsies shuddered as they saw Rasputin call on the power of God on the behalf of the tsarevich.

After praying, Rasputin decided to make his way to the palace. When he got there, he went straight to the sickroom where Alexei was suffering. Rasputin blessed all in the room, including one of the high church officials, the Archimandrite Theophan. He then walked over to Nicholas and Alexandra, and greeted them with a traditional bear hug and triple kiss. The tsar and tsarita were never offended by this show of familiarity, but seemed comforted by it.

Perhaps the most dramatic moment of all was when Rasputin turned to the little boy who was pale and exhausted from the fever that wracked his body. The room was full of people—family members, doctors, and church officials. None could help the boy but one, Grigori Rasputin. Rasputin fell to his knees and, almost as if on cue, everyone joined him in that position. After about ten minutes Rasputin stood to his feet, looked down at the small boy and said, "Open your eyes, my son." The tsarevich's eyelids fluttered and then opened. A smile broke over his face as he looked around at everyone in the room.[23]

Alexandra was more than impressed with Rasputin. She had prayed

---

23. Ibid., p. 134.

fervently for a son; and after he was born her heart was broken by Alexei's illness. Not even the prayers of the archimandrite, along with all the priests of Russia, seemed to have any effect on the boy's health. But in just ten minutes this peasant from Siberia brought about an unbelievable change in her son's condition. The hearts of Nicholas and Alexandra were moved by Rasputin. He responded warmly to their devotion to him. Rasputin came to call the tsar *Batiushka,* "Little Father," and the tsarina *Matushka,* "Little Mother." These were terms of endearment showing the high regard the Russian peasantry at that time had for the absolute ruler of the people.[24]

The tsarina found Rasputin to be a key person in her son's continuing health. Without Rasputin's prayers, Alexei could become ill and die. The tsar, too, came to have a reverential respect for Rasputin and even confided in him regarding matters of state.

At that time, Russia had many legalities. The bureaucracy was pompous and often unyielding—but if you knew the right person, you could get almost anything you wanted. Because of his popularity with the royal family, Rasputin was given the privilege of hearing petitions from the people. "When it came to petitions . . . Rasputin had become the most powerful man in Russia after the tsar." People came from everywhere to his small flat wanting the rules bent in their favor—and he had the power to grant their wishes.[25] Rasputin's connections with the royal family, however, proved to be his undoing.

Though we get glimpses of Rasputin from those who admired him, such as his daughter Maria, others saw him as a very evil man. Around 1910, Prime Minister Stolypin, a close friend of Nicholas, decided to warn the tsar about the rumors he had heard concerning Rasputin and the tsarina. The tsar listened and suggested that Stolypin put together a written document concerning all the things being said and that he also include his personal grievances against Rasputin. When the report was finished, the tsar hardly looked at it, but suggested that the prime minister

24. de Jonge, p. 259.
25. Oakley, pp. 142–143

meet Rasputin personally and judge for himself. Here are a few lines of Stolypin's first impression of Rasputin: "He ran his piercing eyes over me, mumbled mysterious and inarticulate words from the scriptures, made strange movements with his hands, and I began to feel an indescribable loathing for the vermin sitting opposite me. Still, I did realize that the man possessed great hypnotic power, which was beginning to produce a fairly strong moral impression on me, though certainly one of repulsion."[26]

Rasputin grew to dislike Stolypin, whose tragic death, and Rasputin's prediction of his death, raised Rasputin to even greater fame and notoriety. On one occasion, the tsar and tsarina were in the royal carriage, followed by a second carriage carrying Stolypin. They were on their way to the opera house in Kiev. When Stolypin's carriage passed by, Rasputin cried, "Death is after him! Death is after him!"

That night, at the second intermission, something terrible happened to Stolypin. There were two loud sounds, as though something had dropped. Stolypin, who was standing and stretching his legs, slowly turned toward the tsar and made the sign of the cross. Stolypin's right hand and uniform were stained with blood. Stolypin slowly sank to the chair and began to unbutton his tunic. He had been shot twice and died shortly thereafter.[27]

Years of Controversy

The tide began to turn against Rasputin when even those religious leaders who were, at one time, on his side and championed him as a man of God, began to be concerned about his debauched behavior.

The resentment from the religious leaders of Russia grew when Rasputin deeply offended the monk Iliodor. The two were on a nine-day journey. Rasputin boasted to the celibate monk, "I can have any woman I choose," and continued to recount the sordid details of his immoral behavior. Iliodor wondered how God could have given Rasputin such powers and yet not punish him for his debauchery and blasphemy. But even

---

26. Ibid., p. 147; see also Fuhrmann, p. 74.
27. Oakley, p. 141.

more damaging was Rasputin's act of sharing several letters written by Alexandra and her daughters to Rasputin. They were gushing and girlish and were deeply offensive. One of the letters from the tsarina reads as follows:

> My beloved, unforgettable teacher, redeemer, and mentor! How tiresome it is without you. My soul is quiet and I relax only when you, my teacher, are sitting beside me. I kiss your hands and lean my head on your blessed shoulders. Oh how light, how light do I feel then! I only wish one thing: to fall asleep, for ever on your shoulders and in your arms. What happiness to feel your presence near me. Where are you? Where have you gone? Oh, I am so sad and my heart is longing. . . . Come quickly, I am waiting for you and am tormenting myself for you. I am asking for your blessing and I am kissing your blessed hands. I love you for ever. Your M. [*Matushka,* meaning "Little Mother"][28]

When Iliodor released letters like this to the public whose suspicions were growing, particularly because of Rasputin's connection with the regime of the tsar, the sinister conspiracy that everyone feared seemed factual beyond a reasonable shadow of doubt. Rasputin's scandalous behavior was an embarrassment to many. The police even made efforts to keep him from disgracing himself in public and encouraged his favorite restaurant, the Villa Rhode, to reserve a private room for this exclusive use. "Yet," as de Jonge writes, "it was impossible to keep the man out of trouble."[29]

The First Assassination Attempt

Iliodor had become one of Rasputin's most hated enemies. He was a conspirator in the first attempt to remove Rasputin. The plan was for some of Iliodor's female disciples to entice Rasputin, overpower him, and then emasculate him. That initial plan failed, but a later one, in 1914, almost succeeded.

Chiona Guseva, an ex-prostitute whose face was grotesquely disfig-

---

28. de Jonge, p. 261.
29. Ibid.

ured by advanced syphilis, made the long trip to Pokrovskoye. Disguised as a beggar, Guseva approached Rasputin with her hand out, as if asking for alms. As Rasputin was fishing in his pockets for some coins, Guseva drew a knife from her cloak and plunged it into Rasputin's stomach and pulled it up as far as she could. She was about to stab Rasputin again, but with almost supernatural strength he held the angry woman off until bystanders came to his aid.

Rasputin was seriously wounded and bleeding copiously from the gaping wound in his midsection when he was brought back to his house. Some of the onlookers claimed that he was trying to prevent his intestines from coming out of his body cavity. The wound was extensive and extended from his navel to his sternum. Some of his intestines had been severed. Blood and refuse were oozing out of them. The nearest doctor was in Tyumen, a six-hour ride.

Rasputin's wife and daughter tried to stop the bleeding while they awaited the arrival of the doctor. When the doctor did arrive, he did emergency surgery but insisted that Rasputin must go to the nearest hospital. Unbelievably, Rasputin survived the six-hour ride on a *troika,* a wagon without springs, that bounced around on the rutted roads of central Siberia like a cork in a river. Despite the gloomy prognosis given by the doctors, Rasputin survived.[30]

The Attempt That Succeeded

The attempts on Rasputin's life show an increasing hatred of the man and what he stood for. Biographers agree, however, that it was more than hatred that provoked the final assassination attempt. In his monumental study, *The Man Who Killed Rasputin: Prince Felix Youssoupov and the Murder That Helped Bring Down the Russian Empire,* Greg King writes:

> As a group, these men [those who were plotting Rasputin's demise] acted out of misguided patriotism in the belief that only Rasputin's

30. Greg King, *The Man Who Killed Rasputin: Prince Felix Youssoupov and the Murder That Helped Bring Down the Russian Empire* (New York: Birch Lane Press, 1995), p. 139.

death could alter the disastrous course which threatened to overwhelm the Russian Empire. By striking out against Rasputin, the conspirators hoped to diminish the empress's influence over her husband; the tsar would then be free to listen to the warning voices of his ministers and grant the reforms necessary if Russia were to survive the turmoil of the war.[31]

Several men were involved in the murder of Rasputin. On November 20, 1916, Vladimir Purishkevich, a government official, had addressed the Duma. He publicly lamented Rasputin's influence over the imperial family and complained that an obscure peasant was, in reality, governing Russia. Then there was Prince Felix Youssoupov, representing the aristocracy. Rasputin had been his counselor, but the prince came to hate the man and firmly believed that Rasputin was a danger to the empire. Others were involved, but these were the principal players in the final plot.

Before we present the final days of Rasputin's life, we want to digress for a moment and look closely at Prince Felix and his relationship with Rasputin. Felix was one of the richest men in Russia. His mother, Princess Zenaide, had already three sons and longed for a daughter. When Felix was born, she was disappointed, but sought to get over her disappointment by treating Felix as a daughter. Princess Zenaide allowed his hair to grow long, and put him in frilly petticoats and dresses until he was five. Even as a young man, Felix continued to wear women's clothing on occasion. He seemed to enjoy attracting the admiring glances of officers and other young men and even won the approving glance of King Edward VII of England.[32]

Felix had heard much about Rasputin's powers and started to go to him for counsel. Rasputin's daughter, Maria, however, did not like the prince and writes that Felix was really motivated by a perverse desire. In fact, on one occasion Maria found the prince trying to seduce Rasputin, who violently pummeled him for his advances. Rasputin did not believe

---

31. Ibid.
32. Ibid., pp. 178–179.

that homosexual love was holy, nor was it a means to redemption. Some would argue that "once his favors to the man had been refused, then rebuffed, the wealthy prince sought revenge."[33]

Felix met with Rasputin on a regular basis for "treatment," though no one is quite sure what the prince was being treated for. The following account of Rasputin's "treatment," written by Felix, reveals something about Rasputin:

> The *starets* told me to lie down on the couch. He stood in front of me, looked me intently in the eyes and began to stroke my chest, neck, and head. He then suddenly knelt down and—so it seemed to me—began to pray, placing his hands on my forehead.... Then he suddenly jumped to his feet and began to make passes. He was evidently familiar with certain of the processes employed by hypnotists. His hypnotic power was immense. I felt it subduing me and diffusing warmth throughout the whole of my body. I grew numb; my body seemed paralyzed. I tried to speak but my tongue would not obey me, and I seemed to be falling asleep, as if under the influence of some strong narcotic.[34]

The men who were planning to murder Rasputin met on several occasions to discuss possible plans. At first Prince Felix wanted to shoot Rasputin in his own flat, but the others pointed out that Rasputin's flat was nearly always mobbed with petitioners asking favors. After much discussion, the conspirators felt that it would be best if Rasputin would simply disappear and his disappearance be kept a mystery. It was suggested that Dr. Stanislaus Lazovert join with them in the conspiracy. After Rasputin was abducted, he could be poisoned and Lazovert would be able to get the necessary ingredients.[35]

The Plot Succeeds

The final night of Grigori Rasputin's earthly sojourn must have seemed

---

33. Ibid., p. 131.
34. Ibid., pp. 139–140.
35. Oakley, p. 192.

strange indeed. He was ushered into a room in Youssoupov's Moika Palace. Prince Felix had placed potassium cyanide crystals in one of the wine glasses and also in several of the cakes. Upstairs the gramophone was playing "Yankee Doodle Dandy."

Rasputin drank the Madeira wine out of his wine glass with no seeming ill effect. He then ate several of the poisoned cakes—again with no seeming ill effect. Felix became panicky. He wondered what had gone wrong. Had God protected Rasputin, or had evil spirits come to Rasputin's aid? Soon Rasputin claimed that he was experiencing some kind of irritation in his throat. Youssoupov was encouraged in his heart and suggested that Rasputin drink some more wine. Rasputin emptied the glass and said to Felix that it had helped. He was feeling better. Rasputin spied the prince's guitar and asked Felix to sing him some gypsy songs. Felix did, and Rasputin joined in. It was a rather humorous sight: the prince singing and playing, wondering why his victim would not die, and Rasputin getter stronger and stronger by the minute. This continued until 2:30 in the morning.[36]

Rasputin's vigor was causing the prince great concern. Youssoupov realized that something had to be done quickly. As Rasputin was chatting, singing, eating poisoned cakes, and drinking poisoned wine, Felix drew his revolver—a last desperate effort to kill this man who would not seem to die.

Rasputin's ability to ingest great quantities of poison led Felix to conclude that an evil spirit was protecting Rasputin. Felix feared that even if he shot Rasputin, the spirit would deflect the bullet. Felix, therefore, led Rasputin to the crucifix on the wall and even got Rasputin to make the sign of the cross. Believing that the evil spirit had been exorcised in this way, Felix drew his revolver and fired one shot point blank into Rasputin's chest.[37] At this point the account almost becomes humorous:

Youssoupov says that he bent over Rasputin and felt his pulse, which was

36. King, p. 156.
37. de Jonge, pp. 326–327.

lifeless, and then, taken with a fit of rage, he started to shake the corpse before letting it drop. Suddenly, to his horror, he saw Rasputin open first his left and then is right eye, and experienced that paralysis that comes from fear so total that, however hard one tries, one cannot make the muscles move. Suddenly Rasputin leaped to his feet and attacked him with a roar, trying to strangle him, foaming and bleeding at the mouth and repeating his name, "Felix, Felix," over and over again. Eventually Youssoupov tore himself loose, leaving one of his shoulder straps behind him, and ran upstairs, calling to Purishkevich that Rasputin was still alive. The politician saw him, sickly pale, running off to his parents' quarters again. He then heard a second set of footsteps coming up the stairs and the sound of the door into the courtyard being opened. He grabbed his revolver and rushed down in time to see Rasputin moving fast across the courtyard calling, "Felix, Felix. I'll tell the tsarina." Purishkevich, who considered himself a good shot, fired twice and missed; the third shot caught Rasputin in the back and stopped him—he was some twenty paces away—and a fourth sent him to the ground. Purishkevich ran up and delivered a massive kick to the left temple, which left an ugly wound. This time it was finished.[38]

Oakley reports, however, that it was neither the poison, nor the bullets, nor the kick in the head that killed Rasputin. "That only when he was thrown, trussed and wounded, into the subzero temperatures of the frozen river did he finally have to give up his fight for life. The autopsy found that his lungs were full of water, that it was drowning which killed Rasputin."[39]

How Are We To Understand Rasputin?

Though some of the accounts of Rasputin's miracles—if they were indeed that—can be explained by natural means, others of them defy explanation. His ability to withstand the cyanide leaves even a skeptic like de Jonge saying: "Rasputin's resistance to cyanide is one of the most potent

---

38. Oakley, pp. 200–201.
39. Ibid.

elements of his legend, and it has not yet been satisfactorily explained."[40] From where did this man get his power? Was it demonic, hypnotic, or simply attributable to the suggestibility of the subjects with whom Rasputin worked? And how about his seeming power over women?

Others have been known for similar abilities. Giacomo Girolamo Casanova (b. April 2, 1725; d. June 4, 1798) was also known to be able to sway women to do his bidding. Having been expelled as a young man from the Roman Catholic Seminary of St. Cyprian for "scandalous behavior," Casanova joined the Masonic Order in 1750, introduced the lottery to Paris in 1757, and had a legendary reputation as a lover.[41]

Similar accounts abound in fiction as well as history. In George de Maurier's 1894 novel *Trilby,* the main character, Trilby, falls into the hands of Svengali, an unscrupulous and self-seeking Hungarian musician with strange powers. He hypnotizes a beautiful young artist's model into doing all his wishes. The name Svengali has become a synonym for self-seeking individuals who seek to gain sway over people for their own evil ends.

In 1936, one of the most celebrated German criminal cases revealed some shocking details of the life and strange powers of a hypnotist named Franz Walther. He frequently posed as a doctor and took advantage of women over whom he seemed to have some strange powers. One day Walther boarded a train in Heidelberg and entered a room occupied by a young woman who told Walther that she was on her way to see a doctor because of stomach problems. Walther appeared compassionate and sympathized with her. He told her he was a doctor and invited her to have coffee with him. She quickly became frightened by his demeanor and says she wanted to refuse, but when Walther took her hand she seemed to come under his power. The woman later remembered that "it seemed to me as if I no longer had a will of my own." The German authorities report that Walther hypnotized her and then raped her.[42]

Some attribute such "power," if we may call it that, to a "will to domi-

---

40. de Jonge, p. 323.
41. *The New Encyclopedia Britannica* (1988), vol. 2, "Casanova."
42. Wilson, p. 31.

nate" behavior. Zoologists have shown the importance of dominance in the animal world. "In the farmyard, the most dominant chicken can peck all the others; the second most dominant can peck all except the most dominant, and so on." But do we find this sort of dominance in man? One author writes: "Of all creatures, none is so obsessed by the will to power as men. From what we know of magicians, it seems likely that magic developed as an instrument of this will to power."[43]

There are many possible explanations to Rasputin's behavior. The more one reads about his life, the more mysterious—and sinister—he becomes.

---

43. Ibid., p. 26.

The Mystery of the So-Called "Lost Tribes of Israel

Who, or what, are the "Lost Tribes of Israel"? In the first edition of *Marginal Mysteries,* Hutchings cites a publication entitled *Israel, My Glory* which, even with the passing of many years, still gives what is perhaps the most insightful and succinct answer to this question:

> The television series *In Search of the Ten Lost Tribes* is an indication of how fascinated people are about the unanswered questions surrounding the existence of the mysterious, the unknown, and the unexplained. The subsequent history of the remnants of the northern kingdom has fueled the imagination of many travelers, writers, romanticists, and cultists. There are three basic ideas that have emerged about their subsequent identity.
>
> First, one traditional Jewish explanation is that the ten tribes are forever lost, assimilated among their Assyrian captors, and never again will be found. The great second century rabbi, Akiba, expressed this opinion strongly. . . .
>
> Second, another Jewish tradition is that the tribes were living beyond the mysterious river Sambaty on whose rapidly flowing waters prevented their crossing it. The Jewish historian Josephus stated at the end of the first century, "The ten tribes are beyond the Euphrates till now, and are an immense multitude and not to be estimated in numbers." Through the Middle Ages various pseudo-messiahs, like David

Reubeni, appeared in Europe and claimed to be from a Jewish kingdom composed of ten "lost" tribes. Legends circulated that fired the hope of their soon discovery, but no tangible evidence of their existence was ever produced. It was this tradition that motivated Israel's rabbis to declare that the Jews of Ethiopia belong to the lost tribe of Dan.

Third, theories abound which identify various ethnic groups today as being the descendants of the ten lost tribes. The *Encyclopedia Judaica* states, "There is hardly a people from the Japanese to the British, and from the Red Indians to the Afghans, who have not been suggested, and hardly a place, among them Africa, India, China, Persia, Caucasia, the United States, and Great Britain."

The theory attempting to explain the subsequent history of the ten lost tribes that has gained the greatest following is the view known popularly as British Israelism. First propounded in nineteenth century England, the basic premise of British Israelism is that the ten tribes captured by the Assyrians are, in reality, the Saxae, or Scythians, who surged westward through northern Europe and eventually became the ancestors of the Saxons who invaded England. The theory maintains that the Anglo-Saxons are thus the "Israel" of the Bible. Therefore, according to this view, the present-day "Jews" are from the tribe of Judah who are under the divine curse and are not to be identified with Israel at all.

Furthermore, the Anglo-Saxon peoples, including the British (Ephraim) and Americans (Manasseh), are the inheritors of the covenants and promises of the Old Testament. In addition to some scriptural arguments based on the birthright of Joseph (Genesis 29:26) and the promises to his sons Ephraim and Manasseh (Genesis 48:20), British Israelism maintains that the "lost" tribes left landmarks on their trek across Europe. Thus, the Dan and Danube Rivers, as well as the city of Danzig and the country of Denmark, are clear indications to them of the tribe of Dan! ...

Another group today which has adopted British Israelism is the "Identity" movement of white supremacy. A number of groups affirming the Satanic character of Zionism and the so-called worldwide Jewish conspiracy have adopted British Israelism to prove the superiority of the white race over the Jew, Asiatics, and Negroes.

Hutchings refers to Thomas Foster's *British Royal Throne* in which the belief is set forth that the prophet Jeremiah fled to Ireland or England with one or two Hebrew princesses and from their union the royal throne of David was established in England. This view asserts that since the time of Jeremiah the kings and queens of England have been occupying David's throne. The erstwhile claim that "the sun never sets on the British Empire" is supposedly proof that David's throne is being established over planet Earth.

From this it would appear that beliefs regarding what Scripture and history allegedly teach about these "ten lost tribes" has spawned a variety of theories and doctrines that:

1. **Bring people under the yoke of legalism.** If America is the true "Israel," then "American Israelites" must observe all Jewish laws.
2. **Elevate Anglo-Saxons above everyone else.** If America is the true "Israel," then Anglo-Saxons have a favored status in the sight of God.,
3. **Rob Israel of God's promises.** The words of Romans 11:26 now come to mean, "And so all *America* shall be saved: as it is written, There shall come out of *England* the Deliverer, and shall turn away ungodliness from *the United States.*"

Much More Than Meets the Eye

There are several consequences of accepting the idea that the ten tribes have now come to America, one of which is the development of the Christian Identity Movement. "Christian Identity believers think of themselves as living in the 'Last Days,' when history will reach its consummation, an A-millennialist outlook they inherited from British Israelism," writes Michael Barkun. "The latter was concerned not merely with identifying the 'Anglo-Saxon-Celtic peoples' as true Israelites but in drawing from this knowledge inferences about the fulfillment of biblical prophecies. . . ."[1] This has led to an utter disdain for pre-millennial pre-tribulationism, as Barkun notes:

> Even more than British Israelism, Christian Identity rejects the Dispensational pre-millennialism associated with the futurist perspective. Far from constituting an offshoot of Fundamentalism, as is often supposed, Christian Identity rejects the futurist orientation of most Fundamentalists. Its hostility is particularly directed at the rapture, a doctrine it regards as without scriptural foundation. . . . Identity's rejection of the rapture is linked to the disdain for anything that promises to rescue the saved from the rigors of the Tribulation. . . . Identity, however, far from wishing to avoid this period of tumult [the Tribulation], yearns for an opportunity to engage the forces of evil in apocalyptic battle. Hence the rapture smacks of cowardice and retreat.[2]

This disdain for futurism manifests itself in "survivalism," a term which indicates:

> a lifestyle of physical withdrawal and self-sufficiency that has as its aim surviving some imagined future calamity. The survivalist writer Kurt Saxon, who claims to have coined the term in 1976, defines survivalist as "one who anticipates the collapse of civilization and wants to save himself and his loved ones and bring something to the movement, if you would, which will contribute to the advancement of the next generation." Survivalists include individuals with a broad array of beliefs. Some are secularists who believe themselves threatened by nuclear war, environmental pollution, or racial conflict. Some are religionists who adopt the so-called post-Tribulationist position, asserting that saved Christians will have to live through the Tribulation instead of being raptured off

---

1. Michael Barkun, *Religion and the Racist Right* (Chapel Hill:The University of North Carolina Press, rev. ed., 1997), p. 75.
2. Ibid., p. 104.

the earth for this period. Those in this camp, such as Jim McKeever, argue that Christians must be prepared to survive in a hostile and violent world until the Second Coming takes place. But there are also Christian Identity survivalists who anticipate imminent catastrophe and believe that as the self-identified remnant of Israel, they must withdraw from an increasingly dangerous world until such time as their enemies have been defeated.[3]

The Division of the Kingdom

Soon after the death of King Solomon, his kingdom was divided. Solomon had placed such heavy taxation upon the people to support his extravagant endeavors that after his death the people cried for relief; however, Rehoboam, his son, refused to listen. We read the account in 2 Chronicles 10:10–11:

> And the young men that were brought up with him spake unto him, saying, Thus shalt thou answer the people that spake unto thee, saying, Thy father made our yoke heavy, but make thou it somewhat lighter for us; thus shalt thou say unto them, My little finger shall be thicker than my father's loins. For whereas my father put a heavy yoke upon you, I will put more to your yoke: my father chastised you with whips, but I will chastise you with scorpions.

As a result, in about 930 B.C., the twelve tribes of Israel divided into two separate nations. The tribes of Judah and Benjamin, which were located in the southern part of Israel—hence the designation "the Southern Kingdom"—accepted Rehoboam as king and Jerusalem was their capital. The other tribes, which were located in the north—hence the designation "the Northern Kingdom"—took Jeroboam, the son of Nebat, as their king. Samaria was their capital. The books of 2 Kings and 2 Chronicles give the history of the divided kingdom and their kings for the subsequent two hundred years.

---

3. Ibid., p. 213.

The Fall of the Northern Kingdom

The devastating invasion by the Assyrians that finally brought about the destruction of the Northern Kingdom came as the result of a series of political and military events, all within the sovereign control of God. In Isaiah 7:14 we read, ". . . Behold, a virgin shall conceive, and bear a son, and shall call his name Immanuel." These words were spoken by the prophet Isaiah to King Ahaz of Judah.

Rezin, the king of Syria, and Pekah, the king of Israel, the Northern Kingdom, had allied themselves and were advancing on Jerusalem. Isaiah approached Ahaz with the good news that Rezin and Pekah would not prevail and that all Ahaz had to do was to ask for a sign from the Lord. Feigning piety, Ahaz refused and said, ". . . I will not ask, neither will I tempt the LORD" (Isaiah 7:12). When this Syro-Ephraimitic coalition moved on Jerusalem (2 Kings 16:5; 2 Chronicles 28:5–8), Ahaz was desperate and called on the Assyrian king, Tiglath-pileser, for military assistance. The Assyrians made a mighty sweep westward, imposing heavy tribute on Judah, Ammon, Edom, and Moab, and taking numbers of people into captivity from the areas of Galilee and Gilead. It was during this Assyrian campaign that the fortress of Hazor was destroyed and the Northern Kingdom reduced to a tiny vassal state under Assyrian domination. These events took pace in the years 734–732 B.C.

Emboldened with their military successes, the Assyrians launched an attack on Damascus in 732. In this same year, a pro-Assyrian revolt in Samaria led to the death of Pekah. Hoseha ascended to the throne and assumed leadership of the Northern Kingdom. Hoseha submitted his kingdom to Assyria for a time and paid heavy tribute. However, it soon became an unbearable burden and Hoseha sought help from So, king of Egypt. Retribution from Assyria was swift. Shalmaneser V (726–722 B.C.), the new Assyrian king, invaded Israel and besieged both Shechem and Samaria. King Hoseha was captured outside the city of Samaria and deported (2 Kings 17:4). Samaria was under siege for three years. In the late summer of 722 B.C. the city capitulated. Sargon, Shalmaneser's son and successor, claimed the final victory over Samaria. The ancient *Babylonian*

Chronicle claims the destruction of Samaria to be the most notable event of the reign of Shalmaneser, who deported exiles to Assyrian locations like Gozan and Hara (1 Chronicles 5:26). With the passing of time these exiles from Israel reached Nimrud and Nineveh, where Israelite names have been found in written records.

The fall of Samaria marks the end of the Northern Kingdom. Sargon claims it as his victory. In *The Annals of Sargon* we read: "I besieged and conquered Samaria, led away as booty 27,290 inhabitants of it. . . . The town I rebuilt better than it was before and settled therein people from countries which I myself had conquered. I placed an officer of mine as governor over them and imposed upon them tribute as is customary for Assyrian citizens."[4]

It should be observed that Sargon claims that a little more than 27,000 Israelites from the Northern Kingdom were deported. It is impossible to verify the accuracy of this statement, but, if anything, the figure is inflated. Sargon would want to boast of his conquest, not minimize it. Ingraham makes a significant observation on the number of Israelites deported: "If an estimated half million Israelites lived in Ephraim at that time, then only about five percent of the population journeyed east. Their kingdom and nation passed from existence, but the tribes themselves were never lost. Indeed, they were never deported."[5]

Some Observations

It becomes apparent from the above data that all the members of the northern tribes were not deported and taken into captivity. Furthermore, not all the members of the ten tribes lived in the area known as the Northern Kingdom. According to Scripture, some of the members of the northern tribes lived in Judah and were under the authority of Rehoboam, Solomon's son. First Kings 12:17 states: "But as for *the children of Israel which dwelt in the cities of Judah,* Rehoboam reigned over them."

4. Taken from J. A. Thompson, *The Bible and Archaeology* (Grand Rapids: Eerdmans, 1962), p. 135.
5. David Ingraham, "Lost Sheep, But No Lost Tribes," *Gospel Truth* (February 1993), p. 1.

But what happened following the fall of the Northern Kingdom? Is there any evidence in the Bible that there were still *twelve tribes* in existence following the destruction of Samaria?

Second Chronicles 30 relates that King Hezekiah sought to restore the Feast of Unleavened Bread and the Passover which, perhaps since the time of the dividing of the kingdom, had not been properly observed. We will let the Bible speak for itself:

> And Hezekiah sent to *all Israel and Judah,* and wrote letters also to *Ephraim and Manasseh,* that they should come to the house of the LORD at Jerusalem, to keep the passover unto the LORD God of Israel. For the king had taken counsel, and his princes, and all the congregation in Jerusalem, to keep the passover in the second month. For they could not keep it at that time, because the priests had not sanctified themselves sufficiently, neither had the people gathered themselves together to Jerusalem. And the thing pleased the king and all the congregation. So they established a decree to make proclamation throughout all Israel, from Beersheba even to Dan, that they should come to keep the passover unto the LORD God of Israel at Jerusalem: for they had not done it of a long time in such sort as it was written. So the posts went with the letters from the king and his princes throughout *all Israel and Judah,* and according to the commandment of the king, saying, Ye children of Israel, turn again unto the LORD God of Abraham, Isaac, and Israel, and he will return to the remnant of you, *that are escaped out of the hand of the kings of Assyria.* ... So the posts passed from city to city *through the country of Ephraim and Manasseh even unto Zebulun:* but they laughed them to scorn, and mocked them. Nevertheless divers of *Asher and Manasseh and of Zebulun* humbled themselves, and came to Jerusalem. Also in Judah the hand of God was to give them one heart to do the commandment of the king and of the princes, by the word of the LORD. ... For a multitude of the people, even many of *Ephraim, and Manasseh, Issachar, and Zebulun,* had not cleansed themselves, yet did they eat the passover otherwise than it was written. But Hezekiah prayed for them, saying,

The good LORD pardon every one....And all the congregation of Judah,
with the priests and the Levites, and all the congregation *that came out
of Israel,* and the strangers that came out of the land of Israel, and that
dwelt in Judah, rejoiced.

—2 Chronicles 30:1–6, 10–12, 18, 25

A Scythian Connection

The theory that the "ten lost tribes" of Israel migrated from their places
of deportation eastward to Scythia to become known as "the Scythians"
bears some further comment. The Scythians were an ancient people inhabiting an area between the southern shores of the Caspian and Black
seas. But are they the descendants of the Northern Kingdom, and did they
migrate into Europe, then Britain, and then America? Ingraham states that
this view "arose in Britain because of a passionate sense of nationalism. It
survives in America as a parasite of prejudice."[6]

Is there any relationship between the Scythians and the so-called "lost
tribes" of Israel? There are several observations that can be made about the
Scythians that would lead us to answer in the negative. According to Edwin Yamauchi in his book *Foes From the Northern Frontier,* "The Scythians
were among the most skilled horsemen ever known. It was their superb
horsemanship, especially their ability to shoot arrows while riding at a gal-
lop, even at enemies behind them, that gave the Scythians and their later
imitators, the Parthians, a distinctive military advantage."[7]

Hitchcock summarizes what Herodotus, who is known as "the father of history," had to say about the Scythians. Among other things, they
drank the blood of their first enemy slain, used the skins of their victims
to cover their quivers, drank from the skulls of their victims, and scalped
their enemies and used these scalps as "napkins."[8] Even Josephus wrote
that "they take pleasure in killing men, and differ little from brute beasts"

---

6. Ibid.
7. Edwin Yamauchi, *Foes From the Northern Frontier* (Grand Rapids: Baker Book House,
   1982), p. 67.
8. Mark Hitchcock, *After the Empire* (Oklahoma City: Hearthstone Publishing, 1992), pp.
   20–21.

(*Contra Apion,* 2:39, 38). If these were the descendants of the lost exiles of the Northern Kingdom, from where did they get such un-Jewish practices? None of this seems possible for those who had come from Israel. Moreover, the ethnic background of the Scythians does not favor British Israelism. "The Scyths may be regarded as a horde which came down from upper Asia and conquered Iranian-speaking people, perhaps in time adopting the speech of their subjects."[9]

"The Twelve Tribes" and "The Jews"

When we turn to the pages of the New Testament, there is no indication whatsoever that there are any tribes that have been lost. In the first verse of James 1, the author identifies himself and the recipients of his letter: "James, a servant of . . . Jesus Christ, *to the twelve tribes which are scattered abroad."* The tribes were scattered, but none were missing. In New Testament times the "twelve tribes" were considered both a present entity and a future people. Jesus said, ". . . Ye which have followed me, in the regeneration when the Son of man shall sit in the throne of his glory, ye also shall sit upon twelve thrones, judging *the twelve tribes of Israel"* (Matthew 19:28). Likewise, in his defense, the apostle said: "And now I stand and am judged for the hope of the promise made of God unto *our fathers:* Unto which promise *our twelve tribes,* instantly serving God day and night, hope to come. For which hope's sake, king Agrippa, I am accused of the Jews" (Acts 26:6–7).

Paul was certainly not anti-Semitic, anti-Jew, or anti-Judah. Though Paul was a Benjamite and "of the stock of Israel . . . an Hebrew of the Hebrews" (Philippians 3:5), he nevertheless calls himself "a Jew" (Acts 22:3) and also "an Israelite, of the seed of Abraham (Romans 11:1). The blindness that the apostle ascribes to Israel during this present period of the Gentiles is not a blindness that affects only Judah. "For I would not, brethren," Paul writes in Romans 11:25, "that ye should be ignorant of this mystery, lest ye should be wise in your own conceits; that blindness in part is happened *to Israel,* until the fulness of the Gentiles be come in." If

9. *Encyclopaedia Britannica,* "Scythia" (1929).

a partial blindness has come upon all Israel in the present, so God's blessings will come upon "all Israel" (Romans 11:25–26) in the future, not just on "Anglo-Saxon Israelites." The Bible only recognizes three classes of people. "Give none offence, neither to the *Jews,* nor to the *Gentiles,* nor to the *church* of God" (1 Corinthians 10:32). British Israelism, quite contrary to Scripture, recognizes a fourth—the descendants of the so-called "lost tribes."

A few passages in Scripture seem to indicate the disappearance of the Northern Kingdom, and are therefore used to support the idea of "ten lost tribes." Hosea 1:4–6 is an example:

> And the LORD said unto him, Call his name Jezreel; for yet a little while, and I will avenge the blood of Jezreel upon the house of Jehu, *and will cause to cease the KINGDOM of the house of Israel.* And it shall come to pass at that day, that I will break the bow of Israel in the valley of Jezreel. And she conceived again, and bare a daughter. And God said unto him, Call her name Loruhamah: for I will no more have mercy upon the house of Israel; *but I will utterly take them away."*

The prophet Hosea prophesied the overthrow of the dynasty of Jehu, which occurred in 752 B.C., and is depicted as being yet future (Hosea 1:4). When the Lord says that He will "cause to cease the *kingdom* of the house of Israel," this is obviously a reference to the fall of the Northern Kingdom, which occurred in 722 B.C. It's the Northern *Kingdom,* as a separate geopolitical entity, that is going to cease, not the ten tribes. The Roman Empire suffered disastrous defeats in times past but that does not mean that the people who made up that empire were "lost" or somehow "disappeared." Significantly, the Scripture does not predict the disappearance of the northern tribes but rather that they will be brought together with Judah in the Kingdom Age.

Having been dispersed into Assyria and environs, survivors from these northern tribes intermarried with the general population and within a few generations many lost their Hebrew identity. This, however, does not mean that *all* the members of the northern tribes were lost forever or that the division between the north and south was to continue in perpetuity.

When the Assyrian and Babylonian captivities were ended, the rivalries between the northern and southern tribes ceased and the Israelites looked forward to a common destiny that was bound up with God's promises to David, and with Jerusalem as the capital. In Ezekiel 37 we read:

> The word of the LORD came again unto me, saying, Moreover, thou son of man, take thee one stick, and write upon it, For Judah, and for the children of Israel his companions: then take another stick, and write upon it, For Joseph, the stick of Ephraim, and for all the house of Israel his companions: And join them one to another into one stick; and they shall become one in thine hand. And when the children of thy people shall speak unto thee, saying, Wilt thou not shew us what thou meanest by these? Say unto them, Thus saith the Lord GOD; Behold, I will take the stick of Joseph, which is in the hand of Ephraim, and the tribes of Israel his fellows, and will put them with him, even with the stick of Judah, *and make them one stick, and they shall be one in mine hand.* And the sticks whereon thou writest shall be in thine hand before their eyes. And say unto them, Thus saith the Lord GOD; Behold, *I will take the children of Israel from among the heathen, whither they be gone, and will gather them on every side, and bring them into their own land: And I will make them one nation in the land upon the mountains of Israel; and one king shall be king to them all: and they shall be no more two nations, neither shall they be divided into two kingdoms any more at all.*
>
> —Ezekiel 37:15–22, italics added

The symbolism of the passage is striking. The prophet Ezekiel is told by the Lord to take two sticks. They are to be marked with the words "For Judah" and "For Joseph." Taylor comments:

> These represent the two kingdoms of former days, before Samaria fell to the Assyrians under Sargon II (722/1 B.C.), and Israel, the Northern

Kingdom, lost her identity. He is to take one of them in his right hand, concealing one end of it in his clenched fist. Then he is to take the other stick and join it to the first one, end to end. His clenched fist will thus grasp the place where the two sticks meet, and it will appear as if he is holding one long stick in the middle.[10]

The International Diaspora and Jewish Identity

There have been a number of startling proofs regarding Jews in different parts of the world who have maintained their Jewish identity. A recent report indicates that geneticists have confirmed the Jewish roots of the Lemba people of southern Africa. A DNA sequence was found that is distinctive to the priestly tribe of Levi, something that supports the Lemba's longstanding claim that they have Jewish ancestry. The Lemba, who speak the Bantu language, practice ritual circumcision, avoid eating pork, and keep the Jewish sabbath. According to the report, the male Y chromosome remains unchanged from generation to generation, something that contributes to its usefulness in determining ancestry. The Lemba, who live in South Africa and Zimbabwe, have a longstanding tradition that a man named Buba led them out of Judea.[11]

Another report[12] indicates that descendants of the tribe of Manasseh have been found in northeast India. The group numbers about 5 million and believe their ancient tradition that they are the tribe of Manasseh, which was deported from Israel after the destruction of the Northern Kingdom by the Assyrians. The Israeli government may soon send a group to India to meet the communities claiming descendancy from Manasseh for the purpose of learning "everything about them and to investigate how to reunite them with the people of the land of Israel."

Rabbi Eliyahu Avichail was the first to discover the group in 1979 and has traveled to the East on several occasions for the purpose of dis-

---

10. John B. Taylor, *Ezekiel: An Introduction and Commentary,* in *Tyndale Old Testament Commentaries,* Vol. 20, D. J. Wiseman, ed. (Downers Grove, IL: Intervarsity, 1969), pp. 238–239.
11. J. R. Church, "Two Lost Jewish Tribes Found," *Prophecy In the News,* March 2000, p. 20.
12. gershon@templemountfaithful.org

covering the so-called "lost tribes of Israel." According to Avichail, he has discovered descendants of all ten tribes in India and in the high mountains of Afghanistan. He also discovered that they still call themselves by the original names of the ten tribes.

In the first edition of *Marginal Mysteries,* Noah Hutchings reported that at the time there were several hundred Jews residing in China and, according to the *Jewish Press* of January 11, 1985, these Jews have beards. Chinese do not have beards. In a nation where pork is the primary meat, these Jews eat no pork. Of the meat they eat, they still extract the sinew of the thigh, and are known as the "sect which extracts the sinew." They light candles on Jewish holidays and sprinkle the blood of chickens on their doorposts during Passover season. Despite being separated from their ancestral homeland for thousands of years, these Jews still maintain Jewish customs and traditions. If Americans and Europeans are members of the so-called "ten lost tribes," then, we may ask, why don't we look like Jews and act like Jews?

Reports like these show that despite deportations, captivities, immigrations, and migrations, Jews have a unique ability to maintain their "Jewishness" and to cling tenaciously to their ancient traditions. The "lost tribes" theory seems to ignore this, as well as the abundant biblical testimony arguing against it.

Scripture informs us in Revelation 7 that during the coming Tribulation, twelve thousand Israelites out of each of the twelve tribes will be called and sealed to be God's special servants. In Ezekiel the division of the land among the tribes of Israel is explained. Seven of the tribes will be given portions of the land north of the Temple area, and these tribes include Dan, Manasseh, and Ephraim (Ezekiel 48:1–7). If Ephraim is England and Manasseh is America, how do these two modern nations fit into the geography of the land of Israel?

The "mystery of the ten lost tribes" is really no mystery. During the ancient dispersion of the people of Israel, most Israelites lost their tribal identity, but it is not lost to God nor has He given the northern tribes a new geographical inheritance.

In *25 Messianic Signs in Israel Today,* Noah Hutchings documents twenty-five events that were to occur in Israel just before the Lord returns which have already happened. A remnant has returned from all nations, but there are at least 10 million Jews still living in gentile nations, 5 million in New York City alone. But God knows where every Jew in the world is, and He will gather every Israelite left alive to Israel (Mark 13:27).

The "lost tribe" theory is only a theory and, it seems to us, an indefensible one. When God is ready, He will act according to His prophetic timetable and a remnant will return to the land of Israel from all of the tribes. We see the stage being set for the fulfillment of this prophecy in the nation of Israel today.

The Shroud of Turin

Burial Cloth of Jesus, or Garment of Deceit?

The Shroud of Turin is believed by many to be the burial cloth of Jesus Christ. The headlines reporting its significance are dazzling:

> "Scientists Say Shroud of Turin No Hoax"
> "Christ's Shroud Still Mystery"
> "Top Atheist Shaken by Shroud"
> "Proof of Resurrection?"
> "The Last Miracle of the Nazarene?"

Mark 15:46 tells how Joseph of Arimathea received Jesus' body: "And he bought fine linen [*sindon*], . . . and laid him in a sepulchre which was hewn out of a rock, and rolled a stone unto the door of the sepulchre." In this chapter we will try to separate fact from fancy regarding the Shroud of Turn.

A Proper Focus

There have been two extremes regarding the Shroud. On the one hand, evangelicals have generally ignored the Shroud, fearing to give it too much attention lest it be said that the Shroud is being venerated. On the other hand, the Roman Catholic Church views the Shroud, along with a whole host of items allegedly coming from antiquity, as having special powers. *The Catechism of the Catholic Church* states:

> Following the divinely-inspired teaching of our holy Fathers and the tradition of the Catholic Church (for we know that this tradition comes from the Holy Spirit who dwells in her) we rightly define with full certainty and correctness that, like the figure of the precious and life-giving cross, venerable and holy images of our Lord and God and Savior, Jesus Christ, our inviolate Lady, the holy Mother of God, and the venerated angels, all the saints and the just, whether painted or made of mosaic or another suitable material, are to be exhibited in the holy churches of God, on sacred vessels and vestments, walls and panels, in houses and on streets.[1]

The Shroud must never be viewed as a relic possessing some kind of intrinsic spiritual power. At best it is an archaeological artifact. The power of God to save and cleanse is in the Word of God. That Word works effectually in the lives of those who have put their faith in Jesus Christ (1 Thessalonians 2:13). The Bible never approves of the practice of using the objects of biblical antiquity as items for religious veneration. While it is true that handkerchiefs and garments worn by the apostle Paul had healing power (Acts 19:12), this was a first century occurrence connected with the apostolic office and is limited by these two factors. This practice is never presented as something that would continue through the ages, or that believers are to seek out the garments of the apostles and use them in a similar way. We believe that paganism, not biblical Christianity, focuses on relics and objects that have an allegedly sacred association. Jesus said, "God is a Spirit: and they that worship him must worship him in spirit and in truth" (John 4:24). Relics are in no sense "spirit," nor is their reverence in accord with "truth."

The Shroud and the Sudarium

The Shroud of Turin measures fourteen feet, three inches long by three

---

1. *The Catechism of the Catholic Church* (New York: Doubleday, 1995, #1161), pp. 328–329.

feet, seven inches in width. It has a long and interesting history. In try-ing to reconstruct a history of the Shroud, two informative books have been used: Robert K. Wilcox's *Shroud,* and also Ian Wilson's *The Shroud of Turin.*[2]

The Shroud

Our reconstruction takes us back to A.D. 30 when Agbar V, a Turkish king suffering from an incurable disease, sent a royal messenger to Jesus request-ing that He would come and heal him of his malady. It was around that time that Jesus was crucified and resurrected, but the messenger returned with a cloth which was believed to contain the image of Jesus Christ. Tra-dition states that when Agbar saw the image, he was miraculously healed.

In about A.D. 57 Agbar's son, Ma'nu VI, became ruler of Edessa, an ancient city located in the area of the Turkish-Syrian border. Ma'nu re-verted to paganism and bitterly persecuted Edessa's Christians. It is around this time that "the Image of Edessa," as the Shroud came to be known, disappeared. Some five hundred years later, the Shroud is found bricked up in a wall. The historian Evagrius (527–600) refers to "the divinely-made image not made by the hands of man," and calls it *mandylion,* from the Latin *mantile,* meaning "veil" or "mantle."

The *mandylion* remained in Edessa for several hundred years. How-ever, in 943 and 944, a Roman army besieged Edessa and asked for the *mandylion* as the price of peace. The cloth was surrendered and then taken to Constantinople. In 1203 the cloth was on display in Constantinople, where a Frenchman, Robert de Clari, saw it and claimed it was "the sy-doine in which our Lord had been wrapped . . . so that the figure of our Lord could be plainly seen there." However, in 1204 rampaging Crusaders plundered Constantinople and the *mandylion* was lost.

In 1306, a group called the Knights Templar, after having partici-pated in the plundering of Constantinople, began to fall under the suspi-

---

2. Wilson provides several appendices, pp. 214–251, featuring a "Reconstructed Chronol-ogy of the Turin Shroud," along with the texts of several letters from the Middle Ages concerning the Shroud.

cion of the French king. The Templars were rich, and their money would greatly swell France's coffers. Claiming that they were guilty of idolatry, the Templars were all simultaneously arrested, and their properties were confiscated on the order of King Philip the Fair. The charge of idolatry was based on the stories that were circulating about their practice of holding secretive midnight meetings during which they adored and kissed an image which they considered to be that of Christ. It is believed that the Knights carried the *mandylion* from Constantinople to Paris where it was used as an important part of their religious devotion.

On September 19, 1356, French knight Geoffrey de Charnay was killed by the English at the Battle of Poitiers defending his king. In 1357 his widow, Jeanne de Vergy, held an exposition and viewing of what we today know to be the Shroud of Turin, something that attracts huge crowds of pilgrims. Her granddaughter later gave the Shroud to the Italian royal family, the House of Savoy.

In 1532 the Shroud was moved to Chambery, France. A fire broke out in the chapel where it was stored, and the heat melted part of the silver box in which it was stored. Drops of molten silver landed on the Shroud as it lay folded up and holes were burned through the cloth, although the image was unharmed. The wedge-shaped burns were patched in 1534 but the burns and patches are still visible today even in photographs of the Shroud.

From 1578 to the present time, the Shroud has been kept in Turin, Italy, with the permission of King Umberto, head of the House of Savoy. In 1939, the Shroud was taken to the Abbey of Monte Vergine (Avellino) for safety during World War II, but was returned to Turin in 1946 where it now remains.

The Sudarium

In John 20:7 we read of "the napkin" (Gr: *soudarion*) that was placed on the head of Jesus. This Sudarium has an interesting history and ties in with the Shroud of Turin.

According to an account of the Bishop Pelagius (Pelayo) the Sudarium was removed from Jerusalem in A.D. 614 under the name *Sudarium Domini,* "the Sudarium of the Lord." According to tradition, this is the "napkin" referred to in John 20:7. There are several points of similarity between the Shroud and the Sudarium which would strongly suggest that they were both used to cover the same individual. Both are stained with type AB blood, and both show that the victim's nose was pushed to the right, suggesting that he was beaten in the face. The man whose face the Sudarium covered had a beard, moustache, and long hair, tied up at the nape of his neck in a "ponytail." Significantly both the Shroud and the Sudarium show that the left tip of the beard has more hair than the right one, as the right tip is less dense. One of the researchers investigating the Sudarium writes:

> Comparing the life-size photography of the face on the Shroud taken by Enrie with the one I brought with me [the Sudarium] from Oviedo, and putting one on top of the other . . . I was taken aback by the perfect fit of the Shroud image with the macroscopic Sudarium outline. In other words, the superimposition was clear, not only with the first element (the blood at the right hand side of the mouth) by itself, but also with the second, the tip of the beard (on the left). The same is also true for the right hand side of the beard, with less hair—it is the same on the Sudarium. This could be "confirmation" for the hypothesis that both the Shroud and the Sudarium were placed on the SAME FACE.[3]

Unlike the Shroud of Turin, the Sudarium of Oviedo, located in Asturias, northern Spain, has a history that suddenly begins in A.D. 614, as indicated earlier. A question that arises is: "Why the many centuries of silence concerning the Sudarium?" A recent symposium answers the question in this way:

---

3. Guillermo Heras Moreno, Jose-Delfin Villlalain Blanco, Jorge-Manuel Rodriguez Al-
menar, *Comparative Study of the Sudarium of Oviedo and the Shroud of Turin* (Valencia: Centro
Español de Sindonologia, 1998). Translated from the Spanish by Mark Guscin, p. 9.

... It should be pointed out that the information the cloth contributes to understanding the death of the man whose head it covered is awful and shocking. The picture of a corpse hanging on a cross, with blood coming out of its nose and mouth, must have been truly horrible, especially thinking of the Jews. It is therefore understandable that if a cloth were used to cover Jesus' face when he was still on the cross, no mention would be made of it, as it would bring back the memory of that terrible moment. In other words, the idea of the dead body of Jesus of Nazareth, bleeding through the nose and mouth, was impossible to describe for a Jew. This could be an indirect explanation of why the cloth's existence was kept silent up till the time it left Jerusalem. The medieval interest in relics gave rise to the only documents found up to now that speak of the present and past of this cloth.[4]

The Shroud and the Gospel Account

In John 19:39–40 we read: "And there came also Nicodemus, which at the first came to Jesus by night, and brought a mixture of myrrh and aloes, about an hundred pound weight. Then took they [Joseph of Arimathea and Nicodemus] the body of Jesus, and wound it in linen clothes with the spices, as the manner of the Jews is to bury."

Once it had been established by the authorities that Jesus was really dead, Joseph of Arimathea was given permission by Pilate to take possession of the body of Jesus. Joseph was wealthy (Matthew 27:57), devout (Mark 15:43), and a member of the Sanhedrin (Luke 23:51). Joseph furnished the linen wraps for the body of Jesus, as well as the tomb (Matthew 28:60); and Nicodemus furnished the aromatic spices, the mixture of myrrh and aloes. The phrase "an hundred pound weight" is based on a twelve-ounce pound and equals about seventy-two pounds of spices. As the linen was wrapped around the body of Jesus, the spices were strewn in. While the Egyptians embalmed by removing the brain and entrails of the deceased, the Jewish method of burial differed.

A significant question bearing on the authenticity of the Shroud as it

---

4. Ibid., p. 3.

relates to the biblical text is John 19:40, where we are told that Jesus was wrapped in "linen clothes," plural. Since the Shroud is a single piece, how does one explain the plural designation?

In response, it should be pointed out that just two garments—the Shroud and the Sudarium, or "napkin"—would necessitate the plural "linen clothes." Moreover, in New Testament times it appears common practice to use strips of cloth on the hands and the feet of the deceased. For example, regarding Lazarus, John 11:44 states: "And he that was dead came forth, bound *hand and foot* with graveclothes. . . ."

Moving on from John 19, we want to focus on John 20:6–7: "Then cometh Simon Peter following him, and went into the sepulchre, and seeth the linen clothes lie, And the napkin, that was about his head, not lying with the linen clothes, but wrapped together in a place by itself." Though John arrived at the tomb first (John 20:3–4), Peter went in first, perhaps in keeping with his usual impetuosity. Why John did not go in is not stated, but it may be that he was just too shocked by the sight of the empty tomb to do so. We will come back to this point later as we examine the image on the Shroud, but suffice it to say scientific examination of the Shroud reveals that the Shroud was not forcibly pried from the body of the victim it enclosed. This, of course, could be explained by a miraculous resurrection, as occurred with Jesus Christ.

A Forensic Pathologist's Report and the Gospel Accounts

Perhaps the most remarkable result of an objective study of the Shroud is that the evidence shows that the abuse suffered by the man in the Shroud and the abuse suffered by Jesus Christ were similar in many ways, something that suggests the same individual was involved.[5]

We are going to look at eight similarities, with the help of the research of Robert Bucklin, M.D., J.D., a forensic pathologist who has spent many years in Shroud research. We will quote his "An Autopsy on the Man of the Shroud," which can be found at *www.shroud.com/bucklin.htm*.

---

5. See Stevenson, p. 147ff.

Bucklin gives some interesting details about the man whose image is on the Shroud: "In the case of the image on the Shroud, it can be stated that the deceased person is an adult male measuring 71 inches from crown to heel and weighing an estimated 175 pounds. The body structure is anatomically normal, representing a well-developed and well-nourished individual with clearly identifiable head, trunk, and extremities."

In the following comparison of the man in the Shroud and the New Testament descriptions of the passion of Jesus Christ, the quotations from Bucklin's "Autopsy" will be set off in italics.

1. They were both severely beaten.

In Mark 15:15 we read: "And so Pilate, willing to content the people, released Barabbas unto them, and delivered Jesus, when he had scourged him, to be crucified." Scourging was accomplished with a scourge, a cruel implement designed for inflicting pain. It consisted of a short wooden handle to which several thongs were attached. To the ends of these thongs were fastened sharp pieces of lead, brass, and/or bone. The individual that was scourged was often required to kneel with the back laid bare. This kneeling may explain the contusions on the knees of the victim in the Shroud. Generally two men administered the scourging, one lashing the victim from one side, the other from the other side. The back of the victim was quickly lacerated. Bits of skin and muscle would often be seen hanging from the victim's back. If the scourging was of sufficient duration and severity, the inner organs were often exposed. No wonder Jesus was in such poor physical condition that Simon of Cyrene was required to carry the cross after Jesus had carried it but for a short distance (Mark 15:21; Matthew 27:32; Luke 23:26; John 19:16–17).

As the back image is examined, it becomes quite clear that there is a series of traumatic injuries which extend from the shoulder areas to the lower portion of the back, the buttocks, and the backs of the calves. These images are bifid [divided into two parts] *and appear to have been made by some type of object applied as a whip, leaving dumbbell-shaped imprints in the skin from which blood has issued. The direction of the injuries is from lateral toward medial and downward suggesting that the whip was applied by someone standing behind the individual.*

2. They both show wounds to the scalp

Jesus had a crown of thorns put on His head to mock His Kingship, and He was also struck on the head with a reed.

> And when they had platted a crown of thorns, they put it upon his head, and a reed in his right hand: and they bowed the knee before him, and mocked him, saying, Hail, King of the Jews! And they spit upon him, and took the reed, and smote him on the head.
>
> —Matthew 27:29–30

> *. . . The deceased had long hair, which on the posterior image appears to be fashioned into a pigtail or braid type configuration. There also is a short beard which is forked in the middle. In the frontal view, a ring of puncture tracks is noted to involve the scalp. One of these has the configuration of a letter "3". Blood has issued from these punctures into the hair and onto the skin of the forehead. The dorsal view shows that the puncture wounds extend around the occipital* [back] *portion of the scalp in the manner of a crown. . . .*

3. They were both struck in the face

> And the men that held Jesus mocked him, and smote him. And when they had blindfolded him, they struck him on the face, and asked him, saying, Prophesy, who is it that smote thee?
>
> —Luke 22:63–64

> *There is a distinct abrasion at the tip of the nose and the right cheek is distinctly swollen as compared with the left cheek. Both eyes appear to be closed, but on very close inspection, rounded foreign objects can be noted on the imprint in the area of the right and left eyes.*

4. They both carried something on their back

After the abusive treatment mentioned above, Jesus was forced to carry His cross.

And he bearing his cross went forth into a place called the place of a skull, which is called in the Hebrew Golgotha.

—John 19:17

An interesting finding is noted over the shoulder blade area on the right and left sides. This consists of an abrasion or denuding of the skin surfaces, consistent with a heavy object, like a beam, resting over the shoulder blades and producing a rubbing effect on the skin surfaces.

5. *Both feet were pierced through the hands/wrists and feet*

The other disciples therefore said unto him [Thomas], We have seen the Lord. But he said unto them, Except I shall see in his hands the print of the nails, and put my finger into the print of the nails, and thrust my hand into his side, I will not believe. And after eight days again his disciples were within, and Thomas with them: then came Jesus, the doors being shut, and stood in the midst, and said, Peace be unto you. Then saith he to Thomas, Reach hither thy finger, and behold my hands; and reach hither thy hand, and thrust it into my side: and be not faithless, but believing.

—John 20:25–27

By examination of the arms, forearms, wrists, and hands, the pathologist notes that the left hand overlies the right wrist. On the left wrist area is a distinct puncture-type injury which has two projecting rivulets derived from a central source. . . . [T]he medical examiner . . . notes that there is a reasonably clear outline of the right foot made by the sole of that foot having been covered with blood and leaving an imprint which reflects the heel as well as the toes. The left foot imprint is less clear and it is also noticeable that the left calf imprint is unclear. This supports the opinion that the left leg had been rotated and crossed over the right instep in such a way that an incomplete foot print was formed. In the center of the right foot imprint, a definite puncture defect can be noted. This puncture is consistent with an object having penetrated the structures of the feet, and from the position of the feet the conclusion would be reasonable that the same object penetrated both feet after the left foot had been placed over the right.

6. Both suffered a chest wound

But when they came to Jesus, and saw that he was dead already, they brake not his legs: But one of the soldiers with a spear pierced his side, and forthwith came there out blood and water.

—John 19:33–34

As far as the mechanism of death is concerned, a detailed study of the Shroud imprint and the bloodstains, coupled with a basic understanding of the physical and physiological changes in the body that take place during crucifixion, suggests strongly that the decedent had undergone postural asphyxia as the result of his position during the crucifixion episode. There is also evidence of severe blood loss from the skin wounds as well as fluid accumulation in the chest cavities related to terminal cardio-respiratory failure. . . . In this case, it would be determined historically that the individual was sentenced to death, and that the execution was carried out by crucifixion. The manner of death would be classed as judicial homicide.

Those who view a photograph of the image on the Shroud can observe that both the right and left hands have left imprints of only four fingers on each hand. No thumbs can be seen on the hands of the man who was covered by the Shroud. Bucklin states: "This would suggest to the pathologist that there has been some damage to a nerve which would result in flexion of the thumb toward the palm." In a 1980 study of the Shroud, Hutchings refers to a study by Barbet who observed that ". . . at the moment when the nail went through . . . the thumb would bend sharply and would be exactly facing the palm by the contraction of the thenar muscles. . . . And that is why, on the Shroud, the two hands from behind only show four fingers, and why the two thumbs are hidden in the palms."[6]

Who was the individual wrapped in the Shroud? In his "Autopsy," cited above, Bucklin gives his opinion:

In the case of Man on the Shroud, the forensic pathologist will have

---

6. *The Gospel Truth,* June 1980, p. 4.

information relative to the circumstances of death by crucifixion which he can support by his anatomic findings. He will be aware that the individual whose image is depicted on the cloth has undergone puncture injuries to his wrists and feet, puncture injuries to his head, multiple traumatic whip-like injuries to his back and postmortem puncture injury to his chest area which has released both blood and a water type of fluid. From this data, it is not an unreasonable conclusion for the forensic pathologist to determine that only one person historically has undergone this sequence of events. That person is Jesus Christ.

There are several considerations that strongly suggest that Bucklin's conclusion is reasonable. The man on the Shroud suffered no broken legs, as was true of Jesus. Moreover, the man on the Shroud had contusions on his knees. It will be remembered that Jesus had to be relieved of the weight of the cross by Simon of Cyrene. Christ may possibly have stumbled under the weight of the cross, hence the contusions on the knees. It should be remembered that Jesus' burial was in an expensive linen cloth, as was true of the man on the Shroud. This was far different from the usual burial given to the victims of crucifixion who, many times, were simply dumped into a mass grave. Strange coincidence, is it not? Furthermore, there are "no decomposition stains . . . present on the Shroud."[7] This fits the scriptural teaching that the body of Jesus Christ did not go through the normal processes of decay and corruption (Acts 2:22–32).

One scientific study, however, seemed to raise grave questions about the authenticity of the Shroud. In 1988, Oxford University, the University of Arizona, and the Swiss Federal Institute of Technology reported that carbon-14 dating of Shroud samples gave a 95 percent probability that the Shroud should be dated between A.D. 1260 and 1390. This conclusion would indicate that the Shroud, though an ancient garment, is not the burial cloth of Jesus of Nazareth.

As could be imagined, this was contested. Dr. T. Phillips explained this late date by a theory of neutron bombardment. In 1994, Dr. D. Kouznetsov

---

7. Stevenson, pp. 153–154.

and Dr. A. Ivanov claimed the late dating can be attributed to the fire of 1532 which "shifted the mix of surface carbon atoms by 20 percent to 40 percent, thus yielding errors in C-14 measurement." Their experiments led them to conclude that the Shroud is "not less than 1,800 years old."[8]

One can reasonably assume, therefore, that there is a high degree of probability that the Shroud of Turin is the burial cloth of Jesus Christ. Several researchers have investigated the probabilities that the man on the Shroud is *not* Jesus Christ. Stevenson summarizes their findings:

> After studying the irregularities held in common between the Gospels and the Shroud, Francis Filas, late professor of theology at Loyola University in Chicago, concluded that there is a one chance in 1,026 that the man in the Shroud was not Jesus. Vincent Donovan's conclusion was much more conservative, but still estimated only one change in 282 million that the two men were not the same. Engineer and Jesuit Paul de Gail arrived at an even higher figure than Donovan's in spite of the fact that his work was done in 1972, six years before the major scientific investigation. The lowest figure was given by professors Tino Zeuli and Bruno Barbaris at the University of Turin's science facility. In 1978 they concluded that there is a one chance in 225 billion that the two men were different.[9]

The Image That Will Not Go Away

There are many aspects of Shroud research that are intriguing, but perhaps most intriguing of all is: "What caused the image on the Shroud?" Several hypotheses have been advanced by the scientific community, but they all have some major flaws. What are the different answers and how do they stack up against the facts?

Some contend that the image is a *hoax*. They argue that it was created by some foreign material being applied to the linen. However, no paints, dyes, pigments, or stains have been found on the fabric. The image on the

8. Ibid., pp. 255–257.
9. Ibid., p. 151.

Shroud is not the result of some kind of coloring being added to "fake" the appearance of a man. Some have tried to produce a contact image by draping a cloth over a warmed statue or bas-relief to see if, somehow, an image could be transferred to the cloth in some manner, but this, too, did not produce an image on the cloth and leaves grave doubts that someone tried to produce the image.

Others have offered a *natural explanation*. As early as 1902 biologist Paul Vignon advanced the hypothesis that the body under the cloth emitted certain gases that were caused by sweat, blood, burial spices, and other agents interacting, and that these gases diffused upward to make an image on the cloth. It had been believed that an individual going through the excruciating pains of crucifixion would perspire heavily. The area in the perspiration would decompose and give off ammonia which, when combined with the spices used on the body, would produce some kind of a photographic image. However, no one has been able to duplicate the three-dimensional image found on the Shroud. Such chemicals and gases diffuse themselves through linen fibers and produce a vague and blurry image quite unlike that on the Shroud.

A variant on this explanation is the contact thesis. The contact of the body with the Shroud left an image. At first glance, this seems plausible. Contact with the blood of the victim leaves bloodstains. Is it not logical to assume that contact with the victim's body would likewise leave some kind of an image? This, too, has been discounted. If there were chemicals that moved from the body to the Shroud, one would expect that the chemicals would have been absorbed by the fibrils in the cloth, but such is not at all the case. The image on the Shroud shows no saturation. Furthermore, if there had been some kind of a contact transference, the dorsal side would show a more intense image because of the weight of the body laid to rest in the tomb. However, the back side of the image on the Shroud is neither more saturated nor intense than on the front. Indeed, the image on the Shroud is "pressure independent."

The most favored view at present is the *scorch theory*. Many who have studied the Shroud believe that the image has been produced by some kind of a low-temperature scorch, and in this way the image of the body was somehow projected onto the linen. While there is general agreement regarding the scorch theory, there is no agreement whatsoever as to how a dead body under a cloth would produce enough heat to create a scorch.

Supportive of the scorch theory is that the burn marks produced on the Shroud by the fire of 1532 reveal a molecular structure similar to that of the image, suggesting that the image was produced by a heat source. Of course, the source of the heat was different. In the case of the Shroud's image, it was the body itself that produced the heat. One researcher claimed that "the Shroud's image was caused by low-energy X-rays of a secondary nature, which were emitted by the body under the cloth." Various theses have been proposed but, as Stevenson comments, "the question regarding how such heat could emanate from a live or dead human body has no purely scientific answer."[10]

There are several factors that make the Shroud and its image remarkable. Unlike other burial cloths that have been found, there is no hint that the body enclosed in the Shroud went into a state of decomposition. Furthermore, research has demonstrated that the body left the Shroud without disturbing it. Since the cloth was attached to the body by the dried blood from the many surface wounds, any attempt to remove the body would have had an effect upon the stains. However, the bloodstains show precisely outlined borders. This is confirmed by the fact that there is no evidence of damage done to the fibers of the cloth, as would have happened if the body was pried from the cloth. Stevenson's observations are to the point: "Naturalistic hypotheses that would account for the Shroud must explain at least (a) the absence of decomposition, (b) the fact that the body was apparently not unwrapped when it separated from the cloth, and (c) a very possible light or heat scorch from (d) a dead body in a state of rigor mortis."[11]

The image on the shroud is intriguing and has led to further study. In *The Truth About the Shroud of Turin: Solving the Mystery*, Robert K. Wil-

---

10. Ibid., pp. 197–198.

11. Ibid., p. 206.

cox writes that he had "been intrigued by the strange shadow-silhouettes formed on Hiroshima walls at the moment the atomic bomb was detonated about that city in 1945."[12] Of course, if an atomic bomb had been detonated over Jerusalem, there would have been no Shroud and no city. However, the dematerialization of the body at the moment of resurrection could have produced the Shroud image.

Wilcox also mentions Kirlian photography and "bioradiation." Energy fields are generated by living entities which appear on a photographic plate. Kirlian took contact photographs of a leaf that had been picked at various intervals. The gradual withering of the leaf produced a decline in the strength of the aura. Wilcox writes:

> In living things, the emanations appeared to be connected with health. When the aura looked dim and lacking vibrancy, the person being photographed was found to be either already sick or on his or her way to becoming sick. When it looked strong and brilliant, the person was well and feeling good. The aura wasn't restricted to physical health alone. Anger, hate, tenderness, and joy showed up markedly in the photographs and through the viewing machine. An angry person's aura, for example, turned bright red; blue was a sign of tranquility.[13]

With few exceptions most of the research suggests that the Shroud is genuine. Spores from forty-nine different plants have been found in the cloth. Some of these plants are native to Europe, which is not surprising since the Shroud has been exposed to the open air in France and Italy. But thirty-three of these plants are native to the Middle East, which is significant since the Shroud has not left Europe since at least 1357.[14] Pollen from one of the flowers which blooms in Israel from December through April, the *Capparis aegyptia,* was found and there are indications of the time of

---

12. Robert K. Wilcox, *The Truth About the Shroud of Turin: Solving the Mystery* (Washington, D.C.: Regnery, 2010), p. 148.

13. Ibid., p. 155.

14. Stevenson, p. 43.

the day when its stems were picked. Material from the flowers indicates a time of from three to four p.m., the time of the day when the buds of the flowers open.[15]

Some Oft-Asked Questions

There are some questions that are often asked with reference to the Shroud of Turin. One that is very common has to do with whether or not DNA tests have been done on the Shroud.

Researchers in Texas did a DNA study of supposed bloodstains from the Shroud. They concluded that it was the blood of a human male, but some have contested the results on the basis of the origin of the bloodstains. Are they really from the victim enclosed by the Shroud? Complicating DNA studies is the fact that the Shroud has been repeatedly handled by researchers over the last several years, making it impossible to do accurate DNA testing. In addition, church authorities who displayed the Shroud, the Poor Clare nuns who unstitched portions of it, visiting dignitaries including the Archbishop of Turin and the emissary of King Umberto, plus many others who wept over the Shroud and venerated it, all left something on the cloth. DNA studies are therefore inconclusive.

Another question has to do with the hair length of the individual on the Shroud. Both the Shroud and the Sudarium indicate that the individual who was covered by these garments had shoulder-length hair. If this individual really was Jesus of Nazareth, isn't it odd that He would have long hair in violation of 1 Corinthians 11:14? This is certainly a valid question and one that is to be expected. A few comments, therefore, regarding hair length in Scripture is warranted.

The apostle's prohibition of long hair is regarded by some simply as a cultural requirement, or perhaps as a personal opinion on the part of the apostle and was therefore not meant to be binding on others. Against this view, we must point out that there is nothing in the context that suggests that Paul is giving personal opinion. If that interpretation is taken, then why not apply the same idea to the apostle's instructions regarding the

---

15. Ibid., p. 155.

Lord's Supper and view those instructions as mere opinion as well?

In the Old Testament, those who took the Nazarite vow were to re-frain from cutting their hair—which would indicate that after a while the Nazarite's hair would be of considerable length. Numbers 6:5 states: "...he shall be holy, and shall let the locks of the hair of his head grow" (see also Judges 13:5). In the time during which Jesus ministered on Earth, many Jews had long hair, but it was the Romans who were clean-shaven and had short hair. The Romans designated those who wore beards as "barbarians," *barba* being the Latin word for "beard." It is possible that Paul's statement in 1 Corinthians 11:14 was occasioned by the fact that the Corinthians were living in a Roman world and had to abide by Roman conventions in dress and hairstyle. However, this interpretation is problematic because the apostle says, "Doth not even *nature itself* teach you, that, if a man have long hair, it is a shame unto him?" It is hard to see that Paul would speak in such categorical terms of a situation brought about by living in a particular societal arrangement. It may be more in keeping with the general drift of Scripture to understand Paul's condemnation of long hair as really being a condemnation of an effeminate style given to long hair. It is *long hair* on women that is "a glory to her" (1 Corinthians 11:15) and it is that style of long hair on a man that is "a shame" (1 Corinthians 11:14). It should also be kept in mind that "long" and "short" are relative terms. The Bible never specifies what "long" hair really is. A man who has shoulder-length hair may seem to have "long" hair in a society where men get a machine cut and a trim around the ears, but in a society where women rarely cut their hair, and consequently may have had hair that extended almost down the entire length of their backs, shoulder-length hair wasn't all that long.[16]

The Final Word

In the *Toronto Star* for Monday, November 19, 1979, Shroud researcher Dr. Thomas D'Muhala was reported as saying: "Every one of the scientists I have talked to believe the cloth is authentic. Some say maybe this is a love letter, a tool He [Christ] left behind for the analytical mind."

16. For these and other Q&As, see www.shroud.com/faq.htm.

It was dark in the tomb on that first morning of mankind's new spring. A body lay enfolded in a long linen cloth. But suddenly a shaking began in the Earth; a light suddenly shown from within the wrappings. There was an immense earth tremor, and the stone before the tomb fell away. A blinding flash of light filled the tomb as Roman soldiers fled in terror. The glorified body rose through the cloth like water flowing through a sieve. The Son of Man is alive once more, no more to die. Later, His disciples will find the clothes that were left behind. The markings they will find on them will only make them more eager to meet Him when He comes to them as He has promised.

Twenty-five years later, Paul wrote in 1 Corinthians 15:3–4, "For I delivered unto you first of all that which I also received, how that Christ died for our sins according to the scriptures; And that he was buried, and that he rose again the third day according to the scriptures." In verse 14 he said, "And if Christ be not risen, then is our preaching vain, and your faith is also vain."

But Christ did rise on the third day. It is He that says, "I am he that liveth, and was dead; and, behold, I am alive for evermore, Amen; and have the keys of hell and of death" (Revelation 1:18). It is Christ who says, ". . . lo, I am with you alway, even unto the end of the world. Amen" (Matthew 28:20).

The Shroud of Turin may indeed be a love letter He left behind for the analytical mind. There is plenty there for chemists, pathologists, and forensic experts to examine. Its purpose is not as a relic to be honored, but to guide men into a knowledge of the King of Kings and Lord of Lords, who was dead, and is alive for evermore. It is promised in 1 John 3:2, ". . . we shall be like him. . . ."

Those Mysterious Pyramids

People often think of a mystery as something that maybe you might see, and maybe you might not—like the Abominable Snowman, or the Loch Ness Monster. The mystery about the Pyramids, however, is not like that at all. There is no question about their existence. They are too massive to miss. The mystery concerns not their existence, but their purpose and especially their origin.

These mysterious structures raise more questions than they answer. How could primitive Egyptians construct such complex and symmetrically-built structures using blocks of stone that were heavy and unwieldy? Pyramids, like those found at Giza, near Cairo, Egypt, are made of blocks weighing anywhere from two tons to two hundred tons. The blocks had to be loaded on barges, and then unloaded when reaching their destination. In the construction process the blocks had to be lifted a considerable height above the ground as the building of the Pyramid proceeded.[1] How could this be accomplished without the benefit of modern machinery?

Some believe that the designers and builders of the Pyramids had access to advanced knowledge and technology. By their design and location they manifest a knowledge of astronomy and mathematics far beyond that of the age in which they were built. Did the ancient engineers have help from extraterrestrial beings?

There are, to be sure, conflicting reports about the Pyramids. Some believe that they have strange curative powers, and, by their shape and

1. I. E. S. Edwards, *The Pyramids of Egypt* (New York: Penguin, rev. ed., 1985), pp. 272–273.

design, can even contribute to the mummification and consequent preservation of tissue. But what about the mysterious deaths of some of the explorers? Is there some kind of a curse on the Pyramids, or can these deaths be explained by natural means?

Pyramids are found in many parts of the world, most commonly in regions lying within the equatorial belt. The most noted pyramids are those in Egypt, but there are also pyramids built by the Mayans, Incas, Aztecs, and other Indian civilizations of Central and South America. They all seem to have several things in common:

1. **Design and Shape**—Though there are "step" pyramids and "bent" pyramids, the most common shape is the four-sided structure with the sides converging into a point at the apex. Imhotep, Zoser's architect, deliberately built many "steps" into his pyramid. It has come to be known as the "Step Pyramid." The idea has been advanced that he did this because the kings believed that their souls would join the "Imperishable Ones," i.e., the northern stars, at death. These steps may have been envisioned as providing a stairway to the stars.[2] The "Bent Pyramid" was built at Dahshur around 2600 B.C. for King Sneferu. It is given that name because it is not built with true pyramid design and does not have straight sides. Approximately halfway up, the engineers changed the angle of the slope. Some think that this was necessitated by their error of calculation. The angle of the sides was too steep, so the engineers had to change the angle to a more gentle slope. The pyramid looks like it has a bend in it.[3]

2. **Material**—While some pyramids were mad with brick, most were constructed with hewn stone. Archaeologists continue to be amazed at the precision with which the Great Pyramid, in particular, was built. The four sides of the Pyramid face squarely north, south, east, and west with such accuracy that it is almost as if modern surveying instruments had been used. The lengths of the four sides differ by

---

2. Anne Millard, *Pyramids* (New York: Kingfisher, 1996), p. 18.
3. Ibid., p. 19.

only 88/1000 of one percent (.0088).[4] The blocks and stones, therefore, were hewn with amazing precision. One of the greatest technical challenges facing the builders was getting the four sides to meet at a single imaginary point hundreds of feet above the ground. If the gradient slope of one side had been just slightly different than the others, that side would have been over or under the others. Correcting the angle would have produced an unsightly bulge, or bend, as the builders of the Bent Pyramid found when they had to compensate for this error. No such bulge mars the perfection of the Great Pyramid.

3. **Purpose**—Some pyramids, like those in Egypt, were to serve as tombs for the kings and pharaohs. Without a single exception, the Egyptian pyramids were built along the west bank of the Nile. West is the direction of the setting sun at the end of a given day—something associated with the end of earthly life and the beginning of the afterlife. The tomb theory receives additional support from the mastaba, a small pyramid-like mausoleum used for burial purposes in the Old Kingdom period. The association of the mastaba with burials, and the fact that the Pyramids are a later development of the mastaba, would suggest that the Pyramids are, likewise, used for burials and function as tombs.[5]

Because of the intricacy of the Pyramids and the possible significance of the measurements, some have even concluded that the Pyramids were built to pass on secret knowledge and therefore may be connected with the Egyptian mystery religions. These religions hold that there is a body of secret knowledge that is to be understood by a select group of initiates. This secret knowledge is believed to describe the laws and principles governing the universe. Helena P. Blavatsky, in her book *The Secret Doctrine,* described the Great Pyramid as "the everlasting record and indestructible symbol of the Mysteries and Initiations on Earth."[6] Blavatsky believed

---

4. Michael O'Neal, *Pyramids: Opposing Viewpoints* (San Diego: Greenhaven, 1995), p. 24.

5. Ibid., p. 30.

6. Ibid., p. 39.

that the Great Pyramid symbolized the creative principle found in nature and illustrates the principles of geometry, mathematics, and astrology. For many secular humanists, the Great Pyramid seems to be a monument to human ingenuity.

Some pyramids, however, were constructed for observatories, to observe the stars and to determine the dates for the calendar. Some were made to offer human and animal sacrifice to appease a particular deity. But, primarily, they seem to have a religious purpose for their existence.

It appears that the Egyptian pyramids were connected to the Egyptian concept of immortality and the afterlife. It was believed that, in addition to the body, every individual had a spiritual "double" known as the *ka*. According to ancient belief, the *ka* does not have to die with the body and that if, somehow, the body was protected from decay, the *ka* would be immortal and the pharaoh could assume a place of honor among the gods. Bodies were preserved through a process of mummification. By removing the internal organs, soaking the body in certain chemicals, wrapping it with long bandages, and then enclosing the body in a human-shaped coffin, the body would be preserved from decay and the *ka* would continue its existence. Thus the pyramid would play a vital role in guaranteeing the king's immortality. The mummification would preserve it from decay and, by being enclosed in a pyramid with secret chambers and false passages leading to a dead end, the body would be protected from intruders and thieves. The deceased would also have an ample supply of food and water which would be stored in the pyramid's many chambers.

The Wonder of It All

Writers and historians of the ancient world recognized "Seven Wonders of the Ancient World." They were usually listed in the following order: the Pyramids of Egypt, the Hanging Gardens of Babylon, the Pharos (Lighthouse) of Alexandria, the Colossus of Rhodes, the Temple of Artemis (Diana) at Ephesus, the Mausoleum of Halicarnassus, and the Statue of Zeus (Jupiter) at Olympia. The *2000 World Almanac and Book of Facts,* page 578, says this about the Egyptian Pyramids:

The only surviving ancient Wonder, these monumental structures of masonry, located at Giza on the west bank of the Nile right above Cairo, were built from c. 2700 to 2500 B.C. as royal tombs. Three—Khufu (Cheops), Khafra (Chephren), and Menkaura (Mycerinus)—were often grouped as the first Wonder of the World. The largest, the Great Pyramid of Khufu, is a solid mass of limestone blocks covering 13 acres. It is estimated to contain 2.3 million blocks of stone, the stones themselves averaging two tons and some weighing 30 tons. Its construction reputedly took 100,000 laborers 20 years.

All the Egyptian pyramids were built on the west bank of the Nile. The ones located at Giza are the most impressive. They were all built by Khufu, his son Khafra, and his grandson Menkaura. The Great Pyramid, built by Khufu, is the largest, measuring 482 feet tall. It is built with approximately 2.3 million blocks. Khafra's pyramid is shorter by 10 feet, but appears even larger because it is built on higher ground and has some of its original casing on top. Menkaura's pyramid is the smallest, and is only 217 feet tall.[7]

The Great Pyramid is truly a magnificent edifice of imposing size and height. There have been several attempts by writers to illustrate its great size by comparison with other structures made by man. For example, it has been calculated that there is enough room within the Great Pyramid to accommodate the cathedrals of Florence, Milan, and St. Peter's in Rome. Napoleon observed that, according to his calculations, the three pyramids on the Giza plateau contain enough stone to build a wall measuring ten feet in height and one foot in width around the whole of France, and this figure has been later substantiated.[8]

In the mid-nineteenth century, John Taylor, editor of the *London Observer,* spent thirty years doing painstaking pyramid research. Among other things, Taylor was puzzled as to why the builders of the Great Pyramid chose the particular angle of fifty-one degrees, which is the standard for an equilateral triangle. Taylor's research led him to the writings of the ancient

---

7. Millard. p. 26.
8. Edwards, p. 102.

writer Herodotus, who reported what the ancient Egyptian priests had told him. Taylor came to believe that they had been designed to be equal in area to the square of the Pyramid's height. As he continued his research, Taylor found that if he divided the perimeter of the Pyramid by twice its height, it gave him a quotient of 3.144, which is very close to the value of *pi*. "In other words," says Tompkins, "the height of the pyramid appeared to be in relation to the perimeter of its base as the radius of a circle is to its circumference."[9] But why is the value of *pi* built into the Pyramid? Taylor came to believe that perhaps the perimeter of the Pyramid might have been deliberately intended by the designers to represent the circumference of the Earth at the equator, while its height represented the distance from the Earth's center to the pole.[10]

That the builders of the Great Pyramid had a knowledge of the value of *pi* at such an early date is remarkable, because the Rhind Papyrus, dated at 1700 B.C., and therefore much later than the Great Pyramid, has been viewed as the earliest document showing that the Egyptians knew the value of *pi*. What is *pi*? It can be defined as the ratio of the circumference to the diameter of any circle. By just a glance, it is obvious that the circumference is longer than the diameter, but the question is, how many times longer? If we measure the circumference (length around the outside) of a round table, we will find that it is approximately three times longer, more precisely 3.14159. In the Old Testament that value was known as a simple "3" without the added decimals. In the description of Solomon's Temple we read of the "molten sea, ten cubits from the one brim to the other: it was round all about, and his height was five cubits: and a line of *thirty cubits* did compass it round about (1 Kings 7:23).

At any rate, there was too much proof of design for it to have been coincidental, reasoned Taylor. If the base of the Great Pyramid is made in the Hebrew cubit, which is 25.025 inches in length, the length of each baseline is 365.2422 cubits, the exact number of days in the solar year. Our calendars are based on a year of 365 days, but a day has to be added every

---

9. Peter Tompkins, *Secrets of the Great Pyramid* (New York: Harper Row, 1971), p. 70.
10. Taylor, p. 72.

fourth year to allow for the fractional day. Taylor could not but wonder if the Egyptians might have intentionally built the perimeter of the Pyramid into units, the exact number of which would equal the days of the solar year.[11]

Egyptian pyramids were part of a total complex of structures. At the height of the pyramid-building dynasties, when a king died his body was rowed across the Nile to the valley temple to be mummified. From there the body was brought along a causeway which led from the valley temple to the pyramid itself. At the entrance to the pyramid was the temple mortuary, the place where the priests were to make offerings to the king's spirit on a daily basis. Next to the temple mortuary was the queen's pyramid, much smaller than the main pyramid. The actual tomb was set inside the pyramid, where the king and his belongings were buried.[12]

Sites that were considered suitable for building a pyramid were those on the western side of the river—the side of the setting sun. It had to be above the flood level of the Nile, but not so far from the river as to be inaccessible. It was also necessary that there should be a good rock substratum that would not crack with the weight of the pyramid.[13] The positioning of the pyramid was important to the Egyptians. The stars were used to fix the exact position of the sides, which always faced the four compass points. True north was determined by looking into the northern sky and observing the movement of a given star in the northern sky. The locations of the rising and the setting of the star was noted and the angle between the two points was bisected to find true north.[14]

Once the site was chosen, it was made level by the clever use of water. A low, relatively watertight wall was built enclosing the site, which was then flooded with water. Equally-spaced trenches laid out in parallel fashion were cut into the rock and carefully measured. How did the Egyptians know how deep the trenches should be cut? They were chiseled to be

---

11. Ibid.
12. Millard, pp. 20–21.
13. Edwards, p. 262.
14. Ibid., pp. 266–268.

uniformly the same depth below the surface of the water. When the water was drained, the rock between the trenches was cut away providing a level base for the pyramid.[15]

Egyptologists continue to debate precisely how the blocks of rock were cut. Some hold that when huge slabs of rock of consistent uniformity were located, a shallow trench was chiseled out to make the outline of the block. Wooden wedges were then driven into the trench with a wooden mallet. The wedges were repeatedly soaked with water. As they expanded, the swelling wood broke the blocks of stone away from the main mass of stone.[16]

Though not specifically using the term "pyramid," Josephus speaks of great "pillars" that were erected in Siriad, that part of Egypt where the Pyramids are located, and that they were erected *before* the Flood by Seth:

> Now this Seth, when he was brought up, and came to those years in which he could discern what was good, became a virtuous man; and as he was himself of an excellent character, so did he leave children behind him who imitated his virtues. All these proved to be of good dispositions. They also inhabited the same country without dissensions, and in a happy condition, without any misfortunes upon them till they died. They also were the inventors of the peculiar sort of wisdom which is concerned with the heavenly bodies, and their order. And that their inventions might not be lost before they were sufficiently known, upon Adam's prediction that the world was to be destroyed at one time by the force of fire, and at another time by the violence and quantity of water, they made two pillars; the one brick, the other of stone: they inscribed their discoveries on them both, that in case the pillar of brick should be destroyed by the flood, the pillars of stone might remain, and exhibit these discoveries to mankind; and also inform them that there was another pillar of brick erected by them. Now this remains in the land of Siriad to this day.[17]

---

15. Millard, p. 21.
16. Ibid., p. 10.
17. *Antiquities,* I, 2, 68–71.

Josephus is not the only individual of antiquity to make the claim that the Pyramids were erected before the Flood. Von Daniken cites another ancient source and writes:

> In the Bodleian Library at Oxford there is a manuscript in which the Coptic author Mas-Udi asserts that the Egyptian King Surid ruled in Egypt before the Flood. And this wise King Surid ordered his priests to write down the sum total of their wisdom and conceal their writings inside the pyramid. So, according to the Coptic tradition, the pyramid was built before the Flood. Herodotus confirms such a supposition in Book II of his History. . . .[18]

"Prophecy In Stone"

Some writers, both ancient and modern, have also suggested that the Pyramids reveal prophetic truth and that they present prophetic information in stone. Around 300 B.C. the Egyptian historian Manetho wrote about a strange people from the east, "men of an ignoble race," who conquered the Egyptians. Some have taken this to mean that the ancient Hebrews were the actual architects of the Pyramids, rather than the Egyptians, and that these Hebrews were inspired by God to reveal prophetic truth. Supporters of Manetho's contention argue that the Pyramids are so highly complex in structure and perfect in design that the builders must have been enlightened, or instructed, by Deity to accomplish such a feat.[19]

Several Egyptologists have advocated this view. One of the first in more modern times was the London editor and mathematician John Taylor, who published his work *The Great Pyramid: Why Was It Built and Who Built It?* in 1859. Taylor's views were picked up by C. Piazzi Smyth, a professor who held the position of Astronomer Royal to Scotland, and who in 1880 published his near-700–page tome, *The Great Pyramid: Its Secrets and Mysteries Revealed.* In 1928, Basil Stewart wrote another book supportive of the same view, entitled *The Witness of the Great Pyramid.*

---

18. Erich von Daniken, *Chariots of the Gods?* (New York: G. P. Putnam's Sons, 1970), p. 79.
19. O'Neal, p. 37.

According to Stewart, the Great Pyramid "reveals a system of prophetic chronology which runs parallel with—and confirms—biblical prophecy, forecasting events which history has proved correct in the past, are being confirmed today, and are due to take place in the immediate future."[20]

Those holding this view focus particularly on the Great Pyramid. It is the Great Pyramid alone that "proves to be a storehouse of important truth—scientific, historic, and prophetic." It is not to be regarded as a supplement to Scripture, because Scripture is complete in and of itself. However, the Great Pyramid "is a strong *corroborative witness* to God's plan; and few students can carefully examine it, marking the harmony of its testimony with that of the written Word, without feeling impressed that its construction was planned and directed by the same divine wisdom, and that it is the pillar of witness referred to by the prophet in the above quotation, i.e., Isaiah 19:19–20."[21]

But does the Bible make reference to the Pyramids? Several scholars answer this in the affirmative and point to Isaiah 19:19–20: "In that day shall there be an altar to the LORD in the midst of the land of Egypt, and a pillar at the border thereof to the LORD. And it shall be for a sign and for a witness unto the LORD of hosts in the land of Egypt: for they shall cry unto the LORD because of the oppressors, and he shall send them a saviour, and a great one, and he shall deliver them."

Other connections between the Bible and the Pyramids have been suggested. Hutchings cites J. Bernard Nicklin, who wrote:

> The late David Davidson . . . drew attention to the remarkable way the age, or Dynasty, of Enoch is impressed upon the Great Pyramid itself. As Enoch lived 365 years (Genesis 5:23), so 365, or to be more exact 365.242 days, the value of the solar year, forms the basis of all measure-

---

20. Taken from O'Neal, p. 37.

21. This material can be found at *nsbible.org*, and is copyrighted by the North Seattle Bible Students. It is entitled "The Corroborative Testimony of God's Stone and Prophet, the Great Pyramid in Egypt." The text was modified September 18, 1998. Though the author's name is not given, the text is available with an endorsement by acclaimed Pyramid scholar C. Piazzi Smyth, and is dated Clova, Ripon, England, December 21, 1890.

ments. Moreover, by ancient writers, the Great Pyramid is described as "The Pillar of Enoch." Enoch was in the line of Seth, and Josephus ascribes the building of it to the dynasty of Seth. So that Enoch—the year-circle man—who, it should be observed, is referred to as a prophet (Jude 14–15), may well have been the architect, if not the builder, of the Great Pyramid. Now, if God revealed the plan of the tabernacle to Moses, and gave instructions for building the temple to David, could He not also have revealed the design and measurements of the Great Pyramid to the one chosen by Him to superintend its erection? In fact, could He not have inspired and guided all concerned in the task?[22]

Any traveler to Egypt will be amazed at the magnificence of the Pyramids. We may wonder what the Hebrew prophet had in mind when he wrote about the Lord and said: "Great in counsel, and mighty in work: for thine eyes are open upon all the ways of the sons of men: to give every one according to his ways, and according to the fruit of his doings: Which hast set signs and wonders in the land of Egypt, even unto this day . . ." (Jeremiah 32:19–20).

Some may conclude that these "signs and wonders" are a reference not to the Pyramids, but to the Lord's works of deliverance under the leadership of Moses, but the passage says that these signs and wonders remain "even unto this day."

More Than Meets the Eye

The logistics of erecting a pyramid are staggering. Looking down on the pyramid from an aerial view, one sees the four surfaces all coming together at the apex. To say the least, this is a phenomenal achievement. Hutchings cites an earlier observer, who wrote:

Let's assume there are slaves to hack out 2,600,000 giant blocks from the quarries. What kind of tools did they use to carve out the stones? There

---

22. Noah W. Hutchings, *Prophecy in Stone* (Oklahoma City: Hearthstone Publishing, 1996), p. 30.

was no dynamite, no explosives in those days. Where did they get the tools? After the blocks were quarried, how were they dressed? Some of those stones were fitted with seamless joints. Dressing ... would require a minimum pressure of two tons! Where does a primitive workman get the equipment to apply that pressure? Third, how do you get the stones to the building site at Giza? Fourth, how could a small country like Egypt feed all those slaves? Fifth, where did they get the ropes to pull those blocks? In ancient Egypt you didn't dash into town to buy rope! How much rope would you need to handle 2,600,000 stone blocks? These stones weigh a minimum of three tons. Let's assume we need four times as many ropes as stones. Some of the ropes could be used again, so we'd need about two times as many ropes as stones. That's an incredible 5 million pieces of rope—good, sturdy rope. Where did they get it? Sixth, where did the Pharaoh find an architect who could design a building with such precise measurements? ... At the completion rate of ten stones a day, it would have taken 260,000 days to build the pyramid. That is 712 years! Modern builders are pleased when they obtain an accuracy of one-tenth of an inch on their construction projects. Yet, the pyramid is built with far greater precision, despite being honey-combed with tunnels, shafts, and bizarre hidden chambers. . . . Find me a construction company that will guarantee to build a 6.5 million-ton building without settling. It can't be done. There are endless mysteries on how the pyramids were constructed. An example is the remarkable "king's" chamber deep inside the structure with two rows of seventy-ton blocks of rare, red granite formed into a unique roof. These stones could only have been taken from quarries that are six hundred miles from Giza. The horse and cart were not brought to Egypt until the seventeenth Dynasty. How did they transport these stones over such an enormous distance? Historians say the seventy-ton blocks and smaller stones were pushed overland on wooden rollers. Trees were chopped down, dressed out to logs, and used as rollers under the blocks. It's a good theory except for the trees. There are no forests in Egypt. There would have been a loss factor of about ten rollers per stone. The Great

Pyramid would have required 26 million wooden rollers. . . . The theory of primitive people building the pyramid with their hands simply doesn't stand inspection.[23]

But Did They Have Help?

Erich von Daniken believes this last statement emphatically. He believes that there must be some other explanation to the origin of the Pyramids. To say that "primitive people" built the Pyramid is like saying that "primitive people" designed the space shuttle.

Born in Switzerland in 1935, von Daniken was raised a strict Roman Catholic, but came to have many doubts about his faith. In particular, he did not believe the traditional understanding of the origin of man. Consequently, he embarked on a worldwide quest for answers. His travels included Stonehenge, Easter Island, Egypt, Tibet, and Peru. Von Daniken has scrapped all previous explanations for the origin of man and maintains that the Earth was colonized by alien space beings around 500 B.C. He summarizes his view:

Dim, as yet undefinable ages ago an unknown spaceship discovered our planet. The crew of the spaceship soon found that the earth had all the prerequisites for intelligent life to develop. Obviously the "man" of those times was no *homo sapiens,* but something rather different. The spacemen artificially fertilized some female members of this species, put them into a deep sleep, so ancient legends say, and departed. Thousands of years later the space travelers returned and found scattered specimens of the genus *homo sapiens.* They repeated their breeding experiment several times until finally they produced a creature intelligent enough to have the rules of society imparted to it. The people of that age were still barbaric. Because there was a danger that they might retrogress and mate with animals again, the space travelers destroyed the unsuccessful specimens or took them with them to settle them on other continents. The first communities and the first skills came into being; rock faces and

23. Taken from Hutchings, pp. 38–39.

cave walls were painted, pottery was discovered, and the first attempts at architecture were made.[24]

Von Daniken applies this theory to his explanation for the origin of the Pyramids. Highly advanced beings must have been involved in the work. He asks:

> Is it really a coincidence that the height of the pyramid of Cheops multiplied by a thousand million—98,000,000 miles—corresponds approximately to the distance between the earth and sun? Is it a coincidence that a meridian running through the pyramids divides continents and oceans into two exactly equal halves? Is it coincidence that the area of the base of the pyramid divided by twice its height gives the celebrated figure $pi = 3.14159$? Is it coincidence that calculations of the weight of the earth were found and is it also coincidence that the rocky ground on which the structure stands is carefully and accurately levelled?[25]

Von Daniken cannot find a single explanation—religious, logistical, or scientific—as to why the builder of the Great Pyramid chose that particular site for its erection. He finds that all of the traditional reasons given "are against all common sense."[26] In fact, operating on the basis of human reason, the builder and designer could have picked many other "better" locations. For one thing, argues von Daniken, "it would certainly have been more practical to locate the building site nearer the eastern quarries in order to shorten transport distances." But even if the traditional explanations are accepted, von Daniken believes there are still other "proofs" of his theory. Since the Pyramid "divides continents and oceans into two equal halves," and since "it also lies at the center of gravity of the continents," yet it is impossible, on that basis, to explain the fact that the site "was chosen by beings who knew all about the spherical shape of the earth and the distribution of continents."[27]

24. Von Daniken, *Chariots,* pp. 51–52.
25. Ibid., pp. 76–77.
26. Ibid., p. 77.
27. Ibid.

After reading von Daniken, one gets the distinct impression that he has reinterpreted the Bible in the light of his theory. For him, there is no God of Scripture, only godlike spacemen with uncanny abilities. As a matter of fact, von Daniken gives a scientific explanation for the miracles of Scripture. He approaches Exodus 25, for example, as a skeptic. While the Bible says Moses was given instructions from God on the dimensions of the Ark of the Covenant, von Daniken believes that it was so constructed to function as "a condenser with a voltage of several hundred volts. And" he writes, "Second Samuel chapter six tells us about a catastrophe connected with the Ark, which we would immediately diagnose today as an electric shock."[28] In fact, von Daniken believes that there is no hope for religion unless the fear and superstition is removed. Von Daniken states: "I agree with Teilhard de Chardin," the notorious process theologian who believed that even God is in the process of evolving, "when he says that the religion of tomorrow could be a beautiful thing and that it should puts its trust in science."[29]

Von Daniken puts great stock in the Book of Enoch which, he claims, was kept from the people to deliberately suppress the truth. "The editors of the Bible acted as their own censors. They did not allow *all* existing manuscripts to be included in the book of books." However, one can read both the canon, as well as the apocryphal books, and still not find what von Daniken finds. He believes that Enoch 6–16 describe the fall of the rebel angels. The names of the angels are given, but these angels are really "space travelers who couple with the daughters of men against the orders of their God [captain of the spaceship]."[30] He didn't get that from the Book of Enoch.

Furthermore, von Daniken's ideas concerning life on other planets raise many serious issues. Those who believe that there is life on other planets argue in the following way: *Life evolved on Earth. Since the universe*

---

28. Erich von Daniken, *In Search of Ancient Gods* (New York: G. P. Putnam's Sons, 1973), p. 52.
29. Ibid., p. 83.
30. Ibid., pp. 46–47.

is so immense and contains so many heavenly bodies, chances are that life prob-ably evolved in other places as well. While we will readily admit that there are many planets and stars beyond planet Earth, we also affirm that the chances of life evolving spontaneously are infinitesimally slim. For ex-ample, evolutionary biologist Ernst Mayr states that life is highly complex and the chances that it "could have occurred several times is exceedingly small, no matter how many millions of planets there are in the universe."[31]

Exodus 20:11 states: "For in six days the LORD made heaven and earth, the sea, and all that in them is. . . ." In Genesis 1:14 we read: "And God said, Let there be lights in the firmament of the heaven to divide the day from the night; *and let them be for signs, and for seasons, and for days, and years.*" Scripture mentions Heaven and Earth, and heavenly bodies, but no mention is ever made of life on these bodies.

The "Power" of the Pyramid?

Power for Good?

There have been many reports about the mysterious effects of the Pyra-mids on items that were left inside them. One French investigator, M. Bovis, noticed that some trashcans in the King's Chamber contained dead cats and other small animals that had apparently wandered into the cham-ber and died. To his amazement, Bovis observed that there was no smell of decay and putrefaction. Upon examining the dead animals, he found that they had dehydrated in the chamber. Unable to offer a scientific explana-tion, Bovis supposed that it might have something to do with the unique shape of the Pyramid.

In order to validate, or invalidate, his contention, Bovis made a wood-en model of Cheops with a base three feet long, and faced it due north. Inside the model, a third of the way up, to approximate the location of the King's Chamber, he placed a dead cat that had recently expired. To his utter surprise, it mummified in only five days. To further test his theory, Bovis then placed other organic materials in the model pyramid, such as the brains of a calf, something that putrefies very quickly. When these

---

31. *Time* magazine, April 10, 2000, p. 74.

failed to decay, Bovis concluded that there was something about the pyramidal shape that prevented the natural process of decay. Others have made similar conclusions about the pyramidal shape. In Italy and Yugoslavia milk is packaged in pyramidal containers to keep it fresh. A French firm has also packaged a pyramidal container for yogurt.[32]

Other interesting effects were noted. A Czech radio engineer named Karel Drbal noticed that by placing a used razor blade within a six-inch-high cardboard model of the Cheops pyramid, the blade returned to its original sharpness and that he could, in this way, shave some two hundred times with the same blade. Some have speculated that the pyramid might function as some sort of a gigantic lens that focuses energy simply by virtue of its shape.[33]

Some have suggested that the pyramid functions as a Leyden jar, a primitive kind of electric condenser that stores electricity. Tompkins relates that Sir W. Siemens, a British inventor, claimed that one day, while standing on the top of Cheops, it was observed that whenever he raised his hand with his fingers outspread, a strange ringing noise was heard. When he tried to drink water from a bottle that he had brought along, he received a small electrical shock. Siemens got the idea of moistening a newspaper and wrapping it around the bottle to convert it into a Leyden jar. The electrical charge increased as he held it above his head. The Leyden jar is a small jar about the size of a canning jar, with a cork in the opening. Part of the inside and outside of the jar is coated with tinfoil. Siemens' guides concluded that he was demon-possessed when sparks began to issue from the bottle. They accused him of practicing witchcraft.[34]

Power for Evil?

There have been some tragedies associated with Pyramid exploration which have led some to conclude that there is some kind of a "Pharaoh's curse" put on those who enter the Pyramids. This theory is rooted in an

---

32. Tompkins, pp. 276–277.
33. Ibid., p. 278.
34. Ibid., p. 279.

item of history. The Egyptian kings anticipated that there would be grave robbers who would come to loot the Pyramids. Entrances to the tombs were often hidden and the tomb itself could only be reached through deep shafts. Sometimes the builders made false walls to fool would-be robbers. In Seti's tomb the paintings in the outer room were left incomplete to create the impression that the tomb was not being used. Because of the threat of robbery, *Egyptian pharaohs placed curses on their tombs with the warning that anybody who defiled the tomb could expect to die in some horrible way.*

There are many accounts of the effects of "Pharaoh's curse" from ancient times, and also later accounts. In the modern era, Giovanni Belzoni, who was one of the more flamboyant and colorful Pyramid explorers, died a sudden and unexpected death at the age of forty-four.

Born in 1778, Belzoni worked as a theater strong man, a profession which took him all over Europe. While in Malta, he met a man who convinced him that he needed to go to Egypt to find abundant treasures. In 1817, Belzoni went to Abu Simbel to do what many said could not be done.

The heavy digging was extremely fatiguing because of the intense heat. Belzoni and his men had to stop their work at nine a.m. and resume in the late afternoon. After weeks of laborious work, and despite the heat and the frequent work stoppages by the disgruntled work crew, eight huge statues of Ramses II were dug out of the sand. They were part of a giant temple built by Ramses. Inside the temple that Belzoni and his men discovered were statues of Egyptian deities and a huge one of Ramses seated on his throne. On the walls of the temple ancient artists had drawn figures and battle scenes.

In three years of exploration Belzoni made some fantastic finds, but in late 1822 he came down with a fever and was dead within a week. The man who had financed some of Belzoni's explorations, Henry Salt, died of a stomach infection five years later. His young wife also succumbed to a fever.[35]

---

35. Susan Dudley Gold, *The Pharaoh's Curse* (New York: Crestwood House, 1990), pp. 26–29.

Stories such as these, fueled by the pharaohs' practice of putting a curse on their tombs, helped to create horror stories of death and suffering that came to those who violated the Pyramids. But are there other explanations?

Many naturalistic and scientific explanations have been given. One possibility is that a fungal growth in the tombs was the cause of the fevers. Since some of the explorers died of pneumonia and related lung complications, it has been suggested that the mummies bred various bacteria and viruses. Another possibility is that the ancient priests used certain poisonous substances to embalm the dead, or to protect the dead by sickening and killing those who would enter the tombs. Some have even suggested that the illnesses were self-induced and the result of autosuggestion. The explorers brought about their own demise by being convinced that they had been "cursed."

Others, however, have pointed out that many of the explorers lived to ripe old ages and showed no evil effects from being in the Pyramids. Joseph Lindon Smith, who spent more than half a century exploring the Pyramids, lived to be eighty-seven. One of the most notable explorers of the nineteenth century, Sir W. M. Flinders Petrie, died at eight-nine. Though Lord Carnarvon died shortly after finding King Tut's treasury, his partner, Howard Carter, died seventeen years later.[36] We have traveled in Egypt and have been warned about drinking the water and have been told not to eat fresh salads. It has often been said that Egypt has some deadly diseases that have not yet been classified by modern medicine. There are certainly many perfectly natural explanations that could explain the early deaths of some, but—who knows—perhaps there are some unnatural ones as well.

Pyramids in the Heavens?

As was observed in the earlier edition of *Marginal Mysteries,* page twenty-four, there have been reports of pyramids in outer space. There it was reported that a UFO magazine featured a huge stone face found near a large

36. Ibid., pp. 44–45.

pyramid on the planet Mars by Dr. Vincent di Pietro, a NASA technician who was reviewing photos from the 1976 *Viking* orbiter.

More recent reports on the *Viking* probe shows a continuing interest in the Martian face and pyramid. Mac Tonnies, in his "Mars: The Cydonian Imperative" (mactonnies.com/imperative.html), acknowledges that NASA has concluded that the face is really a "hill," but Tonnies says this is "a conclusion I find hasty and, for the time being, based on insufficient evidence." He adds, "One of my first interpretations of the MGS image was of a severely-eroded sculpture. It retains a Sphinx-like aspect that is difficult to deny." Probably the least clear object is the pyramid, if that is what it really is. Tonnies states: "It's come to my attention that a small portion of the D&M Pyramid is also visible in the MGS image-strip. What is visible is, unfortunately, probably the most degraded portion of this unusual landform and nothing can yet be said about the D&M's potential artificiality."

The Mystery Remains

What, then, are we to think of "those mysterious Pyramids"? Gayle Young, CNN correspondent, states that while "people like mystery, they don't like the facts." She asks, "What are the facts about the Great Pyramid?" Well, she claims that the latest research shows that the builders "were neither slaves nor aliens." An archaeological find, mainly of the workers who built the structures, shows that about fifteen thousand skilled craftsmen were responsible for this massive construction project. The find suggests that "the workers like beer, ate lots of bread, and were generally well cared for by the Pharaohs whose tombs they were constructing."[37] However, it is doubtful if beer and bread can explain the Pyramids in all of their complexity.

We naturally expect that as knowledge increases man will do new and amazing feats. That, of course, is true. With the development of the computer, space exploration, genetic engineering, and several new fields that have developed out of new technologies, we are seeing the unbelievable

---

37. CNN.com, August 11, 1996.

become commonplace. Yet, it is also becoming increasingly obvious that the Pyramids of Egypt are obviously not the work of a few uneducated simpletons of yesteryear. Concerning the Great Pyramid, the Lansburgs write:

> Somehow its builders knew that the world was round but flattened at the poles, which caused a degree of latitude to lengthen at the top and bottom of the planet; that it rotated in one day on an axis tilted 23.5 degrees . . . causing night and day, and that this tilt caused the seasons; that Earth circled the sun once in a year of 365 and a fraction days.
>
> The designers must also have known that Earth's celestial North Pole described a slow circle around the pole of the ecliptic, making the constellations in the sky appear to "slip backward" . . . and bring a new constellation of the Zodiac behind the sun at the equinox approximately every twenty-two hundred years in a grand cycle of about twenty-six thousand years. These facts too were part of the internal measurements of the pyramid.[38]

Despite all of the historical records, archaeological examinations, computer calculations, and observations by the most learned of individuals, there are still lots of questions regarding the origin and purpose of the Pyramids. The Great Pyramid, with its flawless design and impeccable workmanship, could very well bear striking testimony to another dimension of existence beyond the gaze of most individuals.

---

38. Alan and Sally Lansburg, *In Search of Ancient Mysteries* (New York: Bantam Books, 1974), pp. 111–112.

The Mystery That Is By No Means Marginal

We have tried to present a fair hearing for all sides in the issues presented in the previous chapters. These are, to be sure, marginal mysteries. Perhaps their truth will never be validated, or invalidated.

Since these are really marginal mysteries, it doesn't really matter. If you can't make up your mind about Atlantis, or about UFOs, or any of the other issues that we have discussed in this volume, there is nothing gained or lost. These are simply items of discussion—interesting in and of themselves, and issues that we would all like to know something about, but they are marginal. However, there is one mystery that is by no means marginal. In fact, it is so important that one's attitude toward this mystery determines where one spends eternity. We are speaking about the bodily resurrection of Jesus Christ. The Bible says, "That if thou shalt confess with thy mouth the Lord Jesus, *and shalt believe in thine heart that God hath raised him from the dead,* thou shalt be saved" (Romans 10:9).

When the Bible speaks about being "saved," it is speaking about being rescued from the wrath to come. God has not appointed His children—those who believe in Jesus Christ—to wrath, but rather, to obtain salvation and complete rescue (1 Thessalonians 5:9). But the Bible says that the condition to salvation is faith in Christ, the Son of God, whom God has raised from the dead. If you believe this, the Bible tells us, "thou shalt be saved." That's why we say that this mystery is not a marginal issue.

> Now if Christ be preached that he rose from the dead, how say some among you that there is no resurrection of the dead? But if there be no resurrection of the dead, then is Christ not risen: And if Christ be not risen, then is our preaching vain, and your faith is also vain. Yea, and we are found false witnesses of God; because we have testified of God that he raised up Christ: whom he raised not up, if so be that the dead rise not. For if the dead rise not, then is not Christ raised: And if Christ be not raised, *your faith is vain; ye are yet in your sins.* Then they also which are fallen asleep in Christ are perished. If in this life only we have hope in Christ, *we are of all men most miserable.*
>
> —1 Corinthians 15:12–19

In this closing chapter of our book we will deal with the resurrection in much the same way as we have dealt with the other mysteries.

The Charge of "Circular Reasoning"

It is clear that the Bible teaches that Jesus was resurrected from the dead, and that all who believe in Him will, likewise, be resurrected from the dead. But do Christians arrive at this conclusion on the basis of circular reasoning?

Circular reasoning is an attempt to prove what is already asserted. Skeptics often claim that Christians are guilty of committing such a logical fallacy. If we say that we believe that the Bible is the Word of God because the Bible says so, many claim that is an invalid form of reasoning because it is an argument that starts with its conclusion. Imagine that a man named Joe says that he is God. It would be natural to want to know why Joe thinks that he is God. If Joe says, "I am God because I say so," that's an example of circular reasoning. But are biblical claims for the resurrection of Christ and other cardinal doctrines of the Christian faith examples of circular reasoning?

While the Bible is the Word of God—something that many people would dispute—it is also true that the Bible is an ancient document—something that none can dispute. By studying its language, contents, and orthography (writing), along with manuscript evidence demonstrating its antiquity, we can prove that the Bible is an ancient document. And this is something that no one can reasonably dispute. We are operating in the realm of the verifiable. Of course, not everything in the Bible can be verified to the satisfaction of the skeptic and we'll say more about that in a moment. However, if the Bible can be shown to be true in areas where independent verification is possible, we have a much greater warrant for believing that it is true when it addresses matters that cannot be verified.

A simple illustration ought to suffice. Abraham Lincoln was assassinated on April 14, 1865, by John Wilkes Booth while attending a performance at Ford's Theater in Washington, D.C. Now supposing you are doing some research for a paper entitled "America in the Civil War Years," and you come across a book written by a certain individual who seems to have firsthand information concerning the Lincoln years. You are excited to have found a source of information that can provide you with a firsthand account of the Lincoln years. In fact, the author of the book makes the statement that Lincoln personally told him about an issue in which you are really interested. You are profoundly elated with this—until you find out that this author was born in 1864. He was only one year old when Lincoln was assassinated! You have every reason to doubt his integrity and the reliability of the information he writes.

If the credibility of the Bible can be undercut in a similar way, we would have every reason to doubt its reliability. But, as we are going to see, the credibility of the Bible in general, and its accounts of the resurrection of Christ in particular, stand up under the most careful of scrutiny.

Skeptics Who Came to Faith

The best legal minds acquainted with the necessities of evidence have found the resurrection of Christ to be entirely credible. Simon Greenleaf, the Royal Professor of Law at Harvard from 1833 to 1848, an important figure in bringing Harvard Law School into world prominence and who has been called the greatest authority in the world on legal evidence, concluded that the resurrection was factual. It really happened the way the Bible says it did.[1]

In the same way, Frank Morison, an unbelieving British attorney who set out to write a book that would once and for all destroy the Christian faith by showing the resurrection of Christ to be a falsehood, was so overwhelmed with the evidence that he became a Christian. Morison's book, *Who Moved the Stone?*, opens with a compelling chapter entitled "The Book That Refused To Be Written." Another skeptic who sought to disprove the resurrection was Lew Wallace. He ended up writing a book that actually defended the resurrection. The book is entitled *Ben Hur.*

More recently, an unbelieving journalist by the name of Lee Strobel wrote a book entitled *The Case for Christ: A Journalist's Personal Investigation of the Evidence for Jesus.* Strobel, who was educated in law at Yale and who was an award-winning journalist at the *Chicago Tribune,* was a skeptic. His wife's conversion in 1979 challenged Strobel to do some serious investigation. This investigation led him to interview several leading scholars. Strobel states in his book . . .

I'll take you along as I interview thirteen leading scholars and authorities who have impeccable academic credentials. I have crisscrossed the country—from Minnesota to Georgia, from Virginia to California—to elicit their expert opinions, to challenge them with the objections I had when I was a skeptic, to force them to defend their positions with solid data and cogent arguments, and to test them with the very questions that you might ask if given the opportunity. In this quest for truth, I've used my experience as a legal affairs journalist to look at numerous categories of proof—eyewitness evidence, documentary evidence, corroborating evidence, rebuttal evidence, scientific evidence, psychological evidence, circumstantial evidence, and, yes, even fingerprint evidence. . . . These are the same classifications that you'd encounter in a courtroom.

1. Simon Greenleaf, *The Testimony of the Evangelists* (1874; reprint ed., Grand Rapids: Baker, 1965), pp. 28–30).

And maybe taking a legal perspective is the best way to envision this process—with you in the role of a juror.[2]

Reasoning from the Evidence

Attorneys and legal affairs journalists have to reason from the available evidence. We have tried to examine the evidence for the various marginal mysteries, and we are examining the evidence for the validity of what the Bible reports. There is good evidence for the claims of Christ, and there is good evidence for the existence of the God of the Bible.

Suppose two men are traveling on the railroad. They are spellbound by the view—snow-capped mountains, rushing rivers, and verdant pine forests. As they travel farther, they both notice large, white stones on the side of a mountain. The stones seem to be arranged so that they form the words *"The Canadian Pacific Railway Welcomes You to the Canadian Rockies."*

One traveler observes that they must have crossed the border into Canada. The other traveler says, "Well, I don't believe so. What makes you think that?" The other traveler points out the window and says, "Look at the stones out there. They are arranged to say, *'The Canadian Pacific Railway Welcomes You to the Canadian Rockies.'*"

"Oh," says the other traveler. "They just rolled down the hill that way. It is pure chance that they are in that pattern."

The traveler who thinks the stones were deliberately arranged that way is mystified. He can't believe that the other fellow is denying something so obvious. But how can he prove to him that the stones were deliberately put into that pattern?

After a few minutes, the man who did not believe that the stones were deliberately arranged says, "I think that I'll get off the train at the next station and exchange my U.S. currency for Canadian money."

Interesting, isn't it? This man claims that he doesn't believe that the stones had any particular message, but he wants to exchange U.S. currency for Canadian money.

---

2. Lee Strobel, *The Case for Christ: A Journalist's Personal Investigation of the Evidence for Jesus* (Grand Rapids: Zondervan, 1998), pp. 14–15.

This may seem to be an oversimplified illustration, but this is what happens every day with millions upon millions of people. Non-Christian scientists will argue that the universe evolved through blind chance, and yet they assume that the cosmos is orderly. Experiments that are duplicated over and over again work the same way. Two plus two is four. The seasons change with amazing regularity. Somehow seeds reproduce after their own kind. Did it all evolve by chance? Do chickens have lips?

While the man who believes that the rocks on the mountainside were deliberately arranged cannot prove it beyond a shadow of a doubt— maybe they did just roll down the hill that way and he somehow ended up in Canada—he can act accordingly, consistent with his belief. He, too, like the other traveler, can exchange American currency for Canadian money, but such an act is, in his case, totally rational. He has a good reason for believing that he is in Canada.

Need Faith Be Separated from Fact?

Many Christians think that historical fact, logic, and reason have nothing to do with the Christian faith. They feel that the best expression of their faith is through subjective experiences. Afraid that someone might "prove" the Bible wrong in some item of history, they deny that history has any relevance to the Christian faith. Why do we believe the Bible to be true? Those in this camp would say, "I believe because I believe it," or "Because it makes sense to me." Very few are asking whether a religious belief is true. Rather, people judge a movement or religious claim by simply saying, "It makes me feel better." With this kind of thinking, we have come to the point where every opinion about religion is right and no opinion is wrong.

T. H. Huxley, the biologist friend of Charles Darwin, argued that this was the only way that Christianity could "survive" the onslaughts of science. Huxley was quite sure that Darwin's "discovery" regarding the survival of the fittest and natural selection would totally demolish the Christian faith—unless faith was separated from fact. Huxley believed that Christianity could survive if faith lived in another dimension than fact.

In this way, the Christian faith could not be proven, but neither could it be disproved. He didn't realize that such a faith would be of no value. It would then "be up to each individual to choose whatever 'faith' was right for him or her. As long as no one asked whether a belief was true, there could be as many different 'faiths' as there are people in the world!"[3]

This is very much unlike the way Jesus and Paul and the early Christians operated. They never retreated into a subjective shell, but always appealed to the evidence. They were willing to share their message publicly and present it in "the marketplace of ideas." They had no doubt that the Gospel would stand the test of careful scrutiny. When asked by the high priest about His doctrine, Jesus said: "I spake openly to the world; I ever taught in the synagogue, and in the temple, whither the Jews always resort; and in secret have I said nothing" (John 18:20). We can talk about our faith and verbalize its truths. The Bible commands: "And be ready always to give an answer to every man that asketh you a reason of the hope that is in you with meekness and fear" (1 Peter 3:15).

Both modern evangelicalism and our post-modern world have ridiculed the place of sanctified human reason. Fancy has been substituted for fact, and esoteric mystical experiences have been embraced in the place of the communication of Bible doctrine. However, we do not have to cast our minds aside in order to embrace the truths of the Bible and the Savior of whom it speaks. Paul sought to reason from Scripture. He wrote: "Knowing therefore the terror of the Lord, we persuade men" (2 Corinthians 5:11). The word "persuade" implies the marshaling of arguments that can be used to convince people to change their minds.

"But Can You Prove To Me the Bible Is True?"

The answer to this question depends on what the questioner means by "prove." Just about anything can be disputed and doubted, even things that are generally accepted universally. We can't prove the Bible to be true beyond the shadow of a doubt, but there is not much else that we can prove

---

3. Erwin Lutzer, *Seven Reasons Why You Can Trust the Bible* (Chicago: Moody Press, 1998), p. 9.

beyond the shadow of a doubt, either.

For example, can the reader prove beyond the shadow of a doubt that human beings have actually landed on the moon as reported by NASA? Believe it or not, some have questioned the reports and have advanced several arguments that they believe demonstrate that the reported moon landings are nothing but a hoax. Kevin Overstreet has a website in which he examines what he believes are "alleged photos of a moon landing" and raises several questions about the photos and about the NASA reports.[4] He examines a rock at the bottom of one of the photos. It has the letter "C" on it. Overstreet comments: "Perhaps a gag left by the props department." But what could be the possible motivation for alleged faked moon landings? His answer:

> If you ever saw the movie *Wag the Dog,* the president has sexual relations with a twelve-year-old. This information goes out to the media one week before elections. So, to get the public's mind off of the little girl, the president stages a war in Albania. The moon shots were the same concept. People did not like what was going on with the Vietnam War, so, to get the public's mind off of all the bad things going on in Vietnam, the U.S. faked a moon landing. If you check your dates, we abruptly stopped going to the moon around the same time the Vietnam War ended.

Overstreet also claims two other motivations for the "faked landing." It is good for business. According to Overstreet, NASA had taken in about $30 million, and showing pictures of an allegedly successful moon landing really brought in the money.

And what about the Holocaust? Does everyone agree that it really happened as generally reported in history books? Well, not everyone. Some Identity groups, for example, link Jews with the devil, and the so-called "Jewish Conspiracy" with Satan's ongoing battle against humanity. Some see the Holocaust as an important part of "the lie" and deny that

---

4. www.batesmotel.8m.com

it ever really happened.[5] National Public Radio aired an interview on Friday, February 4, 2000, relating to a libel trial involving author David Irving and Debra Lipstat, whom Irving says defamed his book. In a book published by Penguin, Lipstat branded Irving a "Holocaust denier." Irving is suing under Britain's libel laws, which place the burden of proof on the accused. Under these conditions Lipstat and Penguin must prove that Irving is wrong about the Holocaust. In particular, Irving argues that there were probably no Jews gassed at Auschwitz, something that is "commonly held to be the historic truth." We present this not to deny history regarding the moon landings and the Holocaust. We present this simply to demonstrate that the most commonly held and accepted beliefs are often challenged. There are, evidently, some who do not believe that commonly held beliefs about the moon landings and the Holocaust can be proved beyond the shadow of a doubt.

Corroboration from Secular Sources

In legal proceedings, corroboration is extremely important. If a witness states that a green pickup ran a red light and hit the couple in the blue van, the veracity of that testimony is strengthened if someone else steps forward and corroborates that testimony. To corroborate a testimony means to confirm and thereby strengthen its credibility. This raises an important question: Is there corroboration for Jesus and His claims outside of the New Testament?

Time magazine, in its December 18, 1995, edition, reported that John Van Seters of the University of North Carolina stated: "There was no Moses, no crossing of the sea, no revelation on Mount Sinai." The radical *Jesus Seminar* published its color-coded edition of the Gospels. The scholars responsible for this work went through the Gospels and assessed the authenticity of each of Jesus' sayings. Each member voted and used colored beads to indicate the likelihood that the passage was genuine. In this edition of the Gospels, the words of Jesus that the committee felt to

---

5. For a thorough survey of this and related issues see Michael Barkun, *Religion and the Racist Right* (Chapel Hill: University of North Carolina Press, 1997), rev. ed.

be genuine were coded in red. Pink was the color given those passages that sounded like Jesus may have spoken them. Gray expressed greater doubt. A black-coded passage indicated that the members of the group did not think that portion was genuine. Very little of the New Testament survived this "death by coloration." This matter of independent corroboration, therefore, becomes an extremely important issue. Let's look at some examples of corroboration from outside of the New Testament.

The "Eclipse" That Wasn't

The Synoptic Gospel writers claim that there was a great darkness of three hours duration that covered the Earth while Jesus was hanging on the cross (Matthew 27:45; Mark 15:33; Luke 23:44). Some have tried to explain this darkness as an eclipse, though it was the wrong time of the year for such a phenomenon. Others have argued that there was no darkness and that it was just figurative language used by the apostles to dramatize the scene for the reader. Is there any corroboration of this darkness outside of the New Testament?

Around A.D. 52 there was a first-century historian named Thallus who wrote a history of the eastern Mediterranean world. Although Thallus' original work has been lost, it is quoted by Julius Africanus in about A.D. 221. Julius writes: "Thallus, in the third book of his histories, explains away the darkness as an eclipse of the sun—unreasonably, as it seems to me." Though Thallus did not connect the darkness with the events recorded in the New Testament, he did at least corroborate the biblical account concerning the sudden darkness in the middle of the day. In 1968, Paul Maier wrote a book entitled *Pontius Pilate* and made some significant comments on the darkness:

> This phenomenon, evidently, was visible in Rome, Athens, and other Mediterranean cities. According to Tertullian . . . it was a "cosmic" or "world event." Phlegon, a Greek author from Caria writing a chronology soon after A.D. 137, reported that the fourth year of the 202nd Olympiad (i.e., A.D. 33) there was "the greatest eclipse of the sun" and

that "it became night in the sixth hour of the day [i.e., noon] so that stars even appeared in the heavens. There was a great earthquake in Bithynia, and many things were overturned in Nicaea."[6]

Josephus on Jesus

Another testimony from outside the New Testament to the person of Christ is a statement by the Jewish historian Josephus, found in his *Antiquities of the Jews,* 18.63–64:

> About this time there lived Jesus, a wise man, if indeed one ought to call him a man. For he was one who wrought surprising feats and was a teacher of such people as accept the truth gladly. He won over many Jews and many of the Greeks. He was the Christ. When Pilate, upon hearing him accused by men of the highest standing among us, had condemned him to be crucified, those who had in the first place come to love him did not give up their affection for him. On the third day he appeared to them restored to life, for the prophets of God had prophesied these and countless other marvelous things about him. And the tribe of Christians, so called after him, has still to this day not disappeared.

Born in A.D. 37, Josephus was a prolific historian. He angered many of the Jewish leaders of his day because he surrendered to the Roman general Vespasian during the Roman War of A.D. 66–74. Many of Josephus' Jewish colleagues refused surrender as an option and took their own lives rather than give up.

But is the above passage in which Josephus speaks of Jesus in such glowing accolades genuine? Edwin Yamauchi, born in Hawaii in 1937 and converted from his Buddhist background in 1952, has done some careful research on the passage. Yamauchi is a world-class scholar in Hebrew and Hellenistic studies and reads some twenty-two languages, including Arabic, Chinese, Egyptian, Russian, Syriac, Ugaritic, and is an expert in

6. Strobel, pp. 84–85.

the Comanche language. Regarding the Josephus passage, Yamauchi states: "Scholarship has gone through three trends about it. . . . But today there's a remarkable consensus among both Jewish and Christian scholars that the passage as a whole is authentic, although there may be some interpolations." Some scholars believe that Josephus' statement regarding Jesus that "He was the Christ" may have been added by Christians, along with the words, "On the third day he appeared to them restored to life."

However, as Yamauchi points out, even with the removal of these phrases, assuming that they are later interpolations, Josephus corroborates important information about Jesus: that He was the martyred leader of the church in Jerusalem and that He was a wise teacher who had established a wide and lasting following, "despite the fact that he had been crucified under Pilate at the instigation of some of the Jewish leaders."[7] Even in the hands of the most hostile anti-Christian polemicists, Josephus still provides abundant extra-biblical testimony to the historical Person of Jesus Christ.

Important reference to Christ from outside the pages of the New Testament comes from the writings of the Roman historian Tacitus. Around A.D. 115 he wrote that Nero persecuted the Christians as scapegoats for the purpose of diverting suspicion away from himself for the devastating fire that brought such destruction to Rome in A.D. 64. Tacitus writes:

> Nero fastened the guilt and inflicted the most exquisite tortures on a class hated for their abominations, called Christians by the populace. Christus, from whom the name had its origin, suffered the extreme penalty during the reign of Tiberias at the hands of one of our procurators, Pontius Pilate, and a most mischievous superstition, thus checked for the moment, again broke out not only in Judaea, the first source of the evil, but even in Rome. . . . Accordingly, an arrest was first made of all who pleaded guilty: then upon their information, an immense multitude was convicted, not so much of the crime of firing the city, as of hatred against mankind.[8]

7. Ibid., p. 79–80.
8. Tacitus, *Annals,* 15.44.

There are several interesting statements in this paragraph penned by a pagan historian. Tacitus was certainly not pro-Christian, and he cannot be charged with conspiring to advance the Christian faith. Nevertheless he writes of Christ ["Christus"] and of His suffering "the extreme penalty during the reign of Tiberias." He gives powerful, though unwitting, corroboration to the New Testament that Jesus Christ was a real Person.

What did Tacitus mean when he wrote that this "mischievous superstition" was "checked for the moment" but that it later "again broke out"? Some hold that this is a reference to the belief of the early church that though Christ had been crucified and the Christian movement seemed to be ready to perish from the scene, that the resurrection of Christ caused the movement to break out "not only in Judaea . . . but even in Rome." Yamauchi states: "Regardless of whether the passage had this specifically in mind, it does provide us with a very remarkable fact, which is this: crucifixion was the most abhorrent fate that anyone could undergo, and the fact that there was a movement based on a crucified man has to be explained."[9]

The "Psychology of Faith"

Skeptics love to psychoanalyze the early disciples and to apply their analytical techniques to modern Christians. We often hear things like, "Christianity is a crutch for the fearful." The skeptic would argue that the modern world is a terribly frightening place, with the threats of nuclear war, biological terrorism, cancer, road rage, and a whole host of potentially life-threatening situations staring us in the face every day. Allegedly, the Christian's psychological need predisposes certain people to faith. We can't live with the thought that there is no God and that we are alone in the world. It is our hidden need to believe something that motivates us to embrace the claims of Christianity.

That's a neat theory, but it can be turned against the skeptic. We can show that the skeptic's own hidden needs have prejudiced him against the faith. We can show that men don't believe not because the evidence

---

9. Strobel, p. 82.

is insufficient, but because the skeptic doesn't like the direction in which the evidence takes him. He doesn't want to believe because faith would call for a radical readjustment in his lifestyle.

There is a good illustration of this in the Scripture. One day Jesus healed a man who was born blind, but the religious leaders were not willing to admit that Jesus was able to perform such a miracle. The Pharisees insisted, "This man is not of God, because he keepeth not the sabbath day." But others were confused and asked, "How can a man that is a sinner do such miracles? And there was a division among them" (John 9:16).

The Pharisees were unrelenting in their attempts to deny the obvious. They even went to the man's parents and questioned them if this individual really was their son who had been born blind. John 9:22 tells us why the Pharisees kept on denying the miracle: "For the Jews *had agreed already,* that if any man did confess that he was Christ, he should be put out of the synagogue."

Here is a demonstration of the fact that opposition to Christ is rooted in the will of man. The religious leaders were not denying that a miracle had happened because the evidence that was presented was insufficient. They had all the evidence they needed. This was indeed the man who had been born blind. They could not deny that fact. Even the boy's parents testified to that fact. Why did they not believe? Because the verdict had already been decided. They hated Jesus and nothing—not even the facts—would persuade them otherwise.

Scripture reveals that man's problem is personal sin, and that the sin nature is endemic to mankind. Moreover, it boldly announces that while salvation is available to all, there is the necessary condition of faith and repentance. We must renounce confidence in self and accept the free gift. "For the wages of sin is death; but the gift of God is eternal life through Jesus Christ our Lord" (Romans 6:23).

Gullible Disciples?

It is customary to challenge the New Testament accounts about the resurrection of Christ on the basis that the disciples were gullible and would "fall for just about anything." Supposedly, because they were living in a pre-scientific age in which magic, spiritism, belief in demons, and so on, was common, the disciples were more than willing to accept another myth and believe it to be true.

However, it is totally false to think that the ancients were gullible ignoramuses. Skepticism was rampant in the Greco-Roman world. Even among the disciples, hard and fast evidence was necessary to convince Thomas (John 20:26–29). The disciples *should* have known because they *could* have known about the resurrection. When Peter made his confession regarding Christ's messianic identity, we read that "from that time forth began Jesus to shew unto his disciples, how that he must . . . be killed, and be raised again the third day" (Matthew 16:21; see also John 2:19; Matthew 17:22–23; 20:17–19; 26:32, et al). And yet, though the resurrection of Christ had been prophesied, the disciples did not believe. Theirs is certainly not the behavior of gullible individuals willing to believe anything.

The early Christians put a premium on eyewitness testimony and careful documentation to establish historical reliability (Luke 1:1–4; John 1:14; 20:30–31; 1 Corinthians 15:5–8; 1 John 1:1–4). Biblical Christianity invites scrutiny. "For I am persuaded that none of these things are hidden from him," Paul said in addressing King Agrippa, "for this thing was not done in a corner" (Acts 26:26). We submit that this evidence proves that something happened that dramatically convinced fearful, timid disciples who were reluctant to believe.

Following the arrest of Jesus, all of the disciples fled in the fear that they, too, would be put to death. Consequently, they met in secret following the crucifixion because they were fearful of Jewish antagonism (John 20:19). So strong was Peter's fear of the authorities and what they might do to him that he denied Christ three times, even though he had earlier said that he would remain faithful (Mark 14:66–72). Whatever happened to change the minds of the disciples must have been terribly real to them and it must have been terribly persuasive.

It is hard for us to believe that the New Testament accounts of Jesus are mythological. Mythologies take many centuries to develop. Enshrouded in ancient traditions, regional lore, and embellished with imaginative wonder stories, mythologies sometimes take centuries to reach their full-blown form. And yet the early Christians were proclaiming the resurrection of Christ shortly after the events recorded in the New Testament occurred. Indeed, not only did the apostles and their followers claim that Jesus was alive, but that He was coming very shortly for His people. Their behavior cannot be explained on the basis of faith in a myth.

Committed to a Lie?

While we are thinking about the psychological dynamics influencing the disciples, let's look at the often-claimed argument that the resurrection and Jesus' miraculous works were simply fabrications. The disciples made it all up. They lied and built their lives around that lie. We find that hard to believe.

There are several historical facts about Christ as they relate to His resurrection. What is significant about these facts is that most historians—whether they are Bible-believing Christians or not—would be willing to admit that they can be demonstrated by historical research and thereby verified:

1. The body of Jesus Christ was placed in a carefully guarded tomb.
2. The disciples were really not expecting the resurrection. When Jesus died on the cross His disciples lost all hope.
3. The tomb of Jesus was found to be empty.
4. Several hundred eyewitnesses saw Jesus alive after the crucifixion.
5. The disciples were so convinced that Christ was resurrected by the power of God that they were willing to stake even their lives on that belief.

We believe that the best explanation for all of this is that Jesus Christ rose bodily from the dead. Significantly, there is nothing that contradicts this conclusion.

What Happened to Change Their Attitude?

Every ancient history, whether written by Christians or non-Christians, will acknowledge the existence of the Christian church. Textbooks in public schools do the same. And they will all acknowledge the life and death of someone called Jesus. No one can escape the connection between the two. Immediately after the death of Christ, there is a new chapter of history that relates the rise of the church, its growth and advance, and its endurance despite hostility and persecution. Effects have causes. The Grand Canyon was not made by a salamander dragging its tail through the mud. That the early church was formed despite overwhelming odds in a hostile world, and that it has continued down to the present hour, in an increasingly hostile world, must have an explanation.

The Bible, with its central theme of the resurrected Lord and Savior, has had a phenomenal ability to endure. In his book *Age of Reason,* Thomas Paine (1737–1809), the leading rationalist of his day, boasted: "Five years from now there will not be a Bible in America. I have gone through the Bible with an axe and cut down all its trees." Paine was terribly wrong. The "trees" took the blade off his axe.

The Church grew through the teaching and preaching of the apostles. One of the central truths of their message was the resurrection of Christ. When confronting the Jewish leaders of his day, Peter focused on a very significant truth concerning Jesus Christ: "This Jesus hath God raised up, whereof we all are witnesses. . . . Therefore let all the house of Israel know assuredly, that God hath made that same Jesus, whom ye have crucified, both Lord and Christ" (Acts 2:32, 36). It wasn't just "someone called Jesus," but the very same Jesus whom they had murdered.

Interesting, isn't it? No one ever went and exhumed the body of Jesus to demonstrate once and for all that this new religion was false. No doubt, those antagonistic to the Gospel would have loved to disprove the claims of the apostles by producing the body of Jesus—but they couldn't.

An Earnest Plea

Meeting and knowing the true and living God is the most exciting experience possible. This is what the Bible calls "eternal life." Jesus prayed to His Father and said: "And this is life eternal, that they might know thee the only true God, and Jesus Christ, whom thou hast sent" (John 17:3).

Christians believe that eternal life is not only possible, but that we should be ready to tell others about eternal life and to give a "reason" for our hope and joy (1 Peter 3:15). This means, among other things, that those who put their faith in Jesus Christ *need not* commit intellectual suicide by taking some kind of a "blind leap in the dark."

Imagine that you have entered a special theme park. You can do anything that your heart desires in this theme park. There are booths offering cotton candy, and others offering a variety of life experiences ranging from drugs to suicide.

There is only one problem with your stay at this theme park: It is limited to three hours. In fact everyone, including you, has been infected with a fatal disease. Everyone will die within three hours of entering the park.

You try to have the best time possible and to make the most of your limited time. But every once in a while someone gets very pale, begins to have difficulty breathing, and falls over dead. Guards come and carry the lifeless body away. Knowing this will happen to you in less than three hours spoils some of the fun. You can't escape the lingering fear that with each tick of the clock your time is getting closer.

This is what life is like. To be sure, most people live more than three hours. Some live to be sixty, seventy, eighty, or more years, but speaking about a "three-hour lifespan" makes the illustration more compelling. Since life is so short and temporary, everything we do in this life is relatively meaningless and unimportant. Even the most wonderful experiences and most precious friendships that we make at the theme park are terribly shortlived.

To get back to our illustration—as you think of the short time you have left, you become depressed. You even think that perhaps you might as well get a jump on things and end your life—now! While you are mulling these thoughts over in your mind, you notice that there is someone who is excitedly waving to you. He is inviting you to come closer. As you draw closer, he says, "Come here, quickly. Some of us have found a door that you can walk through. You will receive a cure and you will be able to live for ever."

You are excited about that possibility. While you want to believe that person because he is sharing some awfully good news, you begin to feel some strong doubts. This is too good to be true. You have been seeing people die all around you and you don't feel too well yourself. Is there really a cure?

No doubt, the *reasonable* thing to do would be to exercise caution after hearing such a claim. But surely, you would want to investigate further. Any *reasonable* person would want to do that.

Where Do You Fit In?

We would hope that this book would help you to reach your own verdict about Jesus Christ and His claims. This is a matter of the utmost importance and it is, therefore, necessary that you make this a front burner issue in your life. What is at stake? Not just the answer to a few questions, but your own personal future. Jesus said, "If ye believe not that I am he, ye shall die in your sins" (John 8:24).

We know that these are sobering words, but this is a terribly important issue. It is all too easy to put really important things off. Life is terribly short and unpredictable. No one knows what tomorrow will bring for us personally. Isn't it strange how people can get so busy with the ordinary affairs of everyday living that they keep on putting off the really important things?

That Christ was raised from the dead will be of no personal benefit to you unless you personally put your faith in Him. We can believe a lot of things about Jesus without ever believing Him. In that case, Jesus is just an historical figure, and the events recorded in the Gospels are items of historical interest.

As we have moved into the twenty-first century, there are wars and rumors of war. We see one global crisis after another. Technology is raising new issues and new dangers. Mankind possesses the technology to change life as we know it on planet Earth. There is even the technology making it possible for a few to enslave the masses.

When Jesus Christ came to Earth some two thousand years ago, He came to take your place. He came to bear the guilt and penalty due for every sin that we've ever committed. It is in this way that He can forgive those who put their faith in Him. Have you put your faith in Him?